Sin and Redemption

Sin and Redemption

WALKING WITH JESUS
VOLUME TWO

An Expository Commentary based upon Paul's Letter to the Ephesians

(CHAPTER TWO VERSES 1-22)

ROBERT B. CALLAHAN, SR.

RESOURCE *Publications* • Eugene, Oregon

SIN AND REDEMPTION
An Expository Commentary based upon Paul's Letter to the Ephesians

Copyright © 2011 Robert B. Callahan, Sr. All rights reserved. Except for brief quotations in critical publications or reviews, no part of this book may be reproduced in any manner without prior written permission from the publisher. Write: Permissions, Wipf and Stock Publishers, 199 W. 8th Ave., Suite 3, Eugene, OR 97401.

Resource Publications
An Imprint of Wipf and Stock Publishers
199 W. 8th Ave., Suite 3
Eugene, OR 97401
www.wipfandstock.com

ISBN 13: 978-1-60899-646-9

Manufactured in the U.S.A.

All scripture quotations, unless otherwise indicated, are taken from the Holy Bible, The King James Study Bible, Copyright ©1983, 1988. (Previously published as the Liberty Annotated Study Bible and as The Annotated Study Bible, King James Version) Copyright © 1988 by Liberty University. Thomas Nelson Publishers.

*For my wife, Ginger,
whose encouragement, faith,
love, and objectivity contributed
significantly to Walking With Jesus*

Ephesians "*brings one into an atmosphere of unbounded spiritual affluence that creates within one's heart deepest peace and assurance. It is impossible to live habitually in Ephesians and be depressed.*"

RUTH PAXSON

Topical Categories in Walking with Jesus
(An Expository Commentary)

Volume One	Volume Two	Volume Three	Volume Four
The Triune God Speaks to the Saints	*Sin and Redemption*	*Christ's Prisoner*	*Walking As Mature Christians*
To the Faithful in Christ Jesus	Sin and God's Wrath	For This Cause— God's Glory	Living in Harmony With Christ
God's Will— Spiritual Blessings	God, Rich in Mercy and Grace	Revealing God's Hidden Truths	Unity in the Triune God The Holy Spirit
Trusting in Him	A Right Relationship With God	Praying to the Father	The Lord Jesus Christ
Praying for Christians	Reconciliation	Believing God's Power	God, the Father
	Praying Through the Holy Spirit		Grace According to Christ's Gifts

	God's Foundation (Apostles and Prophets)		Maturing in Christ
Volume Five *Following Christ*	Volume Six *Walking Wisely*	Volume Seven *Satan and God's Armor*	Volume Eight *Christ's Ambassadors*
Alienated from God	Christ-Like Conduct	Family Relationships	A Call to Discipleship
Ye Have Not So Learned Christ	No Inheritance in the Kingdom of God and Christ	Life's Basic Relationship	Wearing God's Armor
Christ-Like Conduct	Walking in the Light	The Whole Armor of God	Christ's Ambassadors
	Walking Circumspectly	Satan and His Evil Forces	
	The Marriage Relationship		
	Christ and His Church		

Contents

Topical Categories in Walking with Jesus vii
Volume Two: Topical Categories xi
Foreword xiii
Preface xv
Acknowledgments xvii
The Question of Authorship xix
Introduction xxi

1   The Doctrine of Sin   1

2   Death by Sin   14

3   Trespasses and Sins   20

4   The Doctrine of God's Wrath   30

5   But God, Rich in Mercy   41

6   Raised Up Together   50

7   A Remarkable Truth   58

8   God's Kindness Toward Us   65

9   Saved Through Faith   73

10   Created in Christ Jesus   81

11   God's Chastening Grace   87

12   Circumcision and Uncircumcision   91

13   Aliens from the Commonwealth of Israel   99

14   By the Blood of Christ   107

15   Making Peace   114

16 Reconcile Both Unto God 122

17 He Came and Preached Peace 130

18 Through Him By One Spirit 138

19 Christ's Righteousness 145

20 Making Intercession According to the Will of God 150

21 Having Faith in Prayer 157

22 Unity In Christ 163

23 Fellow Citizens with the Saints 172

24 Abraham's Seed 180

25 God's Dwelling Place 185

26 The Foundation of the Apostles and Prophets 192

27 Being Members of Christ's Body 204

Outline Questions 211
Bibliography 265

Volume Two: Topical Categories

Category	Scripture	Chapters
Sin and God's Wrath	Eph. 2:1–3	1–3
But God, Rich in Mercy and Grace	Eph 2:4–10	4–10
A Right Relationship With God	Eph 2:11–13	11–12
Reconciliation	Eph 2:14–17	13–16
Praying Through the Holy Spirit	Eph 2:18	17–21
God's Foundation	Eph 2:19–22	22–27

Foreword

Robert Callahan's multi-volume work of Paul's Letter to the Ephesians is both a welcomed and long-overdue guide for Christian living today. The Apostle's sense of the eternity and greatness of God, his emphasis on the living reality and exaltation of Christ, his devotion to God's grace as an unearned gift of enduring love, and his call to an ardent and faithful discipleship all witness to an urgency and renewal critically needed in our time. Callahan's heart and style rise to meet this challenge and to convey God's message of hope and promise, of presence and courage, to Christian souls of any and every contemporary Christian tradition.

Callahan's format allows for both a devotional and studious usage. One can permit one's soul to savor every spiritual nuance the author uncovers, verse by verse, mark the passage, and return later for further nourishment. Or one can linger from text to text, gleaning with the author both theological and spiritual insight for enhancing personal discipleship, equally applicable in the arena of church and society.

The author draws on an array of insightful theological and spiritual wisdom, garnered from scholars and saints alike, theologians and missionaries. Calvin's Institutes guide Callahan's expositions, as well as the work of Markus Barth – known for his commentary on Ephesians and his delineation of Pauline theology. The author cites frequent and astute observations from Barth's exegesis of this nature. In addition, Callahan makes wise usage of Martyn Lloyd-Jones' emphasis on "experiencing the living Christ." For Lloyd-Jones, as well as the author, mere intellectual knowledge of the Christ fails to undergird one's faith or discipleship, when life's journey truly becomes sore bestead. Callahan also draws from the great 17th century theologian William Gurnall's delightful work: The Christian in Complete Armour. Perhaps students of Church history remember how both John Newton and Charles Spurgeon prized Gurnall's approach and piety and preferred it to many perspicacious studies available in their time. Gurnall's Complete Armour is known for its pithy, fervent, and wise counsel that confronts human vagaries with the truth about the self. In that respect, so too does Robert Callahan's gentle but firm counsel enrich the Christian heart and inspire one to a higher level of discipleship. No one can fail to sense this in Walking With Jesus. Whether encouraged to venture this methodology owing to his own years as a Presbyterian elder, or as an avid member and participant of the bi-annual Calvin's Colloquiums for the past 30 years, or as a fond reader of Ruth Paxson's The Wealth, Walk and Warfare of the Christian, the result is the same: a powerful, inspirational, and theologically heartwarming guide to discipleship today.

Ministers, Christian educators, seminary students, laypersons, and lovers of Jesus' life will find Callahan's work immensely valuable. His volumes deserve our grateful and sincere attention, as we too seek to walk with Jesus.

Benjamin W. Farley
Younts Professor Emeritus of Bible, Religion, and Philosophy
Erskine College, Due West, South Carolina

Preface

Paul's Epistle to the Ephesians shows us the joy and challenge of being united to Christ in his death and resurrection. It takes us from being seated with Him in the heavenlies (chapter 2), down to the battles we must wage, in His armor, with powers of evil (Eph. 6). In a balanced and judicious manner, longtime Presbyterian elder, Bob Callahan, exercises remarkable insight in opening to believers the vital truths of Ephesians; truths that once taken in, transform the attitude towards life, and often set the soul singing!

As a professor of theology, I have carefully worked through one of his multivolumed series, and found it to be theologically sound: evangelical and scholarly at the same time. It has spiritual depth and is extremely practical; it is accessible in good, clear English. It is neither a commentary, nor a series of sermons. In some ways it reminds me of some of the ancient Patristic engagements with a series of texts of Holy Scripture. It brings the reader into the presence of the Most High, and – if considered thoughtfully and prayerfully, is likely to cause him to sit down under the canopy of God's love.

The journey of Christians in today's world is very demanding indeed, and Bob's work is intended to be a guide to help every pilgrim 'Walking with Jesus.' It will be a rich resource for Sunday Schools, Bible studies, as well as for individual devotions.

Douglas F. Kelly
Reformed Theological Seminary
Charlotte, NC

Acknowledgments

THE CRAFTING OF WALKING With Jesus was not a "one man show" but numerous people working together to present a formidable work. Three guiding lights have been paramount in the minds of those making significant contributions: one, presenting the theology in accord with the tenets of the Reformed Faith; two, employing language that presents the Gospel in a meaningful and understandable light; and, three, expounding upon Scripture in a clear, concise, and forthright manner.

It has been God's blessing that the following ministers and theologians have enthusiastically and willingly provided their time and talents to enhance this work. They are:

- Dr. Frank Barker, Founder and Pastor Emeritus of the Briarwood Presbyterian Church, Birmingham, AL
- Dr. Benjamin W. Farley, Younts Professor Emeritus, Bible, Religion, and Philosophy, Erskine College, Due West, SC
- Dr. James C. Goodloe, IV, Executive Director, Foundation for Reformed Theology, Richmond, VA
- Dr. Todd Jones, Senior Minister, First Presbyterian Church, Nashville, TN
- Dr. Douglas Kelly, Richard Jordan, Professor of Theology, Reformed Theological Seminary, Charlotte, NC
- Dr. Norman McCrummen, Senior Pastor, Spring Hill Presbyterian Church, Mobile, AL
- Dr. Mark Mueller, Senior Pastor, First Presbyterian Church, Huntsville, AL
- Dr. Richard Ray, Former Managing Director of John Knox Press, Montreat, NC

Without the knowledge, wisdom, and encouragement of these individuals this work would neither have become a reality nor available to individuals seeking a better understanding of the teachings of the Scripture and the joy of walking daily with the Lord Jesus.

Several others have labored diligently to create this work, and to produce the finished product. Our daughter, Karen Callahan Myrick, made significant contributions during the drafting process through her knowledge of grammar. Ms. Lynn Sledge, as the copy editor, judiciously reviewed the manuscript and made valuable contributions for improving it. Four ladies, Helen Marshall, D'Anne Dendy, Kelly Comferford, and Elizabeth Annan, worked tirelessly, with dedication, to prepare draft after draft and to make positive contributions to the project. In addition, Wick Skinner's attention to detail provided valuable insight as well as enhancements to the manuscript.

It is not possible to thank them sufficiently for their dedication to making this volume a desirable repository of Christian truths, and in so doing to cheerfully work on draft after draft, to recommend enhancements, and to make appropriate changes in the text. Their unselfish contributions are too many to enumerate. May God bless them.

The Question of Authorship

R‍ECENT SCHOLARS HAVE QUESTIONED the authorship of the letter to the Ephesians and have been less convinced that it was the Apostle Paul. However, for the sake of simplicity of expression we will abide by the traditional view and refer to Paul as its author.

Introduction

THE CREATION OF THIS work was the result of unusual developments which some would attribute to happenstance and others to God's providence. You may be the judge after considering the following.

During May 2000 a friend invited my wife and me to visit the Spring Hill Presbyterian Church in Mobile and hear their new minister, Norman McCrummen. We accepted his invitation.

The following March, Dr. McCrummen was preaching on anything but Ephesians when he interrupted his sermon, paused long enough to slowly scan the congregation twice, and said, "I want everyone to read the first and second chapters of Ephesians by next Sunday" and promptly returned to his sermon. The next day I called him and said, "I can't do it" a few times. Finally, his light went on and he said, "What can't you do?" I said, "I can't read the first and second chapters of Ephesians by next Sunday." He asked, "Why can't you? It will only take ten to fifteen minutes." I responded, "I have fifty-eight to sixty expository messages on the first two chapters of Ephesians that took thirty to thirty-five minutes to present." His response was, "I want to read all those and everything else you have on Ephesians." Thus began the long, arduous, and heart-warming journey of converting handwritten notes along with printed ones into the written word. It has been a joyful, though demanding experience.

Paul's Letter to the Ephesians has been described as "The holiest of the holies." My love affair with it began in the 1980's when I read a book containing great sermons of the twentieth century. The most impressive one was written by Martyn Lloyd-Jones. As a result, I read other works of his including his exposition of Ephesians. Thereafter, unexpectedly, I was asked to teach an adult Bible Study Group. They said they would provide the material, but I demurred and said, "I would gather my own material." This set in motion the process of acquiring knowledge through the best expository works available at the time on Ephesians including Martyn

Lloyd-Jones, William Gurnall, Ruth Paxson, Markus Barth, John Calvin, Otto Weber, and others.

The objective was to present the essence of Paul's letter as it was presented to him by the Lord Jesus and the Holy Spirit. Further, to mine the gold available in the fruitful works of those fertile minds that God had cultivated and enabled to expound upon the truths that His only begotten Son had revealed to His apostles and disciples. Therefore, it was a paramount obligation to express God's truths in a simple, straightforward manner according to the dictates of the Holy Spirit so that the reader may grasp it and interpret it according to the will of our Lord and Saviour Jesus Christ.

The need for the truths of the Gospel is as great today as it was in the first century. The conditions are similar and the challenges facing our culture reveal the need for knowing the living God and His Son. Today, the people of faith require the same spiritual nourishment as those brave souls of the early days after the Resurrection, who would rather face death than deny their Lord and Saviour.

There are people in responsible positions in Christ's church who deny Him by: their passivity; seeking secular acceptance; and failing to honor Him in public. These apostasies negatively impact members of organized Christian churches as well as non-believers.

They create an environment in which unrighteousness flourishes. This results in irreverence as aptly described by R.W. Dale, "Where there is irreverence for the divine law the vision of God becomes fainter; as the vision of God becomes fainter the restraints of the Divine Righteousness are lessened and at last the vision of God is lost altogether." May God enlighten us regarding His infallible Word so that we will hunger and thirst for righteousness, and for the vision of God to shine brighter and brighter as we serve Him with courage, wisdom, justice, and self-control.

This expository commentary is designed to bring individuals, whether they are spiritually children, adolescents or adults into a closer, more mature relationship with the Lord Jesus Christ. It begins with the Triune God; presents the doctrines of the Christian faith; reminds us "that we henceforth be no more children, tossed to and fro . . . but speaking the truth in love, may grow up into Him in all things, . . . even Christ." It continues by emphasizing the importance of being renewed in the spirit of your mind; putting on the new man, which after God is created in righteousness and true holiness; using the whole armor of

God to thwart the manifold attacks of Satan; and concluding with the admonition to conduct ourselves as Christ's ambassadors.

The spiritual food contained ranges from milk and honey to tough meat. The flavor of this exposition encompasses all varieties—sweet, sour, pleasant, bitter, tart, tasteless, dry, burned, and succulent. Do not reject the nourishment because of its texture or flavor, but seek to understand it despite your preferences, since it provides food for good health and strength for joyful living. May God's truths flourish in your heart and mind, and enable you to withstand the tests, trials, and tribulations that come your way as you are "Walking With Jesus."

In presenting this work, I realize everyone has different challenges. The fascinating part of God's Word is that it meets us where we are. The question is, will we meet Him there, hear what He has to say, and accept the nourishment He offers?

The words of William Gurnall are appropriate and enlightening in contemplating God's Word. He said prior to expounding upon Ephesians, "The fare that I shall be serving during the coming weeks will be from God's own table. If perchance it does not go down well or should not have the flavor that you desire, please do not despise the provider of the food, but blame the cook who has prepared it and is serving it." To that I say, Amen!

The courses being served by this cook are described herein. May they provide the taste and nourishment you are seeking.

Robert B. Callahan Sr.

1

The Doctrine of Sin

AND you hath he quickened (made alive), *who were dead in trespasses and sins;*
 Wherein in time past ye walked according to the course (age) of this world, according to the prince of the power of the air, the spirit that now worketh in the children of disobedience:
 Among whom also we all had our conversation (conducted ourselves) *in times past in the lusts of our flesh, fulfilling the desires of the flesh and of the mind; and were by nature the children of wrath, even as others* [Eph.2:1–3].

The Apostle Paul was an amazing individual. He was a master at communicating with others. He loved the Ephesians. He wanted them to know and to love the Triune God, Father, Son, and Holy Spirit. He also wanted them to understand and accept the truths concerning God, the Lord Jesus, and the Holy Spirit. He laid this foundation in the first chapter, which he concluded with a magnificent, meaningful prayer.

Why did he do it this way? Because of the Ephesians' background. They had been pagans, worshipping idols or not anything except themselves. However, they had accepted Christ and were new to the Christian faith. They were infants, or adolescents, young adults in the faith, they were not mature Christians. Paul had received word of their condition and through the power of the Holy Spirit felt compelled to write this epistle. Therefore, before continuing he prayed that the Triune God would give unto them *the spirit of wisdom and revelation in the knowledge of him* (Christ) [Eph. 1:17]. Paul prays they will acquire knowledge of Christ through *the spirit of wisdom and revelation*. He wanted the Triune God to open their hearts and minds to this knowledge. What is this knowledge?

> *That, the eyes of your understanding . . . May know what is the hope of his calling, . . . and the riches of the glory of his inheritance in the saints,*
>
> *And what is the exceeding greatness of his power to us-ward who believe, according to the working of his mighty power,*
>
> *Which he wrought, in Christ, when he raised him from the dead, and set (seated) him at his own right hand in the heavenly places* [Eph. 1:18–20].

Paul wanted the Ephesians to know the full glory of Christ their Redeemer. He wanted them to be knowledgeable about God, Christ, and the Holy Spirit. He knew from experience that their faith had to be nourished and strengthened so they would increase in faith and not succumb to the temptations of the secular world and the wiles of Satan. He loved them, therefore, he shared his faith with them so that they would know the Triune God as he did, and walk with Jesus in gratitude, humility, and joy.

The Apostle Paul learned much during his three years in the wilderness with the Lord Jesus. Yes, he learned the truths of the Gospel, but the pinnacle of his learning was to know, to have a deep personal knowledge and relationship with the Lord Jesus, His Father, and the Holy Spirit. It was this learning, this love, this empathy, this Christ-centeredness that enabled Paul to counsel the Ephesians and others in a loving, respectful, and firm manner.

Consider how he moved from his magnificent, majestic prayer to communicating directly with the Ephesians regarding their former condition, their current situation, and what they should know and do. The remarkable Ruth Paxson sums it up beautifully saying, "A wondrous spiritual panorama now unfolds before us; God's grace and power in operation in the creation of a Christian and in the Constitution of the Church; the Master-Workman at work forming 'the New Man.'"

Paul opens this portion of his letter stating,

> *AND you hath he quickened (made alive) who were dead in trespasses and sins;*
>
> *Wherein in time past ye walked according to the course (age) of this world, according to the prince of power of the air, the spirit that now worketh in the children of disobedience* [Eph. 2:1–2].

Paul reminds them of their past in strong, straightforward words speaking the truth in love. He wants them to remember two things: first, that it was God who had intervened and made them alive, when they were mired in their trespasses and sins; and second, he wanted them to acknowledge what God had done, and is doing that had changed their lives for the better.

You will note in these two verses that Paul uses the words "you" and "ye." He is drawing the distinction that while he was a Jew bringing the gospel of Jesus Christ to them, they were *Gentiles*. *They had . . . walked according to the course* (age) *of this world, according to the prince of the power of the air, the spirit that now worketh in the children of disobedience*. What a thought provoking statement! Paul, through the Holy Spirit wanted them to realize their lives had been controlled by Satan and the criteria of the secular world. This meant that they could do whatever they wanted to do as long as it felt good. They were not subject to any rules, standards, or principles, except their own. Sound familiar today?

Then, Paul, under the influence of the Holy Spirit, changes his tune. He discards the term "ye" and substitutes the all inclusive "we," as he firmly states,

> *Among whom also we all had our conversation* (conducted ourselves) *in times past in the lusts of our flesh, fulfilling the desires of the flesh and of the mind; and were by nature the children of wrath, even as others* [Eph. 2:3].

What a statement by Paul! He had told the *Ephesian* Gentiles unequivocally what they had been, how they had acted, and who they had followed. How would you like to hear these words?

However, Paul through the wisdom bestowed upon him softens the blow by saying "we", "we Jews were no better than you Gentiles—both ethnic groups were sinful," according to the King James Study Bible. The faithful Ruth Paxson provides additional clarity regarding the Jews and Gentiles saying that we "as individuals, are in the same position and condition of sin and death . . . The individual Jew is as great a sinner as the individual Gentile . . . 'By nature' both Gentile and Jew are 'the children of wrath,' both facing the same awful destiny." Paul wanted his beloved Ephesian Gentiles to know that their position and condition before God had been the same. They both faced the same challenges and obstacles.

Paul emphasizes in these verses certain truths that have a negative impact upon the Jews and the Gentiles. What are they?

> *Trespasses and sins; . . . the prince of the power of the air* (Satan), *we all had our conversation* (conducted ourselves) *in times past in the lusts of our flesh . . . and of the mind; and were by nature the children of wrath . . .* [Selections from Eph. 2:1–3].

It was Paul's purpose that the Ephesians (and we) grasp and understand what they were without God and the Lord Jesus. These truths are to be taught, so that people will know what may afflict them and keep them from being in a right relationship with God.

Before proceeding, it is prudent to consider Paul's positive words to Timothy in his second letter to him, which are pertinent at this juncture:

> *But continue thou in the things which thou hast learned and hast been assured of, knowing of whom thou hast learned them . . .*
>
> *And that from a child thou hast known the holy scriptures, which are able to make thee wise into salvation through faith which is in Christ Jesus.*
>
> *All scripture is given by inspiration of God, and is profitable for doctrine, for reproof, for correction, for instruction in righteousness:*
>
> *That the man of God may be perfect, thoroughly furnished* (equipped) *unto all good works.*
>
> *I charge thee therefore before God, and the Lord Jesus Christ, who shall judge the quick* (living) *and the dead at his appearing and his kingdom;*
>
> *Preach the word; be instant* (ready) *in season, out of season; reprove, rebuke, exhort with all long-suffering and doctrine.*
>
> *For the time will come when they will not endure sound doctrine; but after their own lusts shall they heap to themselves teachers, having itching ears;*
>
> *And they shall turn away their ears from the truth, and shall be turned unto fables* [2 Tim. 3:14–4:4].

What a contrast between Paul's words to the Ephesians and Timothy! However, they do have similarities. They are God's Word spoken to those He loves under the influence of the Holy Spirit.

Paul loved Timothy, and he wanted to encourage him. But, more importantly, Paul wanted the people, to whom Timothy was ministering, to hear God's word in all its glory and not be distracted or led astray by false doctrine. This truth cannot be stressed too strongly. God's commands and teachings have been belittled, disparaged, stretched, and twisted since Adam and Eve through Abraham, the prophets, the kings, the Pharisees and scribes, up to and including ministers and teachers today.

The challenge regarding The Triune God, and the Word of God is the same now as it has been, and that is to stand firm on the truths revealed in Scripture. There is not to be any compromise with half-truths, the secular culture, and those who ignore or reject the living God. The Word must be proclaimed in all its fullness and glory, and allow the Holy Spirit to interpret it properly in the hearts and minds of the hearers.

Paul tells Timothy that *all scripture is given by inspiration of God, and profitable for doctrine, for reproof, for correction, for instruction in righteousness: . . .* Paul states unequivocally that *all scripture,* not just parts, nor the ones we like or reject, but *all scripture* is inspired by God. Those who preach and teach the gospel of Christ Jesus must accept this truth and abide by it. John Calvin amplifies upon this when he states, "that we owe to the scripture the same reverence as we owe to God, since it has its only source in Him and has nothing of human origin mixed with it."

For what is Scripture profitable? Paul, through the wisdom God bestowed upon him, tells Timothy that Scripture is profitable to those who hear, read, study, and proclaim the Word under the influence of the Holy Spirit. He also tells them how it is to be used and why. It is to be used for declaring the tenets of the Christian faith, for exposing misinterpretations and misrepresentations; and for telling believers and non-believers how to correct the errors of their ways. Finally, Paul wants the people instructed in righteousness as it is portrayed in Scripture, which leads to living "a godly and holy life" as described by John Calvin. This is the purpose of God's Scripture, to bring us into a right relationship with Himself.

Why did Paul say these things in an authoritative manner? The answer is simple, yet profound, some may shrug it off and say what does it matter? Others will grasp it and thank God for His grace, mercy, and love. Paul's reason for counseling Timothy regarding the importance of Scripture in one's life is that they may become perfect and *thoroughly furnished (equipped) unto all good works.* God wants each of us to know Him, His Son, and the Holy Spirit to the fullest. When we do, we will know Him, serve the Lord Jesus, and listen to the Holy Spirit.

Paul firmly instructs Timothy, as well as ministers and teachers ever since, regarding their responsibilities in presenting and proclaiming God's Word. It is an awesome responsibility.

Paul declares forthrightly that all preaching and teaching is *in the sight of God, and of Jesus Christ*. Those who preach and teach should always bear this in mind, since *all scripture is given by inspiration of God*. John Calvin focuses attention on this command stating, "When Paul speaks of the usefulness of scripture, he concludes not only that everyone should read it, but that teachers (ministers) ought to administer it, which is the duty laid upon them." What if they do not perform their duty? Paul is explicit in answering this question saying *God, and the Lord Jesus Christ, who shall judge the quick* (living) *and the dead at his appearing and his kingdom*. Those are strong words for those entrusted with proclaiming the infallible Word.

The Apostle Paul through his God-given wisdom adds a nugget of wisdom, which is as true today as it was when he wrote the letter. He tells Timothy that those hearers of the preaching and teaching *will not endure sound doctrine; but after their own lusts shall heap to themselves teachers* (ministers), *having itching ears*. The *itching ears* describe the people who do not like to hear pure doctrine. They want to hear what they want to hear. They do not want to hear about godliness. "From this we may learn, first, that the more determined men became to despise the teaching of Christ, the more zealous should godly ministers be to assert it and the more strenuous their efforts to preserve it entire, and more than that, by their diligence to ward off Satan's attacks," as forcefully stated by John Calvin.

Paul completes this warning saying the hearers *shall turn away their ears from the truth, and shall be turned into fables*. This is true today. There are people who do not want to hear doctrine proclaimed. They prefer to be entertained. Conversely, there are ministers and teachers who will curry the favor of people with *itching ears*, and not proclaim the full gospel. Several years ago we had an interim minister who began his engagement preaching the Word. Then, he began inserting a little humor, followed by more humor, but little or no doctrine. Finally, the change was discussed with him and the suggestion made that he go back to the truths of the Gospel, since there were members who want to be nourished by God's Word. He responded saying, "The people enjoy being entertained and I intend to keep doing so." Oh, the wiles of Satan.

Thank God for Paul who has appropriately described the hearers, ministers, and teachers regarding the impact of *itching ears*.

The Apostle in these two letters has beautifully described the condition in which individuals find themselves before being redeemed and afterwards. It is important to know not only the truths of Scripture, but to know the challenges we face as we mature in the Christian faith and walk daily with the Lord Jesus.

Further, they do not like the idea of substitution or the doctrine of penal suffering. They cannot bring themselves to start with man in sin. What we are discussing are the great truths of the Christian faith, and we cannot really understand them apart from man in sin. That is you and me!

There is something even more astounding. You cannot understand real life in this real world apart from the Doctrine of Sin. Paul understood it. Is there any wonder Paul praises God and keeps talking about the Lord Jesus Christ? What I am saying applies to people in business, politics, service, as well as ministers and teachers proclaiming the Gospel.

We cannot understand human history, problems, or calamities apart from the Doctrine of Sin. When considering history, we should examine it in the light of man in sin and in a fallen state.

It may sound like an oversimplification, but there are basically two explanations offered as to why man is as he is, why the world is in its current condition, and why it always has been

- the biblical teaching; and
- non-biblical teaching.

The popular teaching in the twentieth century was that things are like they are because man has not had time to develop, to evolve, and to advance to perfection. He just needs more time. Further, the basic problem with people and man in general is time. If man has the time he can acquire knowledge, he can grow, and he can become perfect. He is capable all by himself. That is a non-biblical teaching. Unfortunately, people believe it, and accept it as a biblical truth.

What is the biblical point of view? First, it is realistic. People today talk about hearing the facts, speaking straight from the shoulder, but there are some things they do not want to hear. They prefer to hear how good man is, how he needs a chance and an opportunity.

The Bible, on the other hand, says man is foolish, that people bring problems upon themselves, and that they are *the children of disobedience*. It says that man must face his condition, his shortcomings, and his needs. There is no hope until he does. The Bible presents this truth and calls upon us to face it. Other approaches appeal to our egos. They tell us how good we are and that all we need is time for the potential to be released.

Second, the Bible gets to the heart of the matter. It keeps probing. It dissects and dissects until it gets to the core. However, man's faith needs to be nourished and strengthened daily or he will yield to the secular world's ideas, philosophies, and rationalizations. Why? Because people do not like to face things which are unpleasant or require changes according to God's commands and Christ's teachings. Therefore, they say that the biblical teaching about man is radical whereas, in truth, God's Word opens the door to joyful living in the world and a right relationship with the Triune God.

Third, the biblical teaching is both more pessimistic and more optimistic than the other points of view. Man has been striving forever to reach utopia and to do it on his own. That is an utterly futile striving.

What is the optimistic point of view? The one that tells us that man is in sin, that the power of God can raise him out of it, and that it is accomplished only through the Lord Jesus Christ.

What do these thoughts have to do with us? What is the Apostle Paul saying in these initial three verses of the second chapter? He is describing the condition of man in sin, the results of it, and what God thinks of it. It is all there.

What is man's condition in sin? *And you hath he quickened* (made alive), *who were dead in trespasses and sins*. Do you notice something about this verse? The words *hath he quickened* are in italics in the Bible text which means the translators have added them to help us better understand this verse. Paul is saying you were dead *on account of* or *because of* sins, not that you are dead *in* trespasses and sins.

Paul is talking about being dead spiritually, not physically, because he continues by saying, *Wherein . . . ye walked according to . . .* (and) *among whom also we all had our conversation* (conducted ourselves) *in times past*. Paul is saying life for the non-Christian is a living death. You cannot be much more emphatic than saying *death* or a person is *dead*.

What does this mean? Probably the best way to describe it is to say that the exact opposite and antithesis of life is death. How does the Bible describe life? It always defines it in terms of our relationship to God. Consider: *And this is eternal life that they might know thee, the only true God, and Jesus Christ whom thou hast sent* [John 17:3]. That is life! The opposite of that is death.

God is the author of life, the source of life, the sustainer of life, and the giver of life.

What is life like as God would have us to live it? It is to know God, to enjoy God, to communicate with God, to share with God, and to be blessed by God. Death is the opposite of all that.

A person is dead who is not in a living relationship with God. Paul says to the Ephesians (and to us), you were dead because you did not know God, His promises, or His commandments.

> *That at that time ye were without Christ, being aliens from the commonwealth of Israel, and strangers from the covenants of promise, and having no hope, and without God in the world* [Eph. 2:12].

You were estranged from God. You were not in fellowship with Him.

A person in that condition is ignorant of spiritual things and of the spiritual life. That is the result of man in sin. Paul says to the Romans, *For they that are after the flesh do mind* (set their minds to) *the things of the flesh; but they that are after the Spirit the things of the Spirit* [Rom. 8:5].

This means that those who are interested in the things of the flesh are not Christians and are not interested in the things of the Spirit. They find them boring; they do not enjoy them; and they do not pursue them. Why? Because they are dead spiritually and have no spiritual life.

The person of the flesh, or world, does not like, even hates, the teachings of Scripture. Why? Because he believes they are boring and that Scripture condemns him. He likes to have a religion he can define and control. Further, he is satisfied when he can establish the time frames and parameters.

Note what Paul said to the Romans,

> *For to be carnally minded is death; but to be spiritually minded is life and peace.*
> *Because the carnal mind is enmity against God: for it is not subject to the law of God, neither indeed can (it) be.*
> *So then they that are in the flesh cannot please God*
> [Rom. 8:6–8].

This type person (the one of the flesh) is not like God and does not share God's life. To use the biblical term, he is corrupt.

The ones who are corrupt are outside God and His life. They delight in evil things because their nature is evil. Righteousness is not in them; truth is not in them. They believe lies and enjoy them and follow that way. They are in sin and spiritually dead.

The natural consequence of such a life is not being blessed by God and results in misery. They are always looking, doing, chasing, seeking after something. They get tired of things and pursue changes. Why? Because they do not enjoy spending a few hours with themselves. It is intolerable. So they spend their lives running from themselves. They do not have the resources, reserves, or foundation. Why? Because they are outside the life of God. Paul also says to the Romans, *Likewise reckon* (consider) *ye also yourselves to be dead indeed unto sin, but alive unto God through* (in) *Jesus Christ our Lord* [Rom. 6:11]. Can you see that this is the way to measure salvation?

When you receive the gift of salvation, you become alive unto God and to the things of God, the commands of God, fellowship with God, and communicating with God.

Certainly, we should pray for God to bless us and strengthen us in all these matters. Just as importantly, we should pray for those who are dead in sin and outside a life with God.

What does Paul present next?

> *Ye walked according to the course* (age) *of this world,* . . .
> or as the original says . . . *according to the age of this world.*

He means that a person's life is controlled by the world, its outlook, ideas, and philosophy. "Paul was reminding his readers of what they were before the grace of God touched their hearts," as amplified upon by Rick Renner. He continues saying that "because Paul uses the (Greek) word *kosmos*, he paints a picture of people who have no standard like God's word by which to live; therefore, they are guided by the constantly changing ethics and whims of the times. Sadly, education, entertainment, and fashion are the forces that guide the lost world."

According to the Bible, the *world* is always against God. Consider the word *world* for a moment and how it is used in a biblical sense.

It does not mean what God has provided, such as the mountains, rivers, beaches, and oceans out of his grace, love, and abundance. Basically, it means man trying to establish himself as the creator, controller, and organizer of life. Paul says, *And be not conformed to this world: but be ye transformed by the renewing of your mind, that ye may prove what is that good, and acceptable, and perfect, will of God* [Rom. 12:2]. The Apostle John says,

> Love not the world, neither the things that are in the world. If any man love the world, the love of the Father is not in him.
> For all that is in the world, the lust of the flesh, and the lust of the eyes, and the pride of life, is not of the Father, but is of the world.
> And the world passeth away, and the lust thereof: but he that doeth the will of God abideth for ever [1 John 2:15–17].

Paul says it and John supports it. *Be not conformed to this world.* Love not the world. Lust not. That is the world; it is opposed to God. The Apostle John says the person who is not a follower, a Christian, is a person who is simply governed and controlled by the world and its lusts, since he or she is self-centered, not Christ-centered.

You see it in designs, fashions, peer pressure, travel, and entertainment. Wherever you look it is *conform, conform, and conform*. It also infects the denominations and churches.

People talk about their freedom and emancipation. But in an environment of conformity, we see people doing things and wonder why, until we realize that man is in sin. He is spiritually dead. He is controlled by the mind of the world, and wants to conform to it.

The Apostle continues by saying that the person in the world is controlled by the evil that is in life. In the second verse he says, *Ye walked according . . . to the prince of the power of the air, the spirit that now worketh in the children of disobedience*. Paul says an evil principle is working. Working is a strong active word; it is not passive or inactive. We must realize that there is working in this world a powerful, evil principle.

Do you imagine that all you see and hear about just comes to pass, that it just happens? Do you not see how organized it is, how uniform it is, how subtle it is?

There was a philosopher in England who lived prior to, during, and for a while after World War II. He had been an atheist. However, he came to believe in the reality of God. Why? Because he became convinced that the Second World War occurred due to the principle of evil at work in the world and that the Bible was right about this fact. He could not explain the war except that there was a devilish, evil power at work, *the spirit that now worketh in the children of disobedience.*

We Christians need to recognize that so many people in the world are dominated and controlled by the evil spirit. The Apostle says that evil is governed by the devil and all his powers.

Some people say in various tones, "Do you mean you believe in the devil and his powers?" People are the way they are, and the world is as it is, because of their listening and responding to the devil. The devil is so powerful that he is able to persuade people that he is not dominating them, guiding them, or leading them. Jesus called him the prince of this world:

- he was an angel created by God,
- he rebelled against God,
- he hates God,
- he wants to ruin God's world,
- he beguiled Eve and Adam, and
- he dominates the life of man.

Paul says, *For we wrestle not against flesh and blood, but against principalities, against powers, against the rulers of the darkness of this world, against spiritual wickedness in high places* [Eph. 6:12]. Unfortunately, people are prone to think it is personalities or individuals, that it is a Hitler or Stalin or whomever. However, it is the prince of this world, Satan.

The Bible tells us that there are unseen powers and the devil is the prince of the power of the air. They are not earthly powers; they are spiritual, they are ethereal, and they have no bodies.

Because man cannot see them, he does not believe in them. He cannot see God, and he cannot see the Holy Ghost. Therefore, he does not believe in them. Since he does not have spiritual understanding, he does not believe.

What about those of us who are Christians or profess to be? We have to wrestle. We are not to seek, or think we will have, a life of ease. We cannot think that we will never have to struggle and will be completely free from strife. Not in this world!

We are confronted by the same one who did not hesitate to tempt the Son of God. He is the same one who continually defeated the patriarchs and saints of the Old Testament. He is the one who is opposed to us with all his might, strength, force, and power.

How can we stand against this powerful, evil one? By . . . *the exceeding greatness of his power to us-ward who believe* [Eph. 1:19]. The God who saves us is the God who keeps us. May our eyes of understanding be enlightened.

Remember, *you hath he quickened* (made alive), *who were dead in trespasses and sins.*

May we give the glory to Him.

Amen!

2

Death by Sin

AND you hath he quickened (made alive), who were dead in trespasses and sins;

Wherein in time past ye walked according to the course of this world (age), according to the prince of the power of the air (Satan), the spirit that now worketh in the children of disobedience:

Among whom also we all had our conversation (conducted ourselves) *in times past in the lusts of our flesh, fulfilling the desires of the flesh and of the mind; and were by nature the children of wrath, even as others* [Eph. 2:1–3].

Paul's choice of words at the beginning of the second chapter is in sharp contrast to his writings about the Triune God and the beautiful phraseology in his heartfelt prayer. Why the sudden change? He warns the Ephesians (and us) to fully understand their relationship to the Father, Son, and the Holy Spirit. Paul knew full well his condition prior to walking down the road to Damascus. He could relate to the Ephesians, their plight before accepting Christ and being baptized. He had received reports about their current condition and knew they had questions about life in general and their relationship to God and the Lord Jesus.

Therefore, Paul basically says to them and to others "Wake up, God the Father has made you alive and do not forget it." To make sure they will not forget this truth he continues saying you *were dead in trespasses and sins*. Note, he did not say you had made some mistakes, or you did not know better because you had been deprived. He continues his discourse saying, *ye walked according to the course of this* (secular) *world* (age), *according to the prince* (Satan) *of the power of the air, the spirit that now worketh in the children of disobedience.* How would you like to hear these words from the pulpit, or receive them from a friendly minister or teacher in a letter? Paul had the knack of getting one's attention and remembering his words. He did not shy from telling the truth.

What can we deduce from Paul's statements? The Christians of the First Century, as well as those of this century, had lived according to the customs, teachings, culture, philosophies, values, and life styles of the secular world. When the Ephesians accepted Christ during Paul's three year ministry to them, they changed their conduct, life style, and values according to Christ's commands and teachings. They were walking in the Spirit. Paul reminds them of this. He does not want them controlled by the secular world, Satan, and the *spirit that now worketh in the children of disobedience.*

What does Paul want for the Ephesians, you and me? He wants us controlled by the loving Father, Son, and Holy Spirit. He knows for this to happen that we must have knowledge as well as faith. He realizes that we must know what and who has controlled us, and what and who should control us.

It is clear from this letter that the Apostle wants to share information with Christ's disciples, and he wants each and every one of them to increase in knowledge, understanding, and wisdom. Therefore, it is important for the true believers in Christ to grasp the different doctrines of the Christian faith. This enables them to mature in the faith, and as the apostles know faith and knowledge are intertwined and support each other. If the Christian does not nourish his or her faith or knowledge then one or the other will atrophy and they will return to the ways of the secular world or live *according to the prince of the power of the air*, Satan.

It is evident at this juncture, that Paul has been describing what keeps individuals from having a positive relation with the Father, Son, and Holy Ghost. It is the practices of the secular world, the influence of Satan, and the evil spirit working in *the children of disobedience*, all of which add up to that little three letter word, sin, that is in man from birth. It is hard for some people to accept this truth, especially when they think of the beautiful, precious babies that come into this world.

The renowned reformed theologian, Otto Weber, puts things in perspective when he says, "[S]ince Augustine, the church's doctrine of sin has had at its center the concept of 'original sin' or 'inherited sin'. . . ." [T]he doctrine of 'original sin' goes further in that, first, it seeks the sinful existence as such from our area of decision, . . . declaring, thirdly, that our sinfulness is a condition of man, or of mankind, in an absolute sense. If we understand sin basically as the rebellion against God's goodness and the distortion of the relationship between the Creator and creature, then the doctrine of 'original sin' can only be properly understood when it is seen, not as a given alone, but in terms of that relationship." What a magnificent statement! It helps us to better understand Paul's admonition to the Ephesians and his counsel to Timothy.

Paul, in his letter to the Romans, expounds upon the Doctrine of Original Sin, declaring:

> *Wherefore, as by one man sin entered into the world, and death by sin; and so death passed upon all men, for that all have sinned:*
> *(For until the law sin was in the world: but sin is not imputed when there is no law.*
> *Nevertheless death reigned from Adam to Moses, even over them that had not sinned after the similitude* (likeness) *of Adam's transgression, who is the figure* (a type) *of him that was to come* [Rom. 5:12–14].

Paul affirmed that sin was in the world from the time of Adam and Eve. They were disobedient. They changed the relationship with their Creator. The Apostle says, by one man sin entered into the world, and death by sin; and so death passed upon all men, for all have sinned. This is a profound and all encompassing statement. It was through the act of one man that sin entered into the world and into all mankind. The result of that monumental act was death and all men being infected by that mortal disease, sin. The renowned John Calvin amplifies upon this saying, "to sin, as the word is used here, is to be corrupt and vitiated. The natural depravity which we bring from our mother's womb, although it does not produce its fruits immediately, is still sin before God, and deserves His punishment. This is what is called original sin. As Adam . . . by falling from the Lord, in himself he corrupted, vitiated, depraved and ruined our nature—having lost the image of God, the only seed which he could have produced was that which bore resemblance to him. We have, therefore, all sinned, because we are all imbued with natural corruption, and for this are wicked and perverse."

These are strong words by Calvin, but they provide clarity and understanding which are in accord with the direct statements of Paul. However, this scriptural truth is difficult for some professing Christians to accept, whether babes in the faith or mature in Christ. It falls unto the category of tough meat.

However, the acceptance of this teaching and remaining steadfast in it, will enable each of us to better understand our relationship to God, our Father, and our Lord Jesus Christ as well as the conditions in which we live, and exist throughout the world. A prime example is contained in Paul's letter to the Galatians regarding walking in the Spirit:

> *This I say then, Walk in the Spirit, and ye shall not fulfill the lust of the flesh.*
>
> *For the flesh lusteth against the Spirit and the Spirit against the flesh: and these are contrary the one to the other: so that ye cannot do the things that ye would.*
>
> *But if ye be led of the Spirit, ye are not under the law.*
>
> *Now the works of the flesh are manifest (evident), which are these; adultery, fornication, uncleanness, lasciviousness (licentiousness),*
>
> *Idolatry, witchcraft (sorcery), hatred, variance (contentions), emulations (jealousies), wrath, strife (selfish ambitions), seditions (dissensions), heresies,*
>
> *Envyings, murders, drunkenness, revellings, and such like: of the which I tell you before, as I have also told you in time past, that they which do such things shall not inherit the Kingdom of God.*
>
> *But the fruit of the Spirit is love, joy, peace, long-suffering, gentleness (kindness), goodness, faith (faithfulness),*
>
> *Meekness, temperance (self-control): against such there is no law.*
>
> *And they that are Christ's have crucified the flesh with the affections (passions) and lusts.*
>
> *If we live in the Spirit, let us also walk in the Spirit*
> [Gal. 5:16–25].

Yes, we have *the prince of the power of the air* (Satan) with whom we must contend as mankind has had to do since Adam disobeyed God and committed the original sin. This condition has caused wrack and ruin, and wreaked havoc on mankind since the beginning. Paul wants us to understand this and bear it in mind as we proceed through this "holiest of holies" letter to the Ephesians and equip ourselves *to walk in the Spirit*.

The eminent Otto Weber provides additional insight into original sin stating, "sin is certainly here not merely an act, but above all a power and as such (is) prior to the sinful act. When one compares the other passages in the Bible, especially in the New Testament, it is difficult to conclude that Romans 5:12 says something absolutely unique, when it states, *Wherefore, as by one man sin entered into the world, and death by sin; and so death passed upon all men, for that all have sinned.* This also cannot be said of Psalm 51:5 (*Behold, I was shapen* (brought forth) *in iniquity; and in sin did my mother conceive me.*), the second classical passage for the doctrine of inherited sin. The composer of the Psalm (David) had come, in the depth of his repentance, to the recognition of his original existence as a sinner in his sinful activity, and that leads him automatically back to his individual origin; as John 3:6 (Jesus) expresses it, "*That which is born of the flesh is flesh.*" But there is no negative designation here of conception and birth, but the recognition of sin as personal sin."

There are two things to note from Weber's statement that should be taken to heart, because they are so true and deserve our contemplation. First, he declares, through the revelation of the Holy Spirit, that "sin is certainly, . . . not merely an act, but above all a power." How often do we think of it that way? We are prone to think of it as a temptation, or a lust, or the impact of societal conditions. Why did the Lord Jesus say, "*Get thee behind me, Satan*"? Christ knew the power of Satan and his devious, deceitful, subtle ways, and how he would prey upon His followers. The only One with the power to route Satan and defeat him is the Lord Jesus. Therefore, we are to take our refuge in Him as we encounter the wiles of Satan on our daily *walk in the Spirit.*

Second, we are to focus our attention on Weber's closing words, "the recognition of sin as personal sin." These are simple, but powerful words. It is like they come straight from Scripture. It can be stated unequivocally that they are based on Scripture, the Doctrine of Original Sin, and the personal responsibility of each professing Christian. Sin is personal. It affects each of us. We have to deal with it personally. We cannot foist it off on another. That is why we are to: increase in knowledge and faith; grow in our relationship with the Lord Jesus Christ; and clothe ourselves in His righteousness. It is a personal matter.

Since it is a personal matter, what are the available choices? The Apostle describes them saying, there are those who God quickens, makes alive, and those who walk *according to the prince of the power of the air, the spirit that worketh in the children of disobedience.* They are the ones who reject God and do not want to know Him. They are hostile to the Lord Jesus Christ, His teachings, and the shedding of His blood for them. They are self satisfied, impressed with their own growth and achievements. They believe their knowledge surpasses the wisdom of God, if there is a God. They do not believe they have sinned against God or their neighbor. They do not realize they are the children of disobedience and subject to the wrath of God, because they are self-righteous in their own minds. This is the state of those who have not been redeemed and remain under the control of *the prince of power of the air*.

That remarkable servant of God, Ruth Paxson, sums it up in a meaningful way saying, "So we see that the sinner is wholly out of adjustment with God. If he is set right, it must be with God. If he is set right, it must be with God first. But in (verses) 2:1–3 (of Ephesians) there is not one ray of light or one gleam of hope. Unless God intervenes and takes the initiative, the sinner will forever remain in his sins." That is not a pleasant thought, but a truthful one.

Amen!

3

Trespasses and Sins

AND *you hath he quickened (made alive) who were dead in trespasses and sins;*

Wherein in time past ye walked according to the course (age) of this world, according to the prince of the power of the air, the spirit that now worketh in the children of disobedience:

Among whom also we all had our conversation (conducted ourselves) in times past in the lusts of our flesh, fulfilling the desires of the flesh and of the mind; and were by nature the children of wrath, even as others [Eph. 2:1–3].

Paul writing to the Ephesians wishes to enlighten them regarding the foundational truths of what we now call the Reformed Faith in Christ Jesus. He brings into focus what has been revealed to him by the Lord Jesus, since that dramatic encounter on the road to Damascus. Not only that, he wants to share the memories of his life as a Pharisee, then being forgiven by the Lord Jesus for his trespasses and sins as well as his lusts of the flesh and the mind.

In addition, there is another factor of equal importance—the people to whom he is writing. He knew the people to whom he is writing. He knew the people in Ephesus, he knew their likes and their dislikes. He knew how they conducted themselves before accepting Christ and afterwards. He visited in their homes. Therefore, he knew them intimately, respected them, and had empathy for them. Undoubtedly, he loved them, had great affection for them, and cherished the memories of his three years in Ephesus.

There are two questions to consider: (i) whose homes did he visit? And, (ii) what did they discuss? Apparently, he visited in the homes of all types of people, whether they be merchants, workers, shopkeepers, traders, financiers, farmers, laborers, nurses, or medical practitioners. They had their anxieties, challenges, fears, heartbreaks, illnesses, problems, shortcomings, trials and tribulations. Does any of this sound familiar? They were people like we are today with similar concerns and objectives, and the desire to live joyful lives. They welcomed Paul gladly and the Word he brought them thankfully. May we do the same.

Paul discussed with the Ephesians the facts of his life from studying under Gamaliel, to consenting to Stephen's death by stoning, to life as a Pharisee, to persecuting Christ's church, and to the life changing event on his way to persecute the early believers in Damascus. The Apostle kept nothing back. He knew the best was yet to come.

Paul had a storehouse of information relating to the Lord Jesus Christ, His ministry, His teachings, His relationship with the other apostles, His interaction with other people, His sufferings, His betrayal, and His resurrection. He had a close relationship with his Redeemer, whom he loved, obeyed, and served. He knew that this had happened by the grace of God, who had mercy upon him, called him when he was dead in his trespasses and sins, and cleansed him from the pollution that previously had permeated his mind and body. Paul's mind and heart were filled with gratitude, humility, and joy while in Ephesus and when writing to them. Therefore, he wanted to share the Gospel with them, he wanted them to mature in Christ, and to increase in their faith.

The Apostle knew if the Ephesians increased in faith, that they would trust Christ more fully as they proceeded through life with its uncertainties, unknown pathways, blurred vision, as well as regrettable associations, deeds, and words. Paul wanted the Ephesians, his friends and former associates, to focus on Christ, what He had done for them and what He will do for those who accept Him as their Redeemer and constant companion.

Paul's background, experiences, knowledge, love, and faith enabled him to write to the Ephesians as he did. The truths he enumerated are as true today as they were then. These attributes also enabled Paul to write to the Romans these memorable words:

> THEREFORE being justified by faith, let us have peace with God through our Lord Jesus Christ:
>
> By whom also we have access by faith into this grace wherein we stand, and rejoice in hope of the glory of God.
>
> And not only so, but we glory in tribulations also: knowing that tribulation worketh (produces perseverance) patience;

> *And patience, experience (character), hope:*
> *And hope maketh not ashamed (does not disappoint); because the love of God is shed abroad (has been poured out) in our hearts by the Holy Ghost which is given unto us.*
> *For when we were yet without strength, in due time (at the right time) Christ died for the ungodly.*
> *For scarcely for a righteous man will one die: yet peradventure (perhaps) for a good man some would even dare to die.*
> *But God commendeth* (demonstrates) *toward us, in that, while we were yet sinners, Christ died for us* [Rom. 5:1–8].

These are powerful, revealing words. They are tremendously important to the Reformed Faith. It was the words *being justified by faith* that penetrated Luther's heart, mind, and understanding. He drafted his ninety-five theses and tacked them on the door in Wittenberg. We have been justified by faith according to God's will, love, mercy, and grace upon grace. All our sins and transgressions against Almighty God are cast on the fires of forgiveness, burned and scattered by the four winds until there is no remembrance of them.

The *peace with God* "is not a feeling but a standing. God and the believer are no longer at enmity but have been reconciled. This is a primary result of our justification," as described by the King James Study Bible. Men and women since the First Century have had trouble with *being justified by faith*. They want to do something to earn it. But they cannot. They can respond in faith, but that seems so simple. It does not require giving, but it does require receiving, giving thanks, and asking what can I do? That seems to be the difficult part, since it requires being subservient, acquiring knowledge, obeying commands, and denying oneself.

Paul also describes the fact that we are to *glory in tribulations* due to the benefits they provide. This is also true of the Ephesians and believers today. The Apostle turns a negative into a positive by citing the beneficial traits produced in a person during periods of tribulation: perseverance, character, and hope. The eminent John Calvin provides additional insight saying, "We are stimulated to patience by tribulation, and patience is a proof to us of divine help. This further encourages us to hope, for however we may be beset and seem to be worn out, we do not cease to feel the divine kindness towards us . . . . All things must serve the will of the Creator, who, according to his fatherly favour towards us, overrules all the trials of the Cross for our salvation. This knowledge of the divine love towards us is instilled into our hearts by the Spirit of God, for the good things which God has prepared for those who worship Him are hidden from the ears, eyes and minds of men, and the Spirit alone can reveal them."

There are some truths in Scripture that we read or hear, and then proceed merrily on our way without giving them further consideration. First, there is the phrase, . . . *in due season Christ died for the ungodly.* What a penetrating thought! Of whom do we think when reading these words? Other people? No one I know? Myself? When contemplating Scripture we realize we are all sinners and need God's forgiveness. We are all guilty of disobeying God and not fully abiding by His commands. It is difficult to accept the fact that Christ went to the Cross voluntarily to atone for your sins and mine. Ponder the fact that He suffered a vicarious death for you and me individually. Some will say He died for our benefit. Yes, that is true. But more to the point He was crucified for the sins of each one of us. Calvin further enlightens us saying, "If Christ had mercy on the ungodly, if He reconciled His enemies to the Father, and accomplished this by virtue of His death, He will now much more easily save them when they are justified, and keep in His grace those whom He has restored to grace, especially since the efficacy of His life is now added to His death. . . . We are all born the children of wrath, and are kept under that curse until we become partakers of Christ. . . . When we were completely unworthy and unfit to be regarded by God, at that very time Christ died for the ungodly."

Second, there are Paul's comforting words, *But God commendeth his* (demonstrates his own) *love towards us, in that, while we were yet sinners, Christ died for us* [Rom. 5:8]. The Apostle Paul cannot forget his own past, nor that of those to whom he was writing, regarding being disobedient to the will of God, before they accepted Christ and became His followers. They had all been sinners in need of God's grace, mercy, and love. It is important for each of us to realize that we, like the Romans and Ephesians, have not always been partakers in Christ, but sinners in His sight and thankful for His love in enabling us to walk with Him, increase in faith and knowledge, and obey His commands and teachings.

According to John Calvin, the Apostle Paul states that God in demonstrating His own love toward us "(i) it is not the Apostle's object to arouse us to give thanks, but to establish the confidence and security of our souls. God, therefore, *confirms,* i.e. declares His love toward us to be most certain and true, because He did not spare Christ His Son for the sake of the ungodly. Herein is His love manifested, that without being influenced by any love of ours, He first loved us of His own good pleasure.... The sum of the whole is that if Christ has attained righteousness for sinners by His death, He will now much more protect them from destruction when they are justified.... It would not have been enough for Christ to have once procured salvation for us, were He not to maintain it safe and secure to the end. This is what the Apostle now asserts, declaring that we have no need to fear that Christ will terminate the bestowal of His grace upon us before we have come to our appointed end."

Yes, we have been sinners, just as the ones Paul was writing to in Ephesus and Rome before we and they were redeemed and became partakers in Christ. Paul succinctly states at the beginning of the second chapter, *And you hath he quickened* (made alive) *who were dead in trespasses and sins.* Why did Paul remind them of this? Because they were children in the faith. Why do preachers and teachers need to propound the Gospel of Jesus Christ? To enlighten the hearts and minds of the hearers and to increase their faith. They also proclaim the Word in order to enlighten their own hearts and minds as well as to increase in knowledge and faith. We all need to reflect back on those things in our lives, whether they were words, deeds, or lusts that were in disobedience to God's commands and will, that contributed to our being *dead in trespasses and sins.* This is a valuable lesson to learn.

While considering these words *trespasses* and *sins* and the meaning behind them, it may be helpful to examine sin in more detail, especially according to the New Testament.

The Synoptic Gospels have few direct references to sin. However, the writers describe Christ's work in relation to sin. Consider the following examples: John the Baptist heralds the forgiveness of sins; Jesus calls people to *repent*; forgiving and healing the paralytic; parables explaining Jesus rescuing and finding the lost; and the repentance and the remission of sins preached by Jesus and the apostles.

The people of the land ('Am ha 'arets') were sinners not because they transgressed the law, but because they did not conform to the Pharisaic interpretation of it.

Practically everyone fell into this classification. Is it any wonder *sinners* were seen in the company of Jesus?

The heathen were the Roman soldiers and the Gentiles.

There were those who were separated from God consciously or subconsciously. Usually this category was a self-designation. Jesus did not reject or suppress the distinction between the righteous and the sinner. It is interesting to note that the sinners did not expect to be drawn to Jesus, but because they needed Him, Jesus drew them to Himself.

It is important to grasp the fact that Jesus did not call us to self-contempt and condemnation, but rather that He wanted us to know the whole reality of God. Further, there is no confession of particular sins, but Jesus was aware of them, knew they were offenses, and treated them very seriously. Jesus said,

> *That which cometh out of the man, that defileth the man.*
> *For from within, out of the heart of men, proceed evil thoughts, adulteries, fornications, murders,*
> *Thefts, covetousness, wickedness, deceit, lasciviousness (licentiousness), an evil eye, blasphemy, pride, foolishness:*
> *All these evil things come from within, and defile the man* [Mark 7:20–23].

It may have been that Jesus spoke of specific acts of sin to the disciples. However, He spoke of the state of sin because He realized the hearers needed God. He did not count their self-righteousness as sin, but condemned it for its self-centeredness, confidence, arrogance, and lack of compassion. Jesus turned upside down the idea that sinners are a separated people. He made people realize that everyone is a sinner. He said to the multitude, *Even so ye also outwardly appear righteous unto men, but within ye are full of hypocrisy and iniquity* (lawlessness) [Matt. 23:28].

In Romans, Paul says, *All have sinned, and come* (fall) *short of the glory of God* [Rom. 3:23]. Sin is the condition in which men lack being in the image of God. This condition is universal. Paul says, *As it is written, THERE IS NONE RIGHTEOUS, NO, NOT ONE* [Rom. 3:10].

Satan is that external power which continuously attacks us. Sin is an internal infection we bear as human beings. As a result, a person experiences conflict between his desires and the power that possesses him.

The law of life and *the law of sin and death* are two laws in conflict with one another. Paul explains the law of life and the law of sin as follows: *So then with the mind I myself serve the law of God; but with the flesh the law of sin* [Rom. 7:25]. *For the law of the Spirit of life in Christ Jesus hath made me free from the law of sin and death* [Rom. 8:2]. That is a wonderful, meaningful description!

Death is a comprehensive term for the physical and spiritual results of sin's dominion. Paul rightly states, *For the wages of sin is death; but the gift of God is eternal life through* (in) *Jesus Christ our Lord. For when we were in the flesh, the motions* (passions) *of sins, which were* (aroused) *by the law, did work in our members to bring forth fruit unto death* [Rom. 6:23, 7:5]. To these revealing statements, Paul adds these memorable words to the Corinthians, *O death, where is thy sting? O grave, where is thy victory? The sting of death is sin; and the strength of sin is the law* [1 Cor. 15:55–56].

This condition shows itself in two ways: sin and death entered the world through Adam's Fall. It entered both as an historical fact and exhibiting a mystical influence over mankind. Men have turned away from worshipping God and turned to their own idols, and in so doing are under the influence of evil principalities and powers. What is the result of this? They perceive that God is only a God of wrath against all ungodliness and wickedness.

The primary residence for sin is the flesh, which is weak and easily succumbs to the power and dominion of sin. Flesh in this context means the entire human being. The psalmist said, *Horror* (indignation) *hath taken hold upon me because of the wicked that forsake thy law* [Ps. 119:53].

What is the function of the law? To show sin for what it is by laying down commandments. Therefore, through the law comes the knowledge of sin. When we recognize that the law is holy, just, and good, then we realize that men are sinful by their actual trespasses. From Adam to Moses there was sin in the world, but men were not guilty before the law [Rom. 5:13].

Man's situation is such that the law gives sin occasion for fresh attacks on him. There is also a mystery of lawlessness about it. This close association of *sin* and *trespasses* makes it possible for the word *sin* to be used to identify specific acts of wrongdoing.

Paul always includes himself in the word *sinners*. He cannot look away from himself and his condition in sin. This is a reality for Paul. He recognized that Christ entered into the sphere where sin had proclaimed and established itself, and that Christ had won the victory, not in theory but in fact. Paul rejoices in the fact that Christ had been raised from the dead, and that he had been called to preach this truth. He expresses his overflowing gratitude to God for raising Christ saying, *If Christ be not risen, then is our preaching vain* (futile), *and your faith is also vain* (futile) [1 Cor. 15:14].

After his conversion, Paul was always aware of his sinful condition, the price Christ paid on the Cross, His shed blood that had cleansed him (Paul) from his sinful condition, and God's power in raising Christ from the dead. This he states emphatically to the Corinthians *And, if Christ be not raised, your faith is vain* (futile)*; ye are yet in your sins* [1 Cor. 15:17]. Therefore, we, like Paul, are to be cognizant of this truth, glorify God, and give thanks to Him for His Son Christ Jesus.

The complete liberation of people from the dominion of sin is shown in the sixth chapter of Romans when in baptism we share Christ's dying and rising again. *The Christian is free to present himself to God or to sin.*

Paul repudiates the idea that people living in the spiritual state of grace need not be concerned about their trespasses and transgressions. If a person sins against a brother whom he has seen, he sins against Christ whom he has not seen.

This brings us back to our Scripture: what is meant by trespasses and sins, and the lusts of the flesh and mind? According to Paul, it is life apart from the grace of God. Note that he says, . . . *wherein in time past ye walked . . . among whom also we all had our conversation* (conducted ourselves) *in times past.* Conversation in this context also means "tenor of life." It is also used in Philippians where Paul says, *For our conversation* (citizenship) *is in heaven; from whence also we look for the Saviour, the Lord Jesus Christ* [Phil. 3:20]. This term also was used in the sixteenth and seventeenth centuries.

People express their ideas of life to themselves and others according to the way in which they live and act. This is true of a man in sin. What we see by this are their trespasses and sins. What leads to it are their polluted natures, tenor of life, and lusts of the flesh and mind. That is man's life without the grace of God in Jesus Christ. The Apostle points out that it is true of everyone, it is a universal condition, and it is not selective.

The Apostle says trespasses and sins are the result of the lusts of the flesh and the mind. He subdivides it so there will not be any oversight or exclusion, saying *the desires of the flesh, and of the mind*. Paul does not leave anyone out.

The following points are noted regarding the flesh and the Spirit: the flesh is weak and sinful, it is contrasted with the Spirit, the Spirit is associated with life and peace, and life in the Spirit is not natural for man. Life in the Spirit depends upon the Holy Spirit dwelling within a person. The positive value of the flesh is seen in:

> *Whereof I Paul am made a minister;*
> *Who now rejoice in my sufferings for you, and fill up that which is behind* (lacking) *of the afflictions of Christ in my flesh for his body's sake, which is the church* [Col. 1:23–24].

Paul identifies himself with Christ's sufferings and relates them to his sufferings in the flesh. When he describes fleshly weakness, he speaks of the sinful body. The body is dead because of sin, and its deeds must be put to death. However, the Spirit can make mortal bodies alive by the power that raised Jesus Christ. Jesus came in the likeness of sinful flesh [Eph. 2:15]. The meaning of the following verse should not be misinterpreted: *In the body of his flesh through death, to present you holy and unblameable and unreproveable in his sight* [Col. 1:22]. Paul condemns sins in the flesh. He extols Christ's victory that was won where sin was strongest and man weakest.

Paul describes the results of life after the flesh and life after the Spirit saying, *For if ye live after the flesh, ye shall die: but if ye through the Spirit do mortify* (put to death) *the deeds of the body, ye shall live* [Rom. 8:13]. Calvin amplifies upon Paul's statement, saying, "Although we may still be subject to sin, nevertheless he still promises us life, provided we strive to mortify the flesh. He does not strictly require the destruction of the flesh, but only bids us make every exertion to subdue its lusts."

In closing, may we consider the words of the Apostle John:

> *If we say that we have no sin, we deceive ourselves, and the truth is not in us.*
> *If we confess our sins, he is faithful and just to forgive us our sins, and to cleanse us from all unrighteousness.*
> *If we say that we have not sinned, we make him a liar, and his word is not in us* [1 John 1:8–10].

The wisdom of the Apostle John in presenting the truths of the Gospel. He gives us a choice, as a matter of fact three choices. There are those who believe they have not sinned and do not sin. They compare themselves to others who succumb to the lusts of the flesh, or do not abide by their flexible moral code. However, they disobey God in other ways. The consequences of their choice results in deceiving themselves and not having God's truth in them.

The second choice is, *If we confess our sins*. Why is this important? Consider the alternatives. If we confess our sins, which we all have, then God is faithful to us and clothes us in His righteousness, and we are reconciled to Him. However, we must remember the heart of a confessing sinner is known to God. If he or she is contrite and sincere, then his or her sins are forgiven, and each one is in a right relationship with our heavenly Father. The alternative is not pleasant. Those who choose it will not be cleansed from their disobedience and unrighteousness. Further, they will not be reconciled to God and He will not reform them, correct them, forgive them, and enlighten them until with humility and sincerity they confess their sins and seek His forgiveness. Which alternative do you choose?

Third, does our pride, ego, and self-centeredness lead us to say that we have not sinned? If the answer is "yes", the Apostle under the influence of the Holy Spirit says, *we make him a liar, and his word is not in us.* Those are strong, harsh words, but truthful ones. May we heed them. John Calvin shines additional light on John's words saying, "From this we learn that we only progress properly in the Word of the Lord when we are really humbled, so as to groan under the burden of our sins and learn to flee to God's mercy and rest only in His fatherly kindness.

May we make the right choices, acknowledge our sins, confess them, and have His Word dwell within us.

May God open our hearts and minds to His truths and His commands through the Lord Jesus Christ, and may the Holy Spirit enlighten us.

Amen!

4

The Doctrine of God's Wrath

> *Among whom also we all had our conversation* (conducted ourselves) *in times past in the lusts of our flesh, fulfilling the desires of the flesh and of the mind; and were by nature the children of wrath, even as other* [Eph. 2:3].

Paul deals forthrightly and compassionately with the reality of sin and its effect on man's relationship with God. He addresses God's proclamations regarding sin and man's sinful condition, which affect each and every one of us. However, people want to ignore them. Why? Because they are self-centered, they are protective regarding their own points of view, and they do not want to consider God's truths.

"When considering *we all . . . were by nature the children of wrath, even as others* we should recognize we are dealing with two difficult and perplexing biblical truths. The Apostle says we are all under the wrath of God, and we are by nature" according to Martyn Lloyd-Jones who then asks "Why should we examine these truths?" When acknowledging the Bible as the Word of God, we are tempted to pick and choose, as we do with food, clothes, or cars. The Word is part and parcel of our Christian faith and conduct, and our guide for acquiring knowledge. Therefore, we are to consider all of it, not just the portions that appeal to us.

Paul states that we can never understand the love of God until we understand the Doctrine of God's Wrath. Nor can we understand why the Lord Jesus Christ came into the world unless we come to grips with this important doctrine and obtain an understanding of it.

We love to think and talk about the Virgin Birth, the Parables, the Sermon on the Mount, and other aspects of Jesus' life. However, this question remains: why did He come? It cannot be answered without including the doctrines of God's judgment, God's wrath, and man's sin.

Christ's coming was essential for our salvation, and God's provisioning must be considered—the Cross, the shedding of Christ's blood, His burial, and His resurrection.

These acts were essential. Yet questions are asked: Why do people not believe in Jesus Christ? Why are people not active members of churches? Why do people ignore Jesus Christ in their daily living?

The answer is that they do not see a need for Him; they do not realize their sinful condition, and the need for His grace. Also, they do not realize the truth regarding God's holiness, justice, and righteousness, let alone God as Judge and His wrath against man's sin.

When desiring to understand the Doctrine of God's Wrath, we should examine Scripture, pray for the Holy Spirit to enlighten us, and remember that old bugaboo, self, as we embark on this journey. We should begin by remembering that Paul told the Athenians they were a religious people, since he had noted the inscription *To the unknown God*. But then he proclaimed to them that *God ... dwelleth not in temples made with hands, ...* [Acts 17:23-24] and that they should seek Him, because they are to realize He is not far from each of them. This is important when considering God's wrath and that it is *In him we live, and move, and have our being ... For we are also His offspring* [Acts 17:28].

Paul did not want the Athenians to think that God is unknown, nor is He like gold, silver, stone, graven art, or man's devices. They were to understand that God overlooked their times of ignorance, commands men to repent, has fixed a day when He will judge the world in righteousness, will judge the world by the Man He has ordained, and assured us of His power in raising Christ from the dead. This is the testimony of the Bible. The fact that God *is* does not enter into the thoughts of the biblical writers for one moment. They know He *is*.

The Bible testifies to the fact that God has much to do with man and vice versa. It never says that God has nothing to do with man, nor that man has nothing to do with God. These passages, and others in Scripture, state that man cannot effectively and fully know God without Him providing His own self-revelation. Therefore, all nations come under God's judgment, for no nation is without knowledge of Almighty God. *For the wrath of God is revealed from heaven against all ungodliness and unrighteousness of men, who hold* (suppress) *the truth in unrighteousness* [Rom. 1:18].

God's wrath consists of the fact that He Himself is not remote from man, but actually interacts with him. His wrath meets man, who is guilty and without excuse. Why? Because he has received God's proclamation and ignored it.

Man's guilt is not due to his being intellectually backward.

> *Because that which may be known of God is manifest* (evident) *in* (among) *them; for God hath showed it unto them.*
> *For the invisible things of him from the creation of the world are clearly seen, being understood by the things that are made, even his eternal power and Godhead* (divine nature)*; so that they are without excuse* [Rom. 1:19–20].

There is not even a hint that God could be disclosed by some external evidence or means other than *The heavens declare the glory of God; and the firmament showeth his handiwork* (the work of his hands) [Ps. 19:1]. "What God has given to be known is known," said the remarkable theologian Otto Weber.

When considering this intellectually comprehensible and predictable situation, it is important to realize that man has refused to give God the honor, praise, glory, and thanks He rightly deserves. This means man has not dealt with God as God.

> *Because that, when they knew God, they glorified him not as God, neither were thankful; but became vain* (futile) *in their imaginations* (thoughts)*, and their foolish heart was darkened.*
> *Professing themselves to be wise, they became fools.*
> *And changed the glory of the uncorruptible God into an image made like to corruptible* (perishable) *man, and to birds, and four-footed beasts, and creeping things* [Rom. 1:21–23].

In practice, man denies God and tries to reverse everything. As a result man becomes subject to the wrath of God. What causes it? Not man's insufficiency, but his guilt. Man is guilty toward God who is near to him, not far removed. What did the psalmist say? *Wherever I go thou* (God) *art there.* Barnabas and Paul amplify on this,

> *Saying, Sirs, why do ye these things? We also are men of like passions with you, and preach unto you that ye should turn from these vanities* (useless things) *unto the living God, which made heaven, and earth, and the sea, and all things that are therein:*
> *Who in times past* (past generations) *suffered* (allowed) *all nations to walk in their own ways.*

> *Nevertheless he left not himself without witness, in that he did good, and gave us rain from heaven, and fruitful seasons, filling our hearts with food and gladness.*
>
> *And with these sayings scarce restrained they* (could scarcely restrain) *the people,* (multitudes) *that they had not done sacrifice unto them* (from sacrificing to them) [Acts 14:15-18].

These verses reveal the wrath of God and the inexcusability of man. They apply to those who are under the law and those who are outside the law to both the Jews and the Gentiles.

Scripture reveals that any idea of man being removed from the presence of God is totally lacking. Man is not free from God. He can neither live and move, nor conduct his faith—or lack of it—without dealing with God, regardless of his faith. Even the problematic altar to an unknown God results in proclaiming or discussing a Creator.

What about the two points we are considering, *all* under the wrath of God and under the wrath of God *by nature*? This puts us face to face with a tremendous doctrine, which is unpopular and even hated, that the wrath of God is not incompatible with the love of God. People say it originates from ancient ideas about God, or from tribal practices depicting their gods as being angry and jealous.

A false teaching has developed declaring that the Old Testament emphasizes divine wrath whereas the New Testament emphasizes God's divine love. This false teaching appears to be saying there are two different gods, and we like the one better than the other.

There are people who completely misinterpret the term *wrath*. The dictionary defines it as *violent anger* or *implying rage or indignation and strongly suggesting a desire or intent to avenge or punish*. This is how people think of it. They think of a person trembling, losing self-control, speaking, and acting violently.

That is an erroneous interpretation of the biblical term *wrath*. According to Scripture, wrath is nothing but a manifestation of God's indignation based upon His justice. "The wrath of God is the other side of His love," as appropriately described by Martyn Lloyd-Jones.

Further, it is the unavoidable result of rejecting God's love. Yes, it is true God is a God of love, but it is equally true He is a God of justice and righteousness. When God's love is rejected and spurned, *the impossible possibility*, then there is His justice, righteousness, and wrath. In addition, God's wrath is His grief.

"Every sinner is born with a nature inherently hostile to God and opposed to doing His will. If he refuses the Saviour he thereby hardens himself in his enmity toward God, and so by his own deliberate choice continues to be a child of disobedience. He is therefore under divine displeasure, and is a child of wrath. If the love of God manifested in Christ is rejected, then the wrath of God must be revealed.

"So we see that the sinner is wholly out of adjustment with God. If he is set right, it must be with God first. But in [Eph. 2:1–3] there is not one ray of light or one gleam of light. Unless God intervenes and takes the initiative, the sinner will forever remain in his sins," as forthrightly stated by that insightful disciple of Christ, Ruth Paxson.

What does Scripture reveal? The Old Testament records that when Adam (man) fell in the garden, God visited him, spoke to him, and pronounced judgment. Then what happened? He drove Adam out of the garden and placed the cherubim with the flaming sword at the eastern gate, preventing him from returning.

The sword is the sword of God's justice and wrath. Man was punished for his disobedience to God.

Early in Genesis we see God's righteous judgment and wrath upon sin. It runs throughout the Old Testament. God gave the law to His people and pronounced that if they break it, He will punish them. When He punishes them that is His wrath. It follows in an orderly and predictable pattern.

The Old Testament reveals God's steady, consistent anger against sin in every form. This was true of the people in Israel and those outside her borders. However, this approach was coupled with extreme patience and restraint by God, who said, *I will not execute the fierceness of mine anger, I will not return to destroy* (again destroy) *Ephraim: for I am God, and not man; the Holy One in the midst of thee: and I will not enter* (come with terror) *into the city* [Hos. 11:9].

An excellent example of God's wrath and forbearance is seen in Exodus 32:7–14 when God rebuked the conduct of the Israelites *And Moses besought the Lord his God* [Exod. 32:11] to show favor on the people through His mercy. *And the Lord said unto Moses, I have seen this people, and, behold, it is a stiffnecked* (stubborn) *people* [Exod. 32:9].

Therefore, God's wrath was generated against the people because of their apostasy. However, Moses prayed and pleaded with God and *The Lord repented of the evil* (relented from the harm) *which he thought to do unto his people* [Exod. 32:14]. In this instance, *repented* means that He changed His mind.

What does the New Testament say? It shows exactly the same attitude on the part of God as that revealed in the Old Testament—intense anger against sin, but great forbearance toward the sinner. We need to remember that although He exhibits strong and firm judgment against sin, He also exhibits patience, restraint, mercy, and love toward the sinner.

Who is the first preacher in the New Testament? John the Baptist. What does he say? *Repent ye: for the kingdom of heaven is at hand* [Matt. 3:2]. *O generation* (offspring) *of vipers, who hath warned you to flee from the wrath to come* [Luke 3:7]? Further, he says that *He that believeth on the Son hath everlasting life: and he that believeth not the Son shall not see life; but the wrath of God abideth* (remains) *on him* [John 3:36].

What does this mean? All people, each and every one, are under the wrath of God, and if we do not believe on Jesus the Son of God, then the wrath of God will abide on us individually.

John also records in the book of Revelation *Fall on us, and hide us from the face of him that sitteth on the throne, and from the wrath of the Lamb* [Rev. 6:16]. Do you ever think about *the wrath of the Lamb*? You think of a lamb as being gentle, innocent, and harmless, yet there it is, *the wrath of the Lamb*. The Lamb of God will take away the sins, but He will also judge the world with righteousness.

The false teaching regarding love and wrath being incompatible is a denial of God's essence. If we do not consider the wrath of God against sin, then we cannot fully understand the love of God and His grace toward the repentant sinner. Accepting God's wrath against sin enables us to realize the significance of our salvation.

The Apostle believed and taught that we are under God's wrath until we believe on the Lord Jesus Christ, and that God's wrath expresses His hatred of sin and His punishment of it. The wrath of God finally exhibits itself in hell with those who remain outside the life of God. Those who are under the wrath of God in this life will remain in that condition in the next life. Some people do not like this teaching. They object to it, argue with it, and ignore it. When they do, they are either arguing with Scripture or ignoring Scripture.

Paul "pronounces all men without exception, both Jews and Gentiles, to be guilty until they are set free by Christ. So that outside

Christ there is no righteousness, no salvation, and, in short, no excellence. By 'children of wrath' understand simply those who are lost and deserving of eternal death 'wrath' means the judgment of God; so that 'the children of wrath' signifies those who are condemned before God," as vividly described by John Calvin.

What other truths are presented in the New Testament? The New Testament introduces the realization of God's fatherhood, God being the Father of the Lord Jesus Christ. It is important to know that this realization takes place in the Son, who came *to redeem them that were under the law, that we might receive the adoption of sons* [Gal. 4:5].

The law is the stumbling block that prevents accepting sonship or adoption and an effective knowledge of God's fatherhood. Why? Because the law brings wrath. *Because the law worketh wrath: for where no law is, there is no transgression* [Rom. 4:15].

What does this mean? Man knows God one of two ways: as a partner in a relationship in which *I give in order that you give* according to God's grace and love; or as a God of wrath.

When examining God's wrath it is beneficial to consider it with respect to His grace, that has been described as the *timeless kindliness of God*. Grace was not properly understood until the ministry of Jesus Christ. However, His grace does not abrogate the pronouncement of judgment and wrath.

Grace is not a passive attribute of God that at various times is turned on and goes into motion, and then is turned off. It is a reality! God's grace (unmerited and unconditional favor) is bestowed continuously.

Therefore, His wrath is greatly mitigated by His grief and mercy toward those who are in Christ. The New Testament interprets God's grace, mercy, faithfulness, and patience as attributes of God that bear the character of an event. What is that event? Jesus Christ. Why? Because in Him, God the Father is present with us. Therefore, in Paul and the other New Testament writers, grace is always identified as the grace of Jesus Christ.

When Paul met with the elders from Ephesus in Miletus, he described his mission as that

> *... which I have received of the Lord Jesus, to testify the gospel of the grace of God* [Acts 20:24].

> *And now, brethren, I commend you to God, and to the word of his grace, ...* [Acts 20:32].

The concept of the wrath of God requires further explanation. It is based upon Scripture. *For the wrath of God is revealed from heaven against all ungodliness and unrighteousness* [Rom. 1:18]. This leads to a question. Is wrath just one side of God's righteousness and an attribute of His love? *Yes!* God's wrath can only be understood as His real, uncompromising, strong *no* to sin. Why? Because sin is the rejection of God's love and His will for His people.

When someone rejects God and His righteousness, he naturally wants to explain His wrath in subjective terms. Conversely, when a person comes to know that in Jesus Christ the judgmental righteousness of God attains its goal, then he knows that he is saved from the wrath taking place at judgment. *Much more then, being* (having been) *now justified by his blood, we shall be saved from wrath through him* [Rom. 5:9].

We must also remember that God's wrath rests upon those who are outside Christ and do not have a believing faith in God the Father. The Apostle John says,

> He that believeth on the Son hath everlasting life: and he that believeth not the Son shall not see life; but the wrath of God abideth (remains) on him [John 3:36].

There is a gulf between God and us that is revealed in the law. There is only one way it can be bridged, and that is through the grace in Jesus Christ in whom the *image of God* is revealed. Jesus is the Man for God, out of God, and before God. It is in the grace of the Lord Jesus Christ that our rejection is terminated and our judgment is set aside.

It is in the person of Jesus Christ that man is recreated in the image of God, and He is the One who God sent *in the likeness of sinful flesh* [Rom. 8:3]. Jesus Christ is the One who bore the wrath of God against the sin of the whole human race, and He carried it to the bitter end.

The second point being considered is that we are all under the wrath of God by nature. The Apostle uses the word *were*. He does not say "become." He does not say that we are born into this world in complete innocence and that because we are exposed to sin or bad people or a bad environment that we become sinners under the wrath of God. However, he does say we are born into this world under the wrath of God. It is not something that is going to happen because of some act on our part. He says we are in this position *by birth*.

One great truth Paul presents in Romans is that as believers our relationship to Christ is exactly analogous to our former relationship to Adam. He says, *Wherefore, as by one man sin entered into the world, and death by sin; and so death passed upon all men, for that all have sinned* [Rom. 5:12]. He states that what was true of Adam is not true of Christ.

A careful examination of what Paul says enables us to see our relationship to Adam and to Christ. If we believe the relationship with Adam, then we should believe the relationship with Christ. Adam sinned and death came, not only to him but to all men. Why? Because all men fall as Adam did; the disobedience that occurred in the Garden occurs in every human life.

Paul was not writing to great philosophers but to the community of believers when he revealed

> *(For until the law sin was in the world: but sin is not imputed when there is no law.)*
> *Nevertheless death reigned from Adam to Moses, even over them that had not sinned after the similitude* (likeness) *of Adam's transgression, who is the figure (a type) of him that was to come* [Rom. 5:13–14].

What does Paul want us to understand regarding sin, the law, and God's wrath? He wants to enlighten the Romans (and us) that before God gave the law to Moses, sin was in the world from the time of Adam. The law focuses attention on sin and that, in reality, it is a transgression against God and His righteousness. Until that time sin was not imputed because there was no law.

The purpose of the law was to bring the reality of sin into a person's mind, heart, and conscience. When there is no law, there is no transgression; therefore, there is no punishment. Since there was no law from Adam to Moses, how can the death of all those people be explained? Paul explains it by stating that they died because they were involved in the sin of Adam. No other reason is offered. In other words, they *were by nature the children of wrath*. Calvin adds additional clarity saying, "The distinction between good and evil had been dismissed, and therefore without the warning of the law, the recollection of sin was buried, because sin still prevailed to condemn them. Death, therefore, reigned also then, because the judgment of God could not be destroyed by men's blindness and hardness of heart."

Paul writes that death reigned *even over them that had not sinned after the similitude* (likeness) *of Adam's transgression* [Rom. 5:14]. Also, he says to the Ephesians we *were by nature the children of wrath, even as others* [Eph. 2:3]. What does this mean? It means that death reigned over those individuals who had not actually committed an act of sin or trespass as Adam did.

Who are those people? There appears to be only one possible answer: those who died in their infancy. All others had sinned or will sin. The infants were the only ones who had not sinned in a likeness similar to Adam's, since they were incapable of exercising their will. Why do infants die? Because Adam's transgression involves them.

The judgment (the condemnation) was brought by one. The sin of Adam was transferred to the whole of mankind. Conversely, and this is important, sins are forgiven in the righteousness of One, Jesus Christ.

> *Therefore as by the offense (one false step) of one judgment came upon all men to condemnation; even so by the righteousness (one righteous act) of one the free gift came upon all men unto justification of life* [Rom. 5:18].

That is explicit. Paul continues,

> *For as by one man's disobedience many were made sinners, so by the obedience of one shall many be made righteous* [Rom. 5:19].

We are *all by nature the children of wrath* [Eph. 2:3]. In Adam we fell; in Christ we are raised. In Christ we are redeemed, reconciled, and saved. How? By His action and God's grace. *Not by anything we do!* If you believe the truth about Christ, then you can believe the truth about Adam.

Therefore, carefully consider the Word of God by laying aside philosophies, experiences, and mindsets. Many people who profess to believe the Bible and to regard it as authoritative reject certain doctrines because they cannot reconcile those doctrines with their own mindsets.

Though dead in our trespasses and sins, and under the wrath of God, helpless and hopeless, what happened? God, whom we disobeyed and offended, and against whom we sinned, provided a way for us to be reconciled to Himself.

He sent His own Son to be the atonement for our sins. He sent Him to Calvary's Hill with all the accompanying suffering, shame, and cruelty. God offers us complete deliverance and reconciliation despite the fact that we deserve only His wrath. *That is the Love of God!*

Do you see why we need to know the Doctrine of God's Wrath? It is so we can understand the magnitude of His love. God has done for us what we could never do for ourselves.

Thanks be to God.

Amen!

5

But God, Rich in Mercy

> *But God, who is rich in mercy, for his great love wherewith he loved us,* . . . [Eph. 2:4].

Paul begins this section of his letter to the Ephesians with two simple, powerful words, *But God*. Why did he do this? What was his purpose? Think for a moment about what he was saying to the Ephesians and to us in the first three verses. He was boldly stating what man, you and me, is like without God. It is not a pretty picture for individuals, families, and society. They are *dead in trespasses and sins; walking according to the prince of the power of the air* (Satan); *under the influence of the spirit that now worketh in the children of disobedience; among whom also we all had our conversation* (conducted ourselves) *in times past in the lusts of the flesh, fulfilling the desires of the flesh and of the mind, and were* (are) *by nature the children of wrath* [Eph. 2:2–3]. What a direct, straightforward statement. Paul and the other writers of Scripture do not sugar coat Biblical truths. They want us to think. They want us to examine ourselves. And, they want us to know what life is like without any God given controls.

Therefore, Paul, after vividly describing man's plight when left to his devices, rationalizations, and standards, wants professing Christians and sinners to focus on *God, who is rich in mercy, for His great love wherewith He loved us.*

When examining this portion of Scripture, it is beneficial to ask a few questions:

- How does the Christian message, especially the evangelical message, apply to the circumstances in which men and women find themselves in their daily lives?

- Is the Christian message remote? Is it irrelevant?
- What impact does Satan have today?
- How am I disobedient to the will of God?
- What lusts impact me, my family and society?
- What is required to become the children of God and mature in the Christian faith as Christ's disciples?

The purpose of Christian teaching and preaching, and the exposition of Scripture, can be understood only when God's love and His revelation in Jesus Christ are understood, believed, and applied. We must exert the necessary effort to understand God's Word; we must have faith when we do not understand completely or fully; and we must apply faith with expectation.

The Gospel deals with man and with his whole life. It does not deal with just part of it or selected portions. The biblical approach is to exhibit God's truth and to show how it relates to *different situations. It is not the reverse*; it does not start with a particular situation and then relate it to Scripture.

The Bible reveals God and His purposes to us. It is the story of His love affair with His people and the gracious means He has provided for their (our) salvation. The Bible from Genesis to Revelation is explicit that life, man, and the world can be understood only when everything is seen in the light of God's truth and God's purpose. Therefore, we must start with God.

If man is essentially good, then he needs only a little instruction, knowledge, and information. The solution is fairly simple. However, if what Paul says is true about man without Christ, then the treatment is different. If the treatment is only through instruction, knowledge, and information, then to be rather brutal, it is a hopeless waste of time.

What is true of man as a sinner? He or she is spiritually dead and is governed by the devil, evil spiritual forces, and the natural forces of the world. As a consequence, he or she lives in trespasses and sins and is under the wrath of God. This truth is contra to what is proclaimed by the secular world, by those who ignore or reject the teachings and revelations contained in Scripture. They say the problem is the environment or that man has not had sufficient time to develop. They refuse to realize that there is evil in the world and in individuals, families, and society. Who else is responsible for aggressions, assaults, deceit, self-justification, and self-rationalization? They originate in the hearts and minds of mankind. Why does Paul stress that *the works of the flesh are manifest* (evident), . . . *adultery, fornication, uncleanness, lasciviousness* (licentiousness), . . . *hatred, variance* (contentions), *emulations* (jealousies), *wrath, strife,* (selfish ambitions), . . . *envyings, murders, drunkenness, revellings, and such like* [Gal. 5:19-21]. To these can be added, arrogance, conflicts, egotism, and transgressions. What do they have in common? They all originate within a person.

James, guided by the Holy Spirit, says,

> *FROM whence come wars (conflicts) and fightings, . . .*
> *Ye lust and have not, . . .*
> *Ye ask, and receive not, because ye ask amiss,*
> *Know ye not that the friendship of (with) the world is enmity with God? . . .*
> *Do ye think that the scripture saith in vain? . . .*
> *Submit yourselves therefore to God. Resist the devil, and he will flee from you.*
> *Draw nigh* (near) *to God, and he will draw nigh* (near) *to you*
> [Selections from Jas. 4:1-5, 4:7-8].

James deals forthrightly with issues involving men and women alike, that they are subject to the wiles of Satan. They lust and have not. John Calvin provides additional insight to this saying, . . . "man's spirit is inexhaustible, once it indulges in wicked desires . . . . When a man allows his appetites free rein, he will never come to an end to his lust. Even if he were given the earth, he would long to have new worlds made for him."

James continues by saying, *ye fight*. "He is not thinking of the wars and battles waged among men with bare weapons, but contested arguments of any kind where one party tries to come out on top of the other . . . . God does well to frustrate them, as they do not acknowledge Him as the Author of good. They struggle by means outside the law, more ready to ask favour from Satan than blessing from God", as clearly stated by Calvin.

James concludes this portion of his letter with the commandment to, *Draw nigh* (near) *to God* with the comforting and encouraging words *and He will draw nigh* (near) *to you*. When Scripture commands us to do something it is usually accompanied by a benefit. O' the blessing of the Father.

The cause of all unwarranted aggressions is man's sinful condition. We must realize this. We must be aware of it and accept it. Then we can begin to increase our understanding of events that occur both remotely and in our immediate areas. We can begin to know ourselves better, as well as the things that plague us.

Unfortunately, people like to think one way when establishing standards about nations, governments, corporations, and churches, and another way when thinking about individuals and themselves. However, all organizations involve people.

According to the Bible, man is governed by the desires of the flesh and the mind. He is governed by what he likes, wants, and feels he must have, rather than whether something is right or wrong according to established spiritual principles.

In the 1950s, when Ralph Cordiner was the CEO of the General Electric Company, an issue arose involving millions of dollars paid annually to another company according to an agreement executed in the late 1920s. Several key executives addressed this situation, seeking an escape from continuing to make the costly payments. They submitted their proposal to the executive committee, which was chaired by Mr. Cordiner.

After discussing the matter, Mr. Cordiner asked each of the approximately twenty-five participants how they would vote on the matter. He went around the table soliciting each person's vote. Everyone present voted to stop paying the money. However, Mr. Cordiner said, "Gentlemen, the General Electric Company made a commitment approximately thirty years ago and the General Electric Company will continue to live up to that agreement." Mr. Cordiner stood on principle and was not swayed by rationalization.

Unfortunately, people want to rationalize. People express horror at what governments or organizations do, but will do similar things in their own lives or their own churches. One thing we must recognize is that lust exists, both of the flesh and of the mind.

A second principle to consider is that man will continue to act as he has as long as he is controlled by lusts and accompanying rationalizations from the world, local communities, and homes.

Certainly there is a point to consider. If man's condition in sin has been responsible for recorded history, then what is going to change in the future if man continues in his sinful condition?

Every generation is always confident that somehow, because it is more learned or enlightened, it can get everything together and make it right. We think we are better educated and more cultured, and therefore we can succeed where past generations have failed. However, if our problems are due to man in sin then we should see the fallacy of these ideas. Because if man is in sin, then there will be all the problems identified previously.

Our Lord Jesus gives us a little different view of history in Luke, when he says to His disciples,

> *And as it was in the days of Noah, so shall it be also in the days of the Son of man.*
>
> *They did eat, they drank, they married wives, they were given in marriage, until the day that Noah entered into the ark, and the flood came, and destroyed them all.*
>
> *Likewise also as it was in the days of Lot; they did eat, they drank, they bought, they sold, they planted, they builded;*
>
> *But the same day that Lot went out of Sodom it rained fire and brimstone from heaven, and destroyed them all.*
>
> *Even thus shall it be in the day when the Son of man is revealed* [Luke 17:26–30].

If we grasp this biblical doctrine, we can begin to understand that new approaches and new organizations offering promises of outlawing wars or changing situations are nothing more than empty promises.

Jesus says that in the days of Noah and Lot people did eat, drink, and marry, and that they bought and sold, planted and built. Yes, they did those things, but as Jesus pointed out in the days of Noah *the flood came, and destroyed them all.* He also noted *But the same day that Lot went out of Sodom it rained fire and brimstone from heaven, and destroyed them all.* Then Jesus said, *Even thus it shall be in the day when the Son of man is revealed* [Luke 17:27, 17:29–30].

The Bible says you cannot change man while he remains unregenerate. This may sound depressing, but that is not our main concern. Our concern is to know the truth, which modern man usually does not want to consider. He does not want to consider the facts as they are presented in the Bible. He feels they are depressing, or at best not realistic; but they are true, and they will happen again and again.

What does Scripture say in Ephesians? After the first three verses of the second chapter describing man's condition, Scripture says, *But God, who is rich in mercy.*

Before considering the positive aspects of this Scripture, we should consider a negative. People say we, meaning Christians or the church, should ask the world to adopt and to practice Christian principles. They continue by saying, you Christians preach about personal salvation, peace, and justice, however, why do you not do something about the conditions existing in the world? When you ask them what they would have us do, some will say tell them to practice the Sermon on the Mount, tell them to turn the other cheek, to walk the extra mile, and to give the cloak also. What is the answer to these comments or so-called suggestions?

The answer is basically contained in the first three verses of the second chapter of Ephesians. You can preach the Sermon on the Mount to individuals who are dead in their trespasses and sins until the cows come home, and it will not do any good. You can preach and teach until you are exhausted, and they will be none the wiser. Why? Because they cannot practice it. They do not want to. Again, why? Because they are governed by the lusts of the flesh and mind. Therefore, how can they practice the Sermon on the Mount?

What does Paul say? He says *But God*. Why? Because there is only one hope for man. He needs to be regenerated; he must have a new nature before he can begin to understand the Sermon on the Mount, let alone begin to practice it. But through the preaching and teaching of the Word, the Holy Spirit begins to move a man's heart to repentance. For as Paul says,

> *How shall they call on him in whom they have not believed? and how shall they believe in him of whom they have not heard? and how shall they hear without a preacher* [Rom. 10:14]?

It is a travesty to urge people to follow the Christian message or to ask them to use their own strength to follow Christ and to implement Christian principles. Why? Because it fails to accept the fact that man in his sinful condition cannot possibly implement such things. You cannot expect Christian behavior from people who are not Christians. To expect such conduct is heresy. However, it is important that we have a clear understanding of applying the Christian message to the modern world.

That is why it is important to spend time considering fundamental principles such as the doctrine of man in sin, man in his hopelessness and helplessness.

A summary of the negative principle in the Christian gospel is that the world is under God's condemnation and everyone who dies in that condition will go straight to perdition. The message of the church to the unbelieving world is to describe judgment, to call them to repentance, and to pronounce assurance if they repent and accept Christ. If they do, they shall be delivered.

The Bible explicitly says that God has done something about the unbelieving world. He placed controls upon the power of sin and evil. How has He done this?

He placed the peoples of the world into nations, with some form of government. He ordained that there should be states and governments. Paul describes this very vividly, saying to the Romans,

> *LET every soul be subject unto the higher powers (governing authorities). For there is no power (authority) but of God: The powers that be are ordained (appointed by) of God.*
>
> *Whosoever therefore resisteth the power (authority), resisteth the ordinance of God: and they that resist shall receive to themselves damnation (judgment).*
>
> *For rulers are not a terror to good works, but to the evil. Wilt thou then not be afraid (do you want to be unafraid) of the power (authority)? do that which is good, and thou shalt have praise of the same:*
>
> *For he is the minister of God to thee for good. But if thou do that which is evil, be afraid; . . . for he is the minister of God, a* revenger *(an avenger)* to execute wrath upon him that doeth evil *[Rom. 13:1-4].*

God ordains the powers. Why? To keep evil within bounds and under control. If God had not provided for law and order, then the lusts of the flesh and mind would run rampant. At times, God partially withdraws His restraint on man and gives him over to a reprobate mind. There are times when God seems to relax His restraint on sin and evil in order that man may see the horror of it all.

There is an important message for individuals. It says we can be delivered out of this present evil. It does not say that the world can be put right by implementing Christian teachings; it does not say people should do this or that.

It does say that because of what God has done in, through, and by Jesus Christ that we can be delivered out of this evil, condemned world. *Who gave himself for our sins, that he might deliver us from this present evil world* (age), *according to the will of God and our Father* [Gal. 1:4]. The message states that the world will remain as it is, but you can be delivered out of it.

Paul says we can become citizens of a kingdom not of this world. He continues by saying if you are *in Christ*, and because of His shed blood you are *fellow citizens with the saints* in the kingdom of God. It is a kingdom that cannot be moved. That is the one into which we are to enter.

We are citizens of this city, county, state, and country, and we participate in the things and events of it whether by choice or not, but also we can become citizens of another kingdom, a spiritual kingdom, an eternal kingdom in the heavens with God.

Martyn Lloyd-Jones provides additional light regarding what God did for the Ephesians, and what He does for those He calls and redeems, saying,

"That is not all. That is not the final word. The Christian realizes that though he is living in such a world, Scripture says *But God*. The believer knows he is linked to a power that gives him or her the ability to bear whatever may come and to be more than a conqueror. The Christian does not sit back and passively bear with every situation, nor does he just stick to it and show courage. The Christian knows about *the exceeding greatness of* God's *power to us-ward who believe*.

"He is strengthened and does not lose courage; he is not defeated, and even rejoices in his tribulations. Even though the world does its worst to him, the Christian has resources, comforts, consolation, and strengths about which others are ignorant.

"Finally, and probably most importantly, the Christian is assured that he is safe in God's hands. Hebrews says, *So that we may boldly say,* THE LORD IS MY HELPER, AND I WILL NOT FEAR WHAT MAN SHALL (CAN) DO UNTO ME [Heb. 13:6].

"Indeed the Christian may know and experience insults, persecutions, or ravages, but he knows that nothing can separate him from the love of God which is in Christ Jesus our Lord. He knows that no matter what happens in this world, he is a son of God and an heir of glory.

"The Christian faith and message has one definite thing to say to this world with all its problems and its failings: *But God*. God hath quickened us, He hath raised us, and He hath provided for us. We have not done anything."

The essence of Christianity is what God has done for us through our Lord Jesus Christ by the power of the Holy Spirit. It is not what we have done or are attempting to do. It is what God has done. How has it happened? Paul says God, . . . *hath quickened* (made alive) *us together with Christ, (by grace ye are* (have been) *saved;)* [Eph. 2:5].

The blessings are ours or become ours because we are joined to Christ; we are in Christ. They all come through Him and because of Him, not by anything we have done. This condition is not something we attain one day because of some big or little thing we do. It is something that begins when we are joined to Christ and accept Him by faith, because by His grace we are saved. We can only be Christians by being in Christ. Who hath quickened us? Who hath regenerated us? God and God only.

To be a real follower, to be a member of the community of believers, is to believe and to know that we are joined to Christ and that His life is in us. How it got there is due to the indissoluble, intimate, mystical union with Him. We may not understand it fully, we may not be able to explain it fully, but it is there. Why? As Scripture says,

> *But God, who is rich in mercy, for his great love wherewith he loved us* [Eph. 2:4].

Charles Wesley in his meaningful hymn, Love Divine, All Love Excelling, beautifully expresses God's *great love wherewith He loved us* with these immortal words:

> *Love divine, all loves excelling, Joy of heaven, to earth come down,*
> *Fix in us Thy humble dwelling, All thy faithful mercies crown!*
> *Jesus, Thou art all compassion, Pure, unbounded love Thou art;*
> *Visit us with Thy salvation, Enter every trembling heart.*
>
> *Breathe, O breathe Thy loving Spirit Into every troubled breast!*
> *Let us all in Thee inherit, Let us find the promised rest;*
> *Take away the love of sinning; Alpha and Omega be;*
> *End of faith, as its Beginning, Set our hearts at liberty.*
>
> *Come, Almighty to deliver, Let us all Thy life receive;*
> *Suddenly return, and never, Never-more Thy temples leave.*
> *Thee we would be always blessing, Serve Thee as Thy hosts above;*
> *Pray, and praise Thee with-out ceasing, Glory in Thy perfect love.*
>
> *Finish, then, Thy new creation; Pure and spotless let us be;*
> *Let us see Thy great salvation Perfectly restored in Thee;*
> *Changed from glory into glory, Till in heaven we take our place,*
> *Till we cast our crowns before Thee, Lost in wonder, love, and praise. Amen*

Amen!

6

Raised Up Together

> *But God, who is rich in mercy, for his great love wherewith he loved us,*
> *Even when we were dead in sins, hath quickened (made alive) us together with Christ, (by grace ye are (have been) saved;)*
> *And hath raised us up together, and made us sit together in heavenly places in Christ Jesus:*
> *That in the ages to come he might show the exceeding riches of his grace in his kindness toward us through (in) Christ Jesus* [Eph. 2:4–7].
>
> *And hath raised us up together, and made us sit together in heavenly places in Christ Jesus* [Eph. 2:6].

Isn't that a beautiful verse, a beautiful thought, but most of all a beautiful fact? Note the tense of the verbs. Recall the difference in content between the first three verses and verses 4–7 of the second chapter of Ephesians.

If we grasp hold of these two segments of Scripture, then we should begin to realize two things: the depth of sin and man's condition in it; and what God has done regarding the greatness and glory of our salvation. Too often people think of salvation only as the forgiveness of sins.

It is as if they were little children saying, "I'm sorry," and then thinking everything is okay. People have a fixed mindset that salvation is really saying "I am sorry," and that is all there is to it. That is not what Scripture teaches.

Paul wants us to realize the depths from which we have come and the heights to which we are raised. We are not raised by anything we have done, but by the fact we are joined to Christ Jesus by the gracious work of the Holy Spirit.

Paul writes to the community of believers, not to all the Ephesians. He wants them to understand what is true of them as believers and to know *the exceeding greatness of God's power* [Eph. 1:19]. Our union with Christ makes us Christians.

He is never satisfied with proclaiming once, or even once in a while, the richness of God's grace. He repeats it and emphasizes it, and wants us to know that everything in our salvation must be ascribed to God. So he says that Christ *hath raised us up together, and made us sit together in the heavenly places in Christ Jesus.*

Paul says that even though we have not seen with our eyes these blessings, they are already in our possession and were conferred upon us when we were led from Adam to Christ. "We have been transferred from the deepest hell to heaven itself," as John Calvin expresses in awe God's amazing grace. It helps our understanding to recognize that the Apostle is drawing a comparison. He is telling us that what happened to the Lord Jesus physically when He was raised from the dead is true of us spiritually.

He concludes this verse saying, *in Christ Jesus.* Why? Because what Paul describes appears only in the Head, which is Christ, but does not appear in the members as yet, but it truly belongs to them. This fact should provide us with the richest consolation, because everything we lack in the present will be ours due to the pledge and the first fruits *in Christ*. We are joined to Christ.

He bore our sins on the Cross and He died. His lifeless body was taken down and was buried. A stone was rolled over His grave. All of this is factual. He was dead. He died for our sins, literally. Though He was dead, He was raised.

What happened after He was raised? He appeared to others, He was no longer dead, He was in another realm, He manifested Himself, and He ascended into heaven. We should constantly remind ourselves of these facts. Our salvation, according to Paul, is comparable to that. A complete change in the realm in which our Lord was existing. That is true of us as Christians. We have been raised together with Him and have our union with Him.

What happened to Him physically happens to us spiritually. This same power that raised the Lord Jesus Christ is working in those who believe and continue to do so. What does this mean? How does it apply to members of the community of believers?

What we need to do when considering these questions is to examine Romans. The best commentary on any of Paul's epistles is to read his other letters. If you do not, then sooner or later you will go astray. When doing this, keep another point in mind. If you exhaustively study one of the epistles you will cover the entire spectrum of Christian doctrine, but if you superficially cover the surface you will not acquire a true conception of the Apostle's teaching. To paraphrase something Dr. Henry Mobley used to say, "Mini-studies make mini-Christians."

What can be said about the true believer when approaching this from the negative side? He is no longer spiritually dead. This is another way of saying that regeneration and salvation produce the profoundest change possible in a person. It is the difference between life and death.

What does this mean in practice? Since we are no longer dead, we are no longer under the wrath of God. Paul, writing to the Romans, refers to the Lord Jesus, saying, . . . *who was delivered for* (because of) *our offenses, and was raised again for* (because of) *our justification* [Rom. 4:25]. The Lord died through the bearing of our offenses, our sins, and our transgressions.

How do we know God was satisfied with the offering? The resurrection! Paul states the truth as to what has happened, that due to the resurrection we have been

> *Delivered for* (because of) *our offenses, and was raised again for* (because of) *our justification* [Rom. 4:25].
>
> THEREFORE *being justified by faith, we have peace with God through our Lord Jesus Christ* [Rom. 5:1].

We are raised, we are justified, and we are no longer under the wrath of God.

Paul uses even stronger language, saying, THERE *is therefore now no condemnation to them which are in Christ Jesus, who walk not after the flesh, but after the Spirit* [Rom. 8:1]. There is no condemnation. Condemnation leads to death. We are no longer *dead in sins and trespasses* and no longer *the children of wrath*. Every Christian should know this truth and know that he or she is joined to Christ.

The first point is that we are no longer spiritually dead. We are dead to the law. We *are not under the law, but under grace.*

> WHAT *shall we say then? Shall we continue in sin, that grace may abound?*

God forbid (certainly not). *How shall we, that are dead* (who died) *to sin, live any longer therein* [Rom. 6:1–2]?

The illustration Paul uses is the same regarding our relationship as Christians to the law. We are born under the law. The law condemns us, challenges us. Paul says in his letter to the Romans, *Is the law sin? God forbid* (certainly not). *Nay, I had not* (would not have) *known sin, but by the law: for I had not* (would not have) *known lust* (covetousness) *except the law had said, THOU SHALT NOT COVET* [Rom. 7:7].

Second, when we are joined to Christ, we are no longer *under the law, but under grace*. This does not mean we no longer have to keep God's commands, but it means our relationship to God has changed; it is no longer a legal one. It is a personal one due to the grace of God.

Man in sin is in an alien relationship to God, and as a consequence, God deals with him in a legal manner. But when grace abounds, God deals with man through Christ Jesus. When we are in Christ, *we are no longer under the law*.

Third, because we have been *raised up together* we are now *dead to sin*. What does this mean? Clearly, it does not mean that we are all perfect, without sin, and that we shall never sin again. *If we say that we have no sin, we deceive ourselves, and the truth is not in us* [1 John 1:8].

What does it mean to say we are *dead to sin*? We are no longer controlled, dominated, and governed by sin and the lusts of the flesh and mind. We are out of that realm. *For sin shall not have dominion over you: for ye are not under the law, but under grace* [Rom. 6:14]. Again, this does not mean we are perfect, but that we are no longer in the realm of sin and its various lusts. We are no longer servants or slaves to sin.

Every unregenerate person is a slave to sin and governed by an evil principle. That is not the case with a Christian. The Christian may in his or her folly listen to evil principles, yield to temptation, or respond to sinful impulses, but that does not mean he or she is a slave to sin and controlled by it. That is the principle, and according to it we are *dead to sin*.

Fourth, we no longer belong to the realm of the law, sin, and death. There are times when we should examine our experiences as Christians, especially when considering these principles. Some people do not accept this truth because they cannot distinguish between a temptation and a sin; because evil thoughts penetrate their minds, they think they are in the realm of sin. They are not! The thoughts come from the outside, not from within; and we must realize there are still sinful tendencies in the body and mind, yet one's attitude towards them changes.

Think of it this way. When one country conquers another, there will still be pockets of resistance; there will be some who hold out; there will be some who are defiant. One battle may change the situation and determine who has possession, but it does not settle every question and possibility.

We can throw more light on this matter by *knowing, that our old man is crucified with him* (Christ*), that the body of sin might be destroyed, that henceforth we should not serve* (be slaves to) *sin* [Rom. 6:6].

What does this mean? The old man is the Adamic man, the one who was in Adam. However, we have died with Christ, and when we did the old man died. We are no longer in Adam, but in Christ.

This means that God looks upon us and considers us as being *in Christ*. I am a new person, but still the same personality. However, my whole position, status, and standing has changed. I am still in the flesh, but I belong to a new realm, a new kingdom, where God reigns and rules. Not where Satan has dominion.

The Christian is *in Christ*, not in Adam. The old person is gone, forever. This does not mean that the sin in my being has gone forever. It means that I am no longer in the realm of Adam, but am *in Christ*, and have been raised with Him.

We have considered what we might call negative points as we interpret this sixth verse of the second chapter. Now let's consider the positive aspects of this meaningful verse.

What happens when we share the life of Christ, when we become joined to Him? First, note what Paul says to the Romans: *Likewise reckon* (consider) *ye also yourselves to be dead indeed unto sin, but alive unto God through* (in) *Jesus Christ our Lord* [Rom. 6:11].

Having *raised us up together* now I am alive unto God. Before I was not, before I was dead unto God. That is the tragedy of the natural man. He is dead unto God. He lives as if there were no God, as if he were not conscious of God, as if he had no personal relationship to God, and as if God did not exist.

The believer is *alive unto God*. What does this mean? It means the believer has an entirely new attitude towards God. He is no longer at enmity with God.

The believer desires God. He has come to know Him and wants to know Him better and better. He wants to spend time with Him, and learn more about Him. *Because the carnal mind is enmity against God: for it is not subject to the law of God, neither can* (it) *be. So then they that are in the flesh cannot please God* [Rom. 8:7-8].

The natural man has his own ideas about God. He does not want to stand before a God of justice, or a just and loving God. He wants to avoid that at all costs. But what does the *believer* want to do? He wants to be *alive unto God* and to exhibit other Christlike traits. *AS the hart panteth after* (longs for) *the water brooks, so panteth my soul after thee, O God. My soul thirsteth for God, for the living God: when shall I come and appear before God* [Ps. 42:1-2]?

He desires to be with God, to draw nearer to Him, to have fellowship with Him. The Apostle John states it in a meaningful, revealing way,

> *THAT which was from the beginning, which we have heard, which we have seen with our eyes, which we have looked upon, and our hands have handled, of the Word of life;*
> *(For the life was manifested (revealed), and we have seen it, and bear witness, and show (declare) unto you that eternal life, which was with the Father, and was manifested unto us;)*
> *That which we have seen and heard declare we unto you, that ye also may have fellowship with us: and truly our fellowship is with the Father, and with his Son Jesus Christ* [1 John 1:1-3].

Calvin provides additional clarity to John's words saying, "And we must note carefully that Christ chose as heralds of the Gospel fit and faithful witnesses of everything that they were to declare. He also testifies to their motive; for he says that he was moved to write for the sole reason of inviting those he was addressing to common fellowship in an inestimable blessing. From this it appears how much he cared for their salvation."

Not only is the believer *alive unto God*, but he wants to walk in the newness of life. The Apostle Paul states it clearly and straight to the point,

> *But ye have not so learned Christ;*
> *If so be that ye have heard him, and have been taught by him, as the truth is in Jesus:*
> *That ye put off concerning the former conversation (conduct) the old man, which is corrupt according to the deceitful lusts;*

And be renewed in the spirit of your mind;
And that ye put on the new man, which after God is created in righteousness and true holiness [Eph. 4:20–24].

How does the new man show himself? How does he seek after God who is righteous and holy? It shows in his mind, his heart, and his will. The person who is a Christian, who is raised up together with Christ, is one who walks in the newness of life and does so with his mind, heart, and will.

The believer, as a Christian, has "a new mind." *And be not conformed to this world: but be ye transformed by the renewing of your mind, that ye may prove what is that good, and acceptable, and perfect, will of God* [Rom. 12:2].

The Christian has a new mind and it shows in different ways. He thinks in terms of eternity and does not think in terms of the finite. He realizes that this life is temporary, but the eternal life is permanent. He thinks in terms of the Spirit as well as the body and soul. He realizes there is something that is within himself called the Spirit. Further, he is conscious of belonging to another realm, and that the ruler of that realm rules his life. He develops new standards and values. He assesses things in an entirely new and different way.

He does not consider what "kick" or pleasure he will get out of something, but what will benefit his soul and how it affects his relationship to God and to Christ.

Why does he do these things? Because he has a new mind, one that has been *transformed*. These three points: being alive to God, walking in the newness of life, and having a new mind, have a positive impact upon a Christian.

The believer becomes more interested in the Bible. The Bible becomes his number-one book. Why? Because he realizes it is God's book and it brings him closer to God. Further, it increases his participation in the life of God and brings about an increasing awareness of Him.

The believer spends increasing amounts of time in meditation. He takes time to think about himself and God, thus developing an increasing awareness of Him.

The believer exhibits the manifestations of a new heart. He has new desires. He begins to hunger and thirst after righteousness. He says with David, *Create within me a clean heart, O God, and renew a right* (steadfast) *spirit within me* [Ps. 51:10]. This becomes a great desire. The Christian desires to be clean, pure, holy, righteous, and free from sin.

The Christian begins to realize that sin is not just an offense against the law, or himself, or another person, but an offense against God, who is holy, pure, and just. It is an offense against God, who loved and loves him and sent His Son to die for him. He begins to realize these truths, and they have an impact upon him. The lusts of the flesh and mind are gone. They are replaced by the desires for Christ Himself.

The believer has a strong desire for prayer, communion, and fellowship with God. There is also the desire for fellowship with other saints. Further, there is an increasing concern for those who are outside the fellowship of the saints, for those who are dead in their sins and trespasses. There is a changed heart within the new man.

Lastly, the believer exercises his will in a new direction. What is it? To please Christ and to please God. His questions are not what do I like or want, but what is His will for me. Now he desires the things of Christ.

We have been raised together with Him, and because of this we have a new heart, mind, and will. We are joined to Christ. It is a bond, a forged link.

I say it reverently, I am joined to my wife whether we are miles apart or not. It is actual, real. However, the bond with Christ is even more so.

Christ rules: He rules here and now, not just in some never, never place. The kingdom of God is not a geographical place, but God is the ruler, and Christ is the King.

Amen!

7

A Remarkable Truth

> *Even when we were dead in sins, hath quickened* (made alive) *us together with Christ, (by grace ye are* (have been) *saved;)*
> *And hath raised us up together, and made us sit together in heavenly places in Christ Jesus* [Eph. 2:5–6].
>
> *But God, . . .*
> *. . . hath quickened (made alive) us together with Christ . . .*
> *And hath raised us* (to do what?) [To] *sit together in heavenly places in Christ Jesus* [Eph. 2:4–6].

After Jesus had been raised from the dead, he did not remain on earth for an indefinite period of time. He ascended into heaven. Paul says that this has happened to the believer. Why does Paul say this? Because the Doctrine of Union with Christ insists upon it. We have been quickened with Him, and we have been raised with Him. Therefore, what has happened to Him in the Spirit must happen to us in the Spirit. We will sit with Him *in the heavenly places.*

The past tense refers to something that has happened, not to something that will happen. Therefore, it is not a prophecy, not a prediction. It is a fact. The Ephesians needed to know what was true of them. Why was it true of them in the Spirit? Because of their union with our Lord.

When you really think about it, three phrases contained in these two verses have an impact upon us: *hath quickened* (made alive) *us; hath raised us; and made us sit together in heavenly places.*

Think about these three truths. We should not gloss over them. Paul, under the influence of the Holy Spirit, wrote *to the saints . . . and to the faithful in Christ Jesus* in Ephesus. This salutation applies to each one of us today, wherever we may be. "The grave could not hold Him that was alive. Neither can it hold the quickened sinner. . . . True, the sinner is saved by grace, and by grace alone, that he may ever praise God for His wondrous goodness. But it is equally true that through God's grace the believer in Christ has left forever the old position in sin, and has come into a totally new position in Christ. Indeed the sinner has become a saint. God lifted him altogether out of that awful pit of sin and placed both feet on the solid rock 'in Christ' wherein he is to walk in the future, as in times past he walked 'in sin'. Being raised together with Christ, the saint is now to walk in newness of life. To do this, Christ must become the Life of his life," as candidly expressed by the faithful Ruth Paxson.

This is a wonderful truth. It is an amazing, glorious thing that has happened to those; *who were dead in trespasses and sins*, those who were and are *the children of disobedience*, those who had their tenor of life in the lusts of the flesh and the mind, and those who *by nature* were *the children of wrath*. What is the truth? We are seated with Christ in the heavenly places, in the Spirit.

What does it mean? The Authorized Version says *in heavenly places*. A better translation would be to say, in "the heavenlies." The word 'places' has been added by the translators. Unfortunately, it localizes the interpretation and really does not convey the full meaning in the mind of the Apostle.

What is meant by *in the heavenlies*? Paul describes it in his letter to the Colossians in the following words:

> *I knew a man in Christ above fourteen years ago, (whether in the body, I cannot tell (do not know); or whether out of the body, I cannot tell (do not know): God knoweth;) such a one caught up to the third heaven* [2 Cor. 12:2].

During biblical times people thought differently about heaven, or the heavens, than they do today. The first heaven was the atmosphere, the clouds, and so forth. The second heaven contained the stars, the moon, and the sun. The third heaven was the place where God manifests His presence and His glory. It is the place where the Lord Jesus Christ dwells. It is the realm to which we belong as the result of our regeneration. It is where the glory and presence of God are manifested. They are manifested in a glorious and wonderful manner.

What does this mean? Recall how we were in the first three verses of this second chapter where Scripture says *But God*. Then we became *alive unto God.* We became regenerated, the Spirit dwelt within us. What does this mean in a positive sense?

First, we belong to the kingdom of God. It is not that we will belong at some time in the future, but that we belong now.

What does the Apostle Paul say about some people?

> *(For many walk, of whom I have told you often, and now tell you even weeping, that they are the enemies of the cross of Christ:*
> *Whose end is destruction, whose God is their belly, and whose glory is in their shame, who (set their) mind (on) earthly things.)*
> *For our conversation* (citizenship) *is in heaven; from whence also we look for the Saviour, the Lord Jesus Christ* [Phil. 3:18–20].

Note these phrases: *whose end is destruction, whose God is their belly, whose glory is in their shame.*

But it continues saying *For our conversation* (citizenship) *is in heaven* [Phil. 3:20]. This means our citizenship is in heaven. While we are on earth, we are merely "a colony of heaven." Our homeland is in heaven. We do not belong to a kingdom doomed to destruction. We belong to God the Father of our Lord Jesus Christ, and He shall abide forever. Our citizenship, our tenor of life, is in heaven.

> *Who hath delivered us from the power of darkness, and hath translated* (transferred) *us into the kingdom of his dear Son* (the son of his love) [Col. 1:13].

> *For ye are dead, and your life is hid with Christ in God* [Col. 3:3].

If you are a Christian, then one thing true of you is that you are dead. The old person, the former self is dead. It is hid with Christ. The former person, the Adamic man, is literally dead. He is no longer in existence. However, as Christians we are *alive unto God.* We belong to the kingdom of God.

Second, we are under the control of the Holy Spirit. What happens when we are under the control of the Holy Spirit? What happens to the real Christian? *For as many as are led by the Spirit of God, they are the sons of God* [Rom. 8:14]. They are led by the Spirit of God, not by the mind of the world, not by other people, not by the papers, not by what is in vogue, but led by the Spirit of God.

The Christian is heavenly minded. He is alive to God. His mind is changed. He is no longer governed by the lusts of the flesh and the mind. They may tempt him, try him, and test him, but he is not controlled by them. The Spirit of God deals with him, works with him, moves him, and guides him.

Third, there is the characteristic of the heavenlies. The heavenlies are where God manifests Himself, His presence, and His glory in a special manner. The author of the letter to the Hebrews says, *Let us therefore come boldly* (confidently) *unto the throne of grace, that we may obtain mercy, and find grace to help in time of need* [Heb. 4:16]. One feature of the heavenlies is the *glory of God*, the praising of God. That is a characteristic of the heavenlies.

When we are *in the heavenlies* we are near to God. James says *Draw nigh to God, and he will draw nigh to you* [Jas. 4:8]. As a believer, we can be near to God, we can draw nigh, we can come to the throne of grace, we will obtain mercy, and we will find grace to help in the time of need.

Further, when examining Hebrews we are told through the Holy Spirit that

> *Having therefore, brethren, boldness* (confidence) *to enter into the holiest by the blood of Jesus,*
> *By a new and living way, which he hath consecrated for us, through the veil, that is to say, his flesh;*
> *And having a high priest over the house of God;*
> *Let us draw near with a true heart in full assurance of faith, having our hearts sprinkled from an evil conscience, and our bodies washed with pure water.*
> *Let us hold fast the profession* (confession) *of our faith* (hope) *without wavering; (for he is faithful that promised;)*
> [Heb. 10:19–23].

The Holy Spirit tells us that we are to have boldness to enter the holiest of holies by the shed blood of Jesus. It is a new way of living that was consecrated through the veil, His flesh. It is necessary to have a high priest in order to draw near to God with *the full assurance of faith*, and to hold fast to *the profession of our faith without wavering*.

What else is true about *in the heavenlies*? The letter to the Hebrews reveals the following:

- *Ye are come unto mount Zion,*
- *The city of the living God,*
- *To an innumerable company of angels,*
- *Church of the first-born,*

- *To God the Judge of all,*
- *The spirits of just men made perfect,*
- *To Jesus the mediator of the new covenant, and to*
- *The blood of sprinkling, that speaketh better things than that of Abel* [Selections from Heb. 12:22–24].

We are to have fellowship with God and with Christ. We have been quickened, raised, and made to sit *in the heavenlies.*

Fourth, because we are *in the heavenlies,* we already know something of the heavenly life while we are in the world. We enjoy the first fruits.

Fifth, what about the phrase *And made us sit together in the heavenlies in Christ Jesus* [Eph. 2:6]? This is a most interesting statement, "seated together."

"Dare we believe this glorious truth that He who went down to the very deepest depths of sin for us now carries us up to the very highest heights of glory with Him. That is hardly the way to put the question. Dare we not believe it? God has written both of these truths in His Word and, if we do not believe the latter, we do not really believe the former. God has said it, and to disbelieve is to make God a liar.

"Yes, at home in the heavenlies, where our citizenship really is [Phil. 3:20]. Not visiting this glorious place from time to time as trial, sorrow and conflict drive us to a higher plane, but settling down in the heavenlies in possessive and permanent occupancy as our abiding place," as described by God's servant Ruth Paxson.

Paul affirms this truth in his letter to the Philippians when he says,

> *For our conversation (citizenship) is in heaven from whence also we look for the Savior, the Lord Jesus Christ* [Phil. 3:20].

Yes, our citizenship is in heaven. The Apostle Paul is making a specific point. He has already said to them before stating that their citizenship is in heaven,

> *Brethren, be followers* (join in following my example) *together of me, and mark* (note) *them which walk so as ye have us for an example* (a pattern).
>
> *For many walk, of whom I have told you often, and now tell you even weeping, that they are the enemies of the cross of Christ:*
>
> *Whose end is destruction, whose God is their belly, and whose glory is in the shame, who mind* (set their mind on) *earthly things* [Phil. 3:17–19].

Paul's description and contrast do not leave much to one's imagination. However, he does offer us a choice. The two options are clearly stated. Which do you choose? To follow Paul's example and have your citizenship in heaven, or to reject or ignore God's commands and teachings along with His *rich mercy* and grace and be an *enemy of the cross of Christ?*

What is true of Christ? Scripture tells us that

> *... when he had by himself purged* (cleansed) *our sins, sat down on the right hand of the Majesty on high* [Heb. 1:3].

> *But to which of the angels said he* (God) *at any time, SIT ON MY RIGHT HAND, UNTIL I MAKE THINE ENEMIES THY FOOTSTOOL* [Heb. 1:13]?

Jesus sat down on the right hand of God. He finished His work, therefore He sat down. When a man sits down, he has finished his work. What does this mean regarding Christ? He was victorious. He won the victory. Therefore, our redemption has been completed. There is nothing further to do. It has been accomplished. Remember, *whom he called, them he also justified: and whom he justified, them he also glorified* [Rom. 8:30].

We are to realize that we are in Christ. We are joined to Him in the Spirit. If we are trying to make ourselves Christians, if we are trying to make ourselves acceptable, then we completely misunderstand what has happened and are overlooking the first two words of the fourth verse, *But God* [Eph. 2:4]. God has done it. How has He done it? God has done it in, through, and by the Lord Jesus Christ and the power of the Holy Spirit.

When accepting this fact, a little additional scriptural knowledge can be helpful on our journey with Christ. *Resist the devil, and he will flee from you* [Jas. 4:7]. Why? Because of the Lord Jesus Christ, in whom we live and who lives with us. Peter says, *Be sober, be vigilant; because your adversary the devil, as a roaring lion, walketh about, seeking whom he may devour* [1 Pet. 5:8]. Paul says, *For sin shall not have dominion over you: for ye are not under the law, but under grace* [Rom. 6:14]. These are the positive elements of being *alive unto God*, walking in the newness of life, and having a new mind.

Thanks be to God for His grace, love, and mercy. Martin Luther in his memorable hymn, A Mighty Fortress Is Our God, focuses attention on sin, Satan, Christ's strength, and God's grace. Thank God for these meaningful truths:

> *A mighty Fortress is our God, A Bulwark never failing;*
> *Our Helper He amid the flood Of mortal ills prevailing.*
> *For still our ancient foe, Doth seek to work us woe; His craft and power are great;*
> *And armed with cruel hate, On earth is not his equal.*
>
> *Did we in our own strength confide, Our striving would be losing;*
> *Were not the right man on our side, The man of God's own choosing.*
> *Dost ask who that may be? Christ Jesus, it is He, Lord Sabaoth His name,*
> *From age to age the same, And He must win the battle.*
>
> *And though this world, with devils filled, Should threaten to undo us,*
> *We will not fear, for God hath willed His truth to triumph through us.*
> *The prince of darkness grim, We tremble not for him, His rage we can endure,*
> *For lo! his doom is sure; One little word shall fell him.*
>
> *That word above all earthly powers, No thanks to them, abideth;*
> *The Spirit and the gifts are ours Through Him who with us sideth;*
> *Let goods and kindred go, This mortal life also; The body they may kill:*
> *God's truth abideth still, His Kingdom is forever.*

Amen!

8

God's Kindness Toward Us

> *That in the ages to come he might show the exceeding riches of his grace in his kindness toward us through* (in) *Christ Jesus* [Eph. 2:7].

The Apostle reminds the Ephesian believers of what God has done for them through our Lord and Saviour Jesus Christ. He begins this portion of Scripture saying *But God* and ends it with *through* (in) *Christ Jesus*.

When we were in a hopeless condition God intervened. Why did He? What was His motive? The answer is given in this seventh verse which begins *That*, meaning "In order that," and it is followed by the words *in the ages to come he might show*. The word *That* is important because it reveals once again the importance of considering what the writers of Scripture are saying, and being aware of the different words and thoughts. We are to remember that often our view of Christianity and ourselves as believers leaves much to be desired.

Too often our conception of salvation is incomplete. After having accepted Christ as our Lord and Saviour, we should grasp our justification and regeneration. We need to grasp the truth about what has happened and is happening to us. Most of our troubles as followers of Christ stem from our self-centeredness and the fact that we always start with ourselves. By nature we seem to subjectively approach everything that concerns us instead of objectively from God's point of view as revealed in His Word.

We should thank God for subjective feelings, especially with respect to our salvation. We should be aware of things within ourselves. However, it can be detrimental to approach things *only* in a subjective manner. If we do, we can fail to grasp with our minds the objective presentation of truths contained in Scripture. If we had a true scriptural conception of ourselves as Christians joined to the body of Christ, then we would concentrate on the truths presented and steer away from the less important items.

We often hear people grumble or complain that they are troubled by things. We have all wondered why God allows things to happen and why He does this and that to us. We need to see ourselves objectively according to God's purpose. If we will, then these difficulties and problems will disappear. If we have some conception of the glory and blessings awaiting us, then our outlook would be changed. The cure for self-centeredness, self-pity, introspection, morbidity, and similar afflictions is to know the glory and purpose of God. That is one reason why the Apostle has written this Epistle.

We are to lift up our heads and see ourselves objectively in God's eternal plan. Why has God done all this? *That in the ages to come he might show the exceeding riches of his grace in his kindness toward us through* (in) *Christ Jesus.*

"Paul was in prison when he wrote this epistle, but one would never know it. There is no smell of a prison in Ephesians. As you open the book it is just like going into some vast, open expanse and breathing the fresh air of heaven. There is no clank of prison chains to be heard, for Paul is not bound in spirit. He is there as the prisoner of Rome, but this he will not admit, and claims to be 'the prisoner of Jesus Christ.' What is the secret of such victorious other worldliness? Paul's spirit is with Christ in the heavenlies though his body languishes in that foul Roman prison.

"Oh! My friend, where do you live? 'At' or 'In'? Do you just live down on earth as a Christian all wrought up into a frenzy of anxiety over life's perplexities and problems; its trials and tribulations; its sufferings and sorrows? You will surely have them, for they are permitted, even intended by God for your discipline, growth and training. Or do you daily take afresh by faith your position in Christ in the heavenlies and there find His peace, joy and rest; yes, and the courage and strength to bear and to endure victoriously?" as appropriately described by the devoted Ruth Paxson who also includes some penetrating questions. May we ponder her words and consider her questions.

What is the primary intent and objective of salvation? It is not what most people think. It is not me; it is not you. It is the *glory of God*. God does this in order to provide a witness to His glory.

Do we normally think of our salvation in this context? I do not think so. We usually think of salvation as something we need. We normally start with ourselves and end at the same place.

We are to learn and to understand that our salvation points to the *glory of God*. Please do not misunderstand what I am saying, but the primary intent with salvation is not us. It is to reveal God's love, mercy, and glory. That is the teaching of Scripture.

We are not to start with our own sinful acts, but with our condition in sin. We are to learn and know about the condition of men in sin, the condition that has been true through the ages. We are to realize what has been true of man apart from Christ. We want to think in terms of ourselves and our own importance. We want to believe we are better than our predecessors of one hundred-, five hundred-, one thousand-, or two thousand years ago.

We need to start thinking in terms of sin, the whole problem of man, and the problem of evil in the world. We should begin by thinking of ourselves, our own sins and problems. When taking this approach we begin to see what the Apostle means when he says that the *glory of God* should be the primary intent and objective of our salvation.

Sin is utterly opposed to God. What has happened as the result of sin and the Fall? The resulting consequences are a tremendous concern to God.

However, we continue to think of sin in the terms of particular acts, especially acts which we may not think we are guilty of committing. We want to turn the problem of sin into a social problem, and think that by education, help, money, or whatever, that conditions will improve and the particular offenses against us or our loved ones will go away. We do not want to feel remorse or be moved to repentance because that is too personal. Yet, thankfully, the Holy Spirit invades our conscience, we feel remorse and are moved to repent. The Bible looks at sin differently. The Bible considers sin as an attack upon God.

You may recall that in the first and second chapters of Genesis, God created everything and saw that it was good. Then what happened in the third chapter? The Fall of Man!

Why did the devil tempt Adam and Eve? So they would commit one single act? No, the primary reason was to detract from the *glory of God*, to detract from His majesty and His greatness.

But what do we do? We get caught up in ourselves or get involved in the inconsequential details. We need to remember Satan's objective in what happened in the garden. He wanted to spoil God's work, to spoil the world and man's relationship with God. That is how we should look at sin. It is *not* primarily a social problem. The social problems occur as a by-product of sin.

What then is salvation? Salvation is the work of God's saving grace that we receive through the sacrifice of Jesus on the Cross. It is effective when we repent, turn to Jesus, and confess Him as our Lord and Saviour. *He that committeth* (practices) *sin is of the devil; for the devil sinneth from the beginning. For this purpose the Son of God was manifested, that he might destroy the works of the devil* [1 John 3:8].

The devil could not and cannot affect the being, nature, and character of God. But he did succeed in affecting the attitude of man towards God. Therefore, God initiated his great plan of salvation by which He declares His love for man. Why has He done this? *That in the ages to come he might show the exceeding riches of his grace in his kindness toward us through* (in) *Christ Jesus*. Why did He send His Son? To show His glory, majesty, and greatness, and to declare the truth about Himself.

There is a special way and manner in which salvation vindicates the greatness and character of God. Through salvation we learn things about God that otherwise we would never have known. People ask the question, maybe halfheartedly, maybe seriously: Why did God allow the Fall? Why did He allow man to fall into sin?

We do not know the full answer. However, if God had not allowed the possibility of man's fall then there would have been limitations on man's freedom. If there had been limitations, man would not have been created perfectly by God. Man as created by God had free will, but he lost it by falling into sin. However, no matter what the explanation, it is perfectly clear that God has overruled it through His Redemption and in so doing has displayed certain attributes of His Holy being, nature, and character. Otherwise these things would never have been known.

These attributes of God are to be known. The Apostle says in this verse *in the ages to come*. What does this mean, to what does it lead? That God should be glorified. That the Ephesians should constantly remind themselves of what God has done, and that they should be assured of their salvation, realizing it was due to God's righteousness. "It was the will of the Lord to hallow in all ages the remembrance of so great a goodness," as beautifully expressed by John Calvin. We are to remember this great goodness that God has given us.

Throughout the ages people have attacked the "free calling of the Gentiles." They have tried to crush it, to stamp it out. What happened to these efforts? By God's mercy we have been called, and we should continually remember it is by God's will that we are called.

When you really think of the "free calling of the Gentiles," (you and me), it is *an astonishing work of divine goodness*. This wonderful work of mercy and goodness should be continually handed down from parents to children to grandchildren to great grandchildren and forever to every succeeding generation.

These four verses [Eph. 2:4–7] started with *But God who is rich in mercy*. This raises an interesting question: What would be our conception of God's rich mercy if we had not fallen into our sinful condition? Also, if we do not have some conception of our sinful condition, how can we have any idea of God's mercy, grace, and power? "Amazing grace that saved a wretch like me."

Can we really know the love of God, sending His Son to Calvary's Hill and the Cross, and the power of the resurrection if we do not have some understanding of our sinful condition, the lusts of the flesh and mind? Therefore, Paul says, . . . *that in the ages to come he might show the exceeding riches of his grace in his kindness toward us through* (in) *Christ Jesus*.

These things enable us to have an understanding of God's grace. The display and vindication of God's being, character, glory, and greatness are realized through the church, through the community of believers. How do these tremendous, wonderful things occur? They happen through us, through people like us.

Can you imagine that this holy, almighty, everlasting, creating, omnipotent God reveals Himself and does things in and through us? He works through His followers, through the community of believers. This is something to realize; this is the meaning of church membership and participation. This helps eliminate subjective feelings and enables one to see something of God's plan and purpose, of God's mercy and love.

When we begin to see these things, we begin to see ourselves in God's great plan and what He has done as the result of man falling into sin. Consider further *the exceeding riches of his grace in his kindness toward us*.

Paul demonstrates and confirms that God's love comes to us through His mercy. He shows this richness in His *kindness toward us*. He shows that the love of God was free; it was a gift of His kindness. It was not an ordinary gift. It was an outstanding one.

The renowned John Calvin provides additional clarity and strength to *the exceeding* riches of His grace in His kindness towards us saying, "He now demonstrates or confirms that the love which God shows to us in Christ springs from mercy. 'That He might shew', he says, 'the richness of His grace.' How? 'In kindness towards us', as the tree in its fruit. Not only, therefore, does he assert that the love of God was free, but also that God displayed in it the richness of His grace—and that not ordinary but outstanding."

The Apostle Paul says that everything from God comes through Christ Jesus, by the power of the Holy Spirit. He declares what he was called to do, according to the gift of God, saying,

> Unto me . . . is this grace given, that I should preach among the Gentiles the unsearchable riches of Christ;
> And to make all men see what is the fellowship of the mystery, which from the beginning . . . hath been hid in God, who created all things by Jesus Christ:
> To the intent that now unto the principalities and powers in heavenly places might be known by the church the manifold (many-sided) *wisdom of God,* . . . [Excerpts from Eph. 3:8–10].

We are to pass these truths along to others.

God uses the church to demonstrate and exhibit the principalities and powers of His eternal, amazing wisdom. That is how we are to think as members of the community of believers. The church is where God vindicates Himself through you and me. He works through people like us. He works through human beings despite their fallibilities. He has done it through the ages and will continue to do so in the ages to come. We are being prepared to be used, and we will be used. Artists prepare their paintings, musicians prepare their pieces, and athletes prepare their bodies.

God is preparing us and we are to prepare ourselves. The Apostle John reveals to us what we may expect on that great day, saying,

> SALVATION TO OUR GOD,
> ... *The angels stood round about the throne ... and worshipped God,*
> *Saying, Amen: Blessing, and glory, and wisdom, and thanksgiving, and honor, and power, and might, ...*
> *What (Who) are these which are arrayed in white robes? ...*
> *These are they which came out of great tribulation ... washed their robes and made them white in the blood of the Lamb,*
> *They (are) before the throne of God, and serve him day and night in his temple: ...*
> *They shall hunger no more, neither thirst any more;*
> *... For the Lamb ... shall feed* (shepherd) *them and shall lead them, ... and God shall wipe away all tears* (every tear) *from their eyes* [Excerpts from Rev. 7:10–17].

Who are these people? The ones redeemed by the wisdom, power, glory, love, and grace of God.

- How? Through Christ Jesus.
- In what way? By the church.
- Who is included? You and me!
- Why? Due to the glory of God.

How does He work in and through the church? Remember, God looked upon us as *children of disobedience* and incurring His wrath, who in their conversation (tenor of life) in times past were subject to the lusts of the flesh and mind.

That is the way we were. *But God* had mercy as He looked upon us. He displayed His holy nature by devising a plan for man's salvation and implementing it. God did this, not man. Salvation is completely, entirely, and fully from God. Man had nothing to do with it. By grace ye have been saved. Truly this is a magnificent display of God's being and character.

When considering these wonderful truths, what impact should they have upon us? If we start by thinking of ourselves, our church membership, or our good deeds, then we have missed the point and are going in the wrong direction. We need to start with what God has done, with the intent of God, and God's plan, as revealed in Paul's words: *That in the ages to come he might show the exceeding riches of his grace.* God has done everything and He has done it *in his kindness toward us through* (in) *Christ Jesus.* This is how we should think of it.

What happens as a result of all this? *And every man that hath this hope in him purifieth himself, even as he is pure* [1 John 3:3]. When a person examines himself or herself in light of these truths, his or her priority will no longer be the things of the world, but the things of the Lord and of the Holy Spirit. Therefore, we are to be diligent in growing and maturing in holiness by increasing in faith and knowledge. God will bless us through His grace and mercy, but we must set our priorities and pursue them. Remember, the Lord Jesus said, *Blessed are the pure in heart: for they shall see God.*

What guarantees the certainty of all this? Do I have confidence in my salvation based upon myself, my own energy, desires, purposes, intellect, ability? No. It is based upon God, His being, His character, and His assurance.

If He started to save me, or He claimed one and left the work unfinished or undone, then Satan would have great joy. Satan would be able to say that God began to save a certain one, but He could not; He failed.

It cannot be that a person is born again in truth and the Spirit, and then is lost. Note, I said in the Spirit, in the Holy Spirit, not in his own mind, not as seed on the hard ground or among the weeds, but born of the Holy Spirit.

Why do I say this? Because the being and character of God is involved. The object is not merely to save me, but it is to reveal the mercy, love, grace, and power of God. *It is to glorify God.* Paul says, *Being confident of this very thing, that he which hath begun a good work in you will perform* (complete) *it until the day of Jesus Christ* [Phil. 1:6].

One last observation: think of the privilege of being used by God in this way, to glorify Him and His name. As the elder asks, who are these? Here we are, and we have been chosen: chosen by God; chosen to be part of His great plan; chosen to be part of His purpose; chosen to vindicate Himself; and chosen to reveal His greatness, His glory, His wisdom, His grace, His love, and His kindness.

When you think and meditate upon being chosen for all these things it is bound to have an impact, it is bound to affect you. May you remember,

> *But God . . . through* (in) *Christ Jesus.*

Amen!

9

Saved Through Faith

For by grace are ye (you have been) *saved through faith; and that not of yourselves: it is the gift of God:*
Not of works, lest any man should boast.
For we are his workmanship (creation), *created in Christ Jesus unto* (for) *good works, which God hath before ordained* (prepared) *that we should walk in them* [Eph. 2:8–10].

Once again, Paul focuses on doctrine. He wants the Ephesians (and us) to have a truthful, clear understanding of what makes a Christian. Therefore he says, *For by grace are ye* (you have been) *saved through faith; and that not of yourselves: it is the gift of God.*

This statement impacts a person one way or another, positively or negatively. Also, it impacts people active in church affairs or holding various positions. Our actions are affected, because a person's beliefs and practices are inseparable. You cannot separate a man's point of view from his thoughts and conduct.

Paul was writing to the community of believers in Ephesus. He wanted them to understand what God had done to help them grow in their Christian faith. He was writing to help them in a practical and pastoral way. He was not just writing a treatise. He was communicating with them, in order that they might live as Christ would have them to live, and to do so in the midst of people who had not been quickened, who were still in the lusts of the flesh and the mind. Paul knew that no one can live their life in Christ unless he or she has a true understanding of what a Christian should be and how he or she should conduct themselves. Therefore, Paul starts with doctrine and proceeds to apply it.

Paul prayed that the believer's eyes of understanding might be enlightened, and that they might realize the greatness of God's *power to us-ward who believe*. We need our eyes enlightened and a realization of God's power to us-ward. We need to understand man's condition in sin, and what has been done to bring us into a right relationship with the Father. Paul continues by describing *God's way of reconciliation* in verses 8–10 of this chapter.

He wants us to know what it really means to be a Christian. When considering this, it is important to start properly. If we do not build the proper foundation, then the house or building will have problems. When preparing a meal, if we do not follow the recipes, then the results may not be edible or taste the way we want. When the golfer does not address the ball properly, then the desired results will not occur.

The Apostle's statements in verses eight to ten are explicit. Why then does confusion occur? Perhaps it is because people want to bring to bear their own philosophy, mindset, and ideas instead of accepting the Apostle's statements and seeking amplification or clarification. They either reject or dispute them or say that does not agree with their own experiences or feelings. And if people do not accept Paul's expository statements, they say how could God be a God of love? Basically, there is a fundamental question to face: do we or do we not accept the scriptures as our one and only foundation? *For they being ignorant of God's righteousness, . . . have not submitted themselves unto the righteousness of God* [Rom. 10:3].

When considering these verses, we should examine them as the foundation upon which living as a member of the community of believers is placed and is being built. This is the beginning point. It is critical to one's growth and development as a member of Christ's body. *For by grace are ye* (you have been) *saved through faith; and that not of yourselves: it is the gift of God.* Paul states in a direct and positive way that we are Christians entirely and solely as the result of God's grace.

The Doctrine of Grace appears in both the Old and New Testaments. It binds all Scripture together. The Bible is the story of God's saving power, of God's grace. The word *grace* appears for the first time in Genesis. *But Noah found grace in the eyes of the Lord* [Gen. 6:8]. He found or received the favor of God, not by anything he, Noah, had done or not done, but because there was a covenant between Noah and God.

After God bestowed His grace upon Noah, He embraced him and retained him by His own hand so that Noah would not perish with the rest of the world. The covenant with Noah resulted after he received

God's favor, which was undeserved and without condition or strings attached. The grace of God in the Old Testament is closely related to the covenant God made with man, which is the basis of the Law.

In the Old Testament, the Hebrew word for grace, *chesed*, is normally translated as *loving-kindness*. It stands for God's continuing faithfulness to His covenant people and for His steadfast determination to never let them go. The Old Testament use of the word was incorporated into the belief that God's favor was entirely free. Nothing whatsoever was done to obtain it. It was completely undeserved, and there was no obligation on God's part to bestow it.

The reason for the continued existence of the Israelites in the Old Testament is found in God's grace. If it had not been for this factor, then Israel would have gone the way of the heathen.

In the New Testament, the word *grace* usually denotes God's redemptive love. It is this love initiated by God that saves man, individuals, from their sinful condition and keeps them in a proper relationship with Himself.

Paul did not use the normal Greek word for the equivalent to the Hebrew *chesed*. Why? He knew it was inadequate because it did not emphasize God's long-suffering and His patience. Paul above all others knew the wonder of God's love and the depth of it. He realized that the rejection of Jesus Christ was the climax of the repeated apostasy by Israel throughout their history.

To Paul, and this is important, Christ's death had broken down the partition, the wall, existing between the Jew and the Gentile. What was the result of that event, that happening? The wealth of God's covenant; love is now available to every person. Why? Because God's grace has broken down all the barriers.

In the New Testament a new covenant reaffirms an old one. It reveals that God's plan of grace was implicit from the beginning. The grace of the Old Testament is manifest in the life and work of Jesus Christ. *For in him* (Christ) *dwelleth all the fullness of the Godhead bodily* [Col. 2:9].

Therefore, we can speak of the grace of the Lord Jesus Christ our Saviour, or the grace of God our Father. All of this is involved in how Paul uses the word *grace*. He makes it clear that the righteousness, salvation offered by God, to which the Law and Prophets gave witness has been declared to all who are without the Law.

Where is this salvation found? By and through faith in Jesus Christ. To whom is it available? To all who believe. There is no distinction between Jew and Gentile.

All are saved by the grace of God. *For all have sinned, and come* (fall) *short of the glory of God; Being justified freely* (without any cost) *by his grace through the redemption that is in Christ Jesus* [Rom. 3:23–24]. Through the forbearance of God their former sins were overlooked. Now is the time of salvation.

The New Testament and Old Testament equally emphasize that grace is the free gift of God. Paul writes to the Ephesians and to the Romans confirming this with explicit words,

> *But God, who is rich in mercy, for his great love wherewith he loved us,*
> *Even when we were dead in sins, hath quickened (made alive) us together with Christ, (by grace ye are (have been) saved;)* [Eph. 2:4–5].

> *Being justified freely* (without any cost) *by his grace through the redemption that is in Christ Jesus* [Rom. 3:24].

> *And if by grace, then is it no more of works: otherwise grace is no more grace. But if it be of works, then is it no more grace: otherwise work is no more work* [Rom. 11:6].

Further, it is not because man is deserving, as Paul made abundantly clear in a letter to Timothy saying, *Who hath saved us, and called us with a holy calling, not according to our works, but according to his own purpose and grace, which was given us in Christ Jesus before the world* (time) *began* [2 Tim. 1:9].

In addition, Paul is certain that his own call was due to God's good pleasure and by His grace, as he expressed in his letter to the Galatians when he said, *But when it pleased God, who separated me from my mother's womb, and called me by his grace* [Gal. 1:15]. Even faith and the condition of salvation is due to the grace of God. Everything from first to last, from Alpha to Omega is by God's grace.

Once we have been called, we must be persistent. Paul tells the Philippians that they have a responsibility regarding their salvation and describes it in explicit detail saying,

> *Wherefore, my beloved, as ye have always obeyed, not as in my presence only, but now much more in my absence work out your own salvation with fear and trembling.*
>
> *God ... worketh in you both to will and to do of (according to) his good pleasure.*
>
> *Do all things without murmurings (grumbling) and disputings:*
>
> *That ye may be blameless and harmless (innocent), the sons (children) of God, without rebuke (fault), in the midst of a crooked and perverse nation (generation), among whom ye shine as lights in the world;*
>
> *Holding forth* (fast) *to the word of life* [Phil. 2:12–16].

Paul, in his inimitable fashion, stresses important truths to the Ephesians and us. He begins by thanking them for their obedience, and encouraging them to *work out your own salvation with fear and trembling*. He knows they have started their journey on life's path with the Lord Jesus, but he does not want them to become distracted, falter, or lazy in pursuing their life with Christ and increasing in faith and knowledge. He wants them "to *work out* the salvation God has already wrought in them ... for their own profit, but for the good of others as well ... (and to) live lives worthy of the gospel in harmony with each other ... and make the appropriate sacrifices in obedience to God, as did Jesus. In doing all this they will work out or express the new life they have through Christ," as appropriately stated in the King James Study Bible.

The solution is found in the Christian experience. There is an important observation to be made: the less a person knows regarding God's saving grace, the more he or she will emphasize the human element; and the more a person knows regarding God's saving grace, the more he or she realizes that it is the decisive factor in his or her life. Everything that reveals or identifies grace in the human heart should be recognized as being the work of the Holy Spirit.

There is a second point to ponder. The fact that we are Christians, members of the community of believers, does not allow us to boast about what we have done. The Apostle says two things in these verses: *not of yourselves* and *lest any man should boast* [Eph. 2:8–9]. This leads to certain questions: What do you think about yourself as a Christian? How did you become a follower, a member of the community of believers? What happened to bring this about? What is the reason?

Do you have any ideas or thoughts about what you have done to become a Christian? If the answer is yes, then you are on the wrong road. You are going in the wrong direction. Remember Paul's admonition, *Where is boasting then? It is excluded. By what law? of works? Nay: but by the law of faith* [Rom. 3:27]. Boasting is excluded. This is what Paul says under the influence of the Holy Ghost.

Paul knew something about boasting before traveling the road to Damascus. He was self-satisfied and self assured; he was proud, proud of his nationality, his tribe, his religion, his morality, and his knowledge. He was also proud of having studied under Gamaliel and being a Pharisee [Phil. 3:4–7].

What did Paul say about all this? One of the most amazing revelations ever recorded, *For whom I have suffered the loss of all things, and do count them but dung, that I may win Christ* [Phil. 3:8]. What is Paul saying? It was all wrong, filthy, and foul. It is excluded.

Paul continues expounding upon his thoughts and reveals there are two areas where we tend to boast.

> First, *Not of works, lest any man should boast.* That is a point where we are all tempted. We want to do something, we want to think we have done something, we want works to count for something. That was why the Pharisees fell out with Jesus. Not because they were just talkers, but because they did certain things: they fasted, and they gave tithes.
>
> *The greatest opponents of the evangelical faith have been good, religious people. Why? Because of their works!*
>
> Second, THERE IS NONE RIGHTEOUS, NO, NOT ONE [Rom. 3:10]. This does not sit well with the person who thinks he or she has done something, just a little something, to merit God's favor. However, the Gospel makes it plain, there is no difference between the Jew and the Gentile.

However, no matter of what we want to boast—our works, our good deeds, our good living, our church attendance, our work in the church, our religious activities, or whatever—to all of these things, Scripture says, No, no, no!

There is an innate drive in people whereby they want to say their good works make them Christians. However, Paul says it is the other way around. We are His workmanship, created in Christ Jesus unto good works. Unfortunately, people want to think that if they do certain things or avoid some things, live a good life, and offer help to others that they will become Christians. That is not the case. God makes us Christians so that we may do good works. That leads to considering the word *faith*.

In Scripture, faith denotes a right relationship to God. It is important to realize and understand that in the biblical context this word does not even intimate "believing what we cannot prove." Normally, the term refers to the full actuality of the relationship established by God for Christians in Christ. Faith to the Hebrew is firmness, reliability and steadfastness. To believe or to have faith is to hold on to something firmly, with conviction and trust. "Faith is holding on to what you believe to be true, despite your emotions," simply, yet firmly stated C. S. Lewis.

There are two aspects to the faith which a person has and exercises. First is the confident reliance upon God, which exhibits itself in how a person grabs hold of God, becomes obedient to God, and trusts Him completely; and second is the abandonment of all self-interest and self-reliance.

Loyalty to God, complete dependence upon Him, is found in a person of faith. These attributes are the result of God acting, not of anything we have done. God makes a person a firm believer and a trustworthy follower. The efficacy of faith for salvation and a right relationship with God is not in the act itself, but in the person who holds firm by believing. It is a right relationship to God.

Faith is not the cause of salvation. Jesus Christ, the embodiment of God's grace, is the cause of salvation. What is faith? It is the instrument by which salvation comes to me. Belief does not save. Faith does not save. Christ saves! Nothing I do saves, only Christ saves.

In the Synoptic Gospels, the faith to which Jesus calls us is the conviction that God through Christ was able to do what He had promised. It reveals a decisive response to the resources available from God through Christ. Therefore, boasting is excluded; whether it be boasting of works or boasting of faith, it is excluded. Salvation is entirely, completely, and only of God. Finally, our being a Christian is strictly the work of God; it is the gift of God: God began to work within me, God began to deal with me, and God began to remake me.

It was not that I decided to do something. Once again, Paul clarifies the issue with strong, easily understood words, stating a fundamental truth, *Being confident of this very thing, that he which hath begun a good work in you will perform* (complete) *it until the day of Jesus Christ* [Phil. 1:6]. It was God that began the good work. He came when you were dead and gave you life. It was not your works, your decision, or your effort. It was the gift of God.

In these verses, the Apostle embraces the sum and substance of his arguments in Romans and Galatians, that righteousness (salvation) comes to each of us because of God's mercy and His mercy only. It is offered in Christ through the Gospel. It is received by faith alone. There are no works involved.

Paul's statement in these verses cannot stand unless all the praise is rendered unto God and His mercy. Some people when considering these verses want to say that the word *gift* as it is used refers to faith only and not to salvation which is given through the grace of God. Paul means that salvation *is* the gift of God and that the only way to obtain it is as a gift. It is completely undeserved and unmerited.

In conclusion: what is a Christian? He is like Christ, and he is conformed to the image of God's Son. How does this happen? *By grace are ye* (have been) *saved*. It is Christ living in you. If it were not for God's grace, then it could not, or would not happen. Thank God it is not of works, or of anything that I can boast. God forbid that I glory save in the Cross of our Lord Jesus Christ.

By grace—through faith!
Amen!

10

Created in Christ Jesus

> *For we are his workmanship* (creation), *created in Christ Jesus unto* (for) *good works, which God hath before ordained* (prepared) *that we should walk in them* [Eph. 2:10].

The Apostle Paul in a direct, straightforward manner states that grace and faith are the gifts of God. And through them we are brought into a right relationship with God. Then he says,

> . . . *we are his workmanship* (creation), *created in Christ Jesus unto* (for) *good works, which God hath before ordained* (prepared) *that we should walk in them* [Eph. 2:10].

When reading this verse carefully, observe the following:

- *we are his workmanship* (creation),
- *created in Christ Jesus,*
- *unto* (for) *good works,*
- *which God hath before ordained* (prepared),
- *that we should walk in them.*

This puts certain truths in their proper perspective and should put us in our proper place.

Our works have nothing to do with our salvation. The Apostle tells us that even our good works are ordained beforehand. We are saved by the grace of God. It is His gift to us. No works, no merit, no payment, nothing on our part. The good works we perform are the fruit of regeneration. The works are part of grace. When Paul says we are the workmanship of God, he is saying we are made of God. We are His creation.

What does he mean? He is not talking of our physical birth. But he is asserting that we are new creatures and have been formed unto righteousness. How? By the spirit of Christ Jesus, not by our own strength or power. This applies to the believers, to those spiritually regenerated by God's grace who become new people. Therefore, everything that is good in us is the work of God. We are God's work because we have been created in Christ; we are no longer in Adam.

This is a wonderful yet profound statement. We cannot gloss over it. Think for a moment of the many, many things you do in a day, week, or year, and how many times you gloss over items, or take the hit-or-miss approach. Yet here is God in all His majesty and splendor, and what does He do? He works within us; He makes us His workmanship. He performs a creative act within us through Christ Jesus unto good works. What a wonderful statement!

We are his workmanship (creation)! Hallelujah! We should understand that the Apostle does *not* say that our will is prepared and proceeds along its own course under its own strength, nor that the power of making the right choices is given to us. Yet this is what some people would have you believe.

However, the Apostle does say that we are God's work; that everything good in us is His creation, not ours; that the whole person is formed by God's power to become good; that the right will is bestowed by God; and that *we are his workmanship* (creation).

"When he (Paul) says that we are the work of God, it is not to be taken of general creation, by which we men are born, but he asserts that we are new creatures who are formed to righteousness by the Spirit of Christ and not by our own power. This applies only to believers, who, although they are born of Adam wicked and perverse, are spiritually regenerated by the grace of Christ, and begin to be new men. Everything in us that is good, therefore, is the supernatural work of God . . . for he adds that we are God's work because we have been created, not in Adam, but in Christ, and not to any kind of life, but to good works.

"Let godly readers weigh carefully the apostle's words. He does not say that we are assisted by God. He does not say that the will is prepared, and has then to proceed in its own strength. He does not say that the power of choosing aright is bestowed upon us, and that we have afterwards to make our own choice. This is what those who weaken God's grace (so far as they can) are accustomed to babble. But he says that we are God's work, and that everything good in us is His creation. By which he means that the whole man is formed by His hand to become good. It is not the mere power of choosing aright, or some indefinable preparation, or assistance, but the right will itself, which is His workmanship . . . He means to prove that man does not in any way procure salvation for himself, but obtains it freely from God. The proof is that man is nothing but by divine grace," as simply but eloquently revealed by the esteemed John Calvin.

Paul wants us to understand that salvation is the complete and free gift of God; man does not procure it for himself. Man is nothing, we are nothing, but by the divine grace of God. Whether we realize it or not, most of our troubles result from the fact that we fail to grasp the truth about ourselves and our status as Christians.

Why is this true? Because we are creatures of tradition and retain the mindset of the natural man. We begin by taking the wrong path and continue in that direction. The natural man starts with the wrong conception of the community of believers. People want to think it is being good, doing good, or committing some generous act, then receiving God's blessings, such as forgiveness. They do not want to give up these self-centered ideas, which fall far short of the New Testament concept of being Christ's followers.

The New Testament believers are continuously reminded: of their position and the privilege of it; of their destiny; that they are a handful in a pagan society; that they are to rejoice; and that they are to go forth boldly and triumphantly.

We fail to remind ourselves of these things. We have a strong tendency to think if we belong to a church or attend church services we are Christians. What is the common understanding of being a Christian? It is in human terms: thinking of God's church as a human institution, working on committees, attending functions or gatherings, and contributing or tithing. These thoughts certainly can be part of the activities and ideas relating to a church and being a member.

However, they do not constitute the church and certainly they do not make a church a church, nor do they make an individual a Christian. The questions to consider are: Do we realize the joy and privilege of being a Christian, of being a member of the community of believers? Do we realize we are part of God's great plan? Do we realize the power of God to us-ward? Do we realize our inheritance? Do we praise His glory?

We are to know the truths regarding these questions as presented by Paul in this tenth verse. They reveal much about our relationship to God the Father, the Lord Jesus Christ, and God's workmanship. This is the first thing to recognize about ourselves. We always want to think about what we have done, the work we have performed, and the effort we have exerted. We did not make ourselves Christians.

We may be too wrapped up in what we are doing, our work, our social life, our families, our church, our politics, and all the things we are doing, but not what God is doing. Therefore, it is difficult to accept the fact that God is active, that we are His handiwork, and that we are of His making. We like to think of what we have been or are doing.

It is a thrilling thought that we are being fashioned and made by God in Christ. This catches us by surprise. Our whole background and mindset is formed by what we have done: we have joined the church; we have made a profession of faith; we attend church; we pray; we read Scripture. We think of ourselves as being active and of God as being passive. We think God waits until we do something. However, it is God who pricks us and causes us to act. He is active, and we are passive until He acts within us.

How often do we hear the following: I decided for Christ; therefore, I am justified; I wanted to be sanctified, so I asked God and He responded; I want something, so I ask God for it. In other words, He is just waiting until I ask Him, and then He accommodates me. These responses are contrary to Scripture. The emphasis of Scripture is that Christianity is the result of God's activity, not ours. God is the workman. We tend to forget that the Bible is a record of what God has done: in the beginning God made man; God made the world; God called Abraham; God gave the Law; God made the Kings; God called the prophets; God gave instructions; God sent His Son; and God sent the Holy Spirit. Does that sound like a passive God? God is the workman. We are His workmanship.

What does the Apostle say? *We are his workmanship, created in Christ Jesus.* When we consider this thought, it takes us right back to Genesis, the first chapter, God created!

A good question: what is creation? The essential idea is that something is made out of nothing. There was not anything there before, but now there is something. God makes something out of nothing. What does this fact do to the idea of self-improvement?

Think now that the Christian is a new creation, a new creature. Something is brought into my life that was not there previously. Something has been created within me out of nothing. It is God's action.

It is a specific action. Paul says to the Corinthians, *For God, who commanded the light to shine out of darkness, hath shined in our hearts, to give the light of the knowledge of the glory of God in the face of Jesus Christ* [2 Cor. 4:6]. God commanded the light to shine out of darkness. He hath shined it in our hearts.

Why? To give us light regarding *the glory of God in the face of Jesus Christ.* That is what it means to be a Christian. The real travesty in life is to think that we are Christians because of something we are, or something we have done or are doing. We are to remember that we are the creation of His workmanship. We are the clay in the hands of the Potter.

How does God perform this wonderful work? Created in Christ Jesus. The work is performed in and through the Lord Jesus Christ by the power of the Holy Spirit. It is all in and through Christ. Through Him we receive the benefits of His life and death. It is through Christ that all the good comes to us. God forms the Lord Jesus Christ in us. *My little children, of whom I travail* (labor) *in birth again until Christ be formed in you* [Gal. 4:19]. That is the New Testament teaching—Christ formed in you.

God performs this wonderful work by employing different ideas or tools to work within us. He uses the Holy Spirit. God the Father, and Christ the Son, send the Holy Ghost to work within us and to fashion us. We cannot be Christians without the Holy Spirit working within us. God works through His Holy Word, which lifts us up and strengthen us.

"Our salvation is not the result of anything we are or know or do. This leaves no place for pride. Our new life and new position in Christ, even the faith by which on the manward side these unsearchable riches become our possession, are all the outright gift of God," as appropriately described by Ruth Paxson.

> *Sanctify* (set) *them* (apart) *through thy truth: thy word is truth* [John 17:17].

> *Of his own will begat he us with the word of truth, that we should be a kind of firstfruits of his creatures* [Jas. 1:18].

> *Being born again, not of corruptible* (perishable) *seed, but of incorruptible* (imperishable), *by the word of God, which liveth and abideth for ever* [1 Pet. 1:23].

God uses His Word in order to give us life. When we think about God working within us, we need to think about His Word and be thankful for it. Reading Scripture is important. God planned to use the Holy scriptures; therefore, He brought them into being. He enlightened the writers, He gave them understanding, and He enabled them to convey His truths. God also uses the preaching and teaching of the Word. God gave gifts unto men. He gave some to be apostles, prophets, evangelists, pastors and teachers.

Why did He do this? For the perfecting of the saints. The gifts given to these different people are for their benefit. He uses all these people to fashion Christians. God calls and places people in different offices so He can use them. The gifts are given to further the kingdom of God, and you are part of that kingdom. Remember these truths and rejoice in them!

Amen!

11

God's Chastening Grace

> *And ye have forgotten the exhortation which speaketh unto you as unto children,* MY SON, DESPISE NOT THOU THE CHASTENING OF THE LORD, NOR FAINT WHEN THOU ART REBUKED OF HIM:
> FOR WHOM THE LORD LOVETH HE CHASTENETH, AND SCOURGETH EVERY SON WHOM HE RECEIVETH.
> *If ye endure chastening, God dealeth with you as with sons; for what son is he whom the father chasteneth not* [Heb. 12:5–7]?

The Hebrew followers of Christ tended to grumble and to complain. Why? Because they were having trials, tribulations, and troubles. The writer does not sympathize with their plight, but says,

FOR WHOM THE LORD LOVETH HE CHASTENETH, . . . [Heb. 12:6].

If the good parent chastises the child, why should not God chastise us? Scripture contains an explicit teaching that God chastises His children. He does it in order to perfect them. God uses different methods to achieve His ultimate goal. If some ways do not work, then He will chasten us. He will make us experience challenges or ordeals in order for us to develop and mature.

God deals with us in various ways because *we are his workmanship*. He brings us to the point where we are aware of a new nature being placed within us, or realizing we are no longer what we once were. He is the Potter; we are the clay. Consider Paul's design. The Apostle states that we have presented nothing to God that obliges Him to do something for us, and even the good works we do come from Him. Scripture says, . . . *created in Christ Jesus unto* (for) *good works, which God hath before ordained* (prepared) *that we should walk in them* [Eph. 2:10]. There is a design for the individual members of the community of believers, and God has planned it.

What is this design? We are to conform to the life of our Lord Jesus Christ in this world; and we are to live our lives, as He lived His, in obedience to God according to the Sermon on the Mount, the four Gospels, and the Epistles. That is the kind of life we are to live. That is how we are to be formed and fashioned.

You do not achieve perfection in a moment. There are trials and tribulations. There are setbacks. However, God puts us through the sanctification process. He provides the way for us to proceed:

> *That he might sanctify* (set it apart) *and cleanse it with the washing of water by the word,*
> *That he might present it to himself a glorious church, not having spot, or wrinkle, or any such thing; but that it should be holy and without blemish* [Eph. 5:26–27].

No blemishes will remain.

In bringing to a close our consideration of Ephesians 2:10, we direct our attention to *He which hath begun a good work in you will perform* (complete) *it until the day of Jesus Christ* [Phil. 1:6]. When God begins a good work, you can be sure that He will continue it. If He has started to fashion and form you, then He will continue to do so. He will continue until there is no spot, blemish, or wrinkle left. However, if you resist His will, then be prepared to be chastised. And be prepared for trials, tribulations, and troubles. Keep in mind that we are His workmanship, and He will mold us, one way or another.

The King James Study Bible provides additional light regarding God who *hath begun a good work in you will perform* (complete) *it until the day of Jesus Christ,* saying " . . . the Lord will keep working in these believers until Jesus returns to earth, at which point He will finish His work, . . . For God had a purpose in view when He began His saving work in the Philippians, and that purpose will neither be abandoned nor unrealized." Meditate upon that statement. How long does it take someone to become a proficient athlete, musician, or scientist and then to maintain that proficiency? Have you ever heard of someone becoming a proficient Christian, other than the Lord Jesus? However, Paul assures us that when God begins a good work in us He will complete it. The life of a Christian is not always easy. There will be joy and sorrow, laughter and tears, ecstasy and heartbreak along life's pathway. Just look at Christ's journey on earth.

The phrase *which God hath before ordained* (prepared) is important. Do not interpret this phrase as meaning that God has commanded in detail what is just, and has laid down all the necessary rules for living a proper, holy life. Paul emphasizes that salvation is the complete gift of God and has nothing to do with anything we may have done. The only way we are able to lead a holy life is by being formed and fashioned by the Potter.

Do you begin to see that we are His workmanship, created in Christ Jesus; that salvation is the complete, total free gift of God; and that God hath prepared the good works? If a person does not desire to be holy and obedient to God, then how can he be a Christian? If a person thinks that the forgiveness of sins is the key element in God's plan of salvation, then he or she is on the wrong path.

There is no value in making a profession of faith unless it is accompanied by a desire to be like Christ Jesus, a desire to be formed and fashioned, and a desire to be rid of the lusts of the flesh and the mind.

God is active; *we are his workmanship* (creation), *created in Christ Jesus unto good works*. Do we desire to be more Christlike? Are we hungering and thirsting after righteousness?

The first chapter of Genesis uses the term *bara* which signifies "to create." The author does not use *Yatsar* which signifies "to frame or to form." Therefore, it means the world was made out of nothing. The world was created by God. It is God's gift. What is it? What does it consist of? Not works and not boasting. It consists of workmanship, by a Workman who created it in Christ Jesus out of nothing.

But it does not stop there, which is where many like to stop. The thought process continues, the idea continues, and the gift continues. It consists of good works, not just works, but good works, which God hath prepared (*before ordained*); and we should walk in them and practice them. We need to tie it all together. We are not to pick and choose.

Consider verse seven below, which closes out what God does, and is doing through Jesus Christ. It says that *he might show the exceeding riches of his grace in his kindness toward us through (in) Christ Jesus* [Eph. 2:7]. The word *kindness* basically means "usefulness."

Salvation is not just sometime in the future. It is not just the forgiveness of our sins. It is more than that. We are to know that we are His workmanship. To know we are created in Christ Jesus unto *good* works. These have been prepared beforehand that we should walk (engage) in them. We are to walk and to do as was stated a long time ago. Please note: being a Christian is both easy and difficult. We can make a profession of faith, but then we are to live the Christlike life. How can we do it?

By God's grace, by His power to us-ward, and by obedience to His will. It is through faith that we receive salvation. It is a gift.

The Gospel can be described as the saving power of God at work in the world. Paul says, under the influence of the Holy Spirit, *For I am not ashamed of the gospel of Christ: for it is the power of God unto salvation to every one that believeth; to the Jew first, and also to the Greek* [Rom. 1:16]. Paul tells the Romans that the promise is available to all who receive it in their hearts by faith. Why? That it might be by grace. This is further stated by Paul, *If thou shalt confess . . . and shalt believe in thine heart . . . thou shalt be saved* [Rom. 10:9]. Also, consider *Who are kept by the power of God through faith unto salvation ready to be revealed in the last time* [1 Pet. 1:5]. All of these passages are tied together. They support and amplify upon one another.

What emphasis is usually placed upon salvation? It is thought of as being saved from sin. Please consider, *For he shall save his people from their sins* [Matt. 1:21]. That is an explicit statement. However, we need to consider it in close connection to specific dangers, troubles, and disobedience to God. In that respect, this text expresses the New Testament Doctrine of Salvation.

We are also to thank God for the confirmation expressed in the following:

> *In whom we have redemption through his blood, even the forgiveness of sins* [Col. 1:14].

> *To give knowledge of salvation unto his people by the remission* (forgiveness) *of their sins, . . .* [Luke 1:77].

> *For God hath not given us the spirit of fear; but of power, and of love, and of a sound mind* [2 Tim. 1:7].

> *For we wrestle not against flesh and blood, but against principalities, against powers, against the rulers of the darkness of this world* (age), *against spiritual* (hosts of) *wickedness in high places* [Eph. 6:12].

God hath given us a spirit of power, love, and a sound mind.

Therefore, we can proceed boldly from the fear of hostile powers to liberty, assurance, and the love of God in Christ. Each of these truths is included in our salvation. May we increase in faith, perform good works according to the will of God, and give thanks to Him for His grace, mercy, and love.

Amen!

12

Circumcision and Uncircumcision

> *Wherefore remember, that ye being in time past Gentiles in the flesh, who are called Uncircumcision by that which is called the Circumcision in the flesh made by hands;*
>
> *That at that time ye were without Christ, being aliens from the commonwealth of Israel, and strangers from the covenants of promise, having no hope, and without God in the world:*
>
> *But now in Christ Jesus ye who sometimes* (once) *were far off are made nigh by the blood of Christ* [Eph. 2:11–13].

The Apostle Paul WAS remarkable in many, many ways. He was dedicated to serving Christ, working tirelessly and ceaselessly proclaiming God's Word. But, one of his greatest attributes was penetrating the heart, mind, and soul of each individual and having them understand not only God's grace, love, and mercy, but their need to examine themselves regarding their relationship to the Lord Jesus Christ, past, present, and future. He knew that relationship had to be enlightened, nourished, and sustained in each believer as they continued walking with Jesus, or they might yield to the temptations of the world. Therefore, Paul speaks to the believers reminding them of their past, telling them they prefer the standards of the world to the revelations of God, and declaring they *are made nigh by the blood of Christ,* and that they are to obey His commands and teachings.

What is the status in today's world among professing Christians? Apparently, there are two divergent teachings regarding the Gospel that impact both believers and non-believers. One group abides by a literal interpretation of Scripture, and the other espouses a liberal interpretation according to their assessment of man's needs. Once again, we have the eternal clash between God's wisdom and man's evaluation. God focuses on the individual separated from Him by sin and needing to be in a right relationship with Himself. Man focuses on society in general and the need to make the environment better in order to improve man's relationship with his fellow man.

God's servant, Ruth Paxson, provides further clarification to this issue saying, ". . . the first work of salvation is to bring the sinner out of hiding into real and joyous fellowship with the Lord. This necessitates preaching the Gospel of redemption to the sinner, that he may get right with God. For, if he is out of adjustment with God, he will most certainly be out of alignment with men. . . . He (God) has used His church as a powerful and effectual factor in the remaking of society, as the unprejudiced study of any mission field will prove. Ephesians has place for a social gospel, but it follows the individual gospel as fruit rather than taking precedence over it as the root."

Remember, we are not examining something that happened only in the past. It is just as true today as it was then. Scripture always speaks in the present tense. It is concerned with people in the midst of their lives, who are living in the real world.

Unfortunately, there is a different teaching that takes place in some of our seminaries today. It is that man is different than he was two thousand years ago, that he is confronted with different situations. Frankly, the lusts of the flesh and mind have not changed. There has not been a new sin for six thousand years, and there isn't likely to be a new one.

Paul wanted the Ephesians to know that their becoming Christians was a tremendous development. He wanted them to understand something of the greatness of God's power. Why? Because you cannot realize the greatness of God's power until you recognize some of the obstacles He has overcome.

Today, there are people who see nothing significant about salvation. Further, they are not amazed about Christianity. Why? Because they are ignorant about sin and know nothing about the blessings and wrath of God. Paul knew, and he wanted to share his knowledge.

Consider certain conditions existing in the first century. The people were divided into groups, groups that were opposed to one another till death. Jews and Gentiles, Greeks and barbarians. These groups were bitterly divided by culture, heritage, and religion. Reconciliation between them was considered nearly impossible, if not absolutely impossible. But it happened. The Ephesian Gentiles and Jews became members of the community of believers. How did it happen? By the exceeding greatness of God's power.

What is the Apostle saying to the Ephesian Gentiles in this verse? *Wherefore remember, that ye being in time past Gentiles in the flesh, who are called Uncircumcision by that which is called the Circumcision in the flesh made by hands.* Paul wants the Ephesians to know what had been their calling previously. He wants them to remember that they did not have any reason for pride. Therefore, Paul reminds them they are *Gentiles in the flesh*. It is a fact. Also, they had not been circumcised. By this statement Paul did not mean that the Gentiles were not sound in the spirit. He meant that the Gentiles did not have the mark or sign of the Jews, which is circumcision, made by hands.

The Jews had taken what was a simple, silent fact and developed it into a problem. Due to misunderstanding Scripture they had come to the point where the only thing that mattered was circumcision of the flesh. That point was critical. The Jews had misunderstood the entire purpose of circumcision. As a result, they created a barrier in the ancient world.

Paul says you were *Gentiles in the flesh*. The Jews talked of themselves as the circumcision people and called the Gentiles the uncircumcision and erected a barrier between the two. It is probably the best example of people speaking only in the terms of the flesh and what man has done with his hands. As a result they held themselves apart, saying we are the *Circumcision*, and you are the *Uncircumcision*.

It was true when Paul wrote this Epistle that the Gentiles had not been circumcised. However, it was equally true that the Jews had exaggerated the fact, emphasizing the importance of their circumcision. Consequently, they erected a wall between the Gentiles and themselves, a barrier that seemed insurmountable. Note what Paul says, *For we are the circumcision, which worship God in the Spirit, and rejoice in Christ Jesus, and have no confidence in the flesh* [Phil. 3:3].

At this juncture it is important to consider why Paul raises this idea and proceeds to discuss it. Recall that during this time there were two obstacles prevalent in the first century that had to be overcome concerning the Gentiles. First, there was the attitude of the Jews toward the Gentiles. Second, there was the perceived attitude of God toward the Gentiles since they had not been circumcised. Therefore, they were not of Abraham's seed.

Paul states *the flesh made by hands*. He is making the point that God overcame dual obstacles. He overcame them through Christ. The attitude of the Gentile towards the Jew and the Jew towards the Gentile changed for only one reason: God through Christ and in Christ.

Why do we discuss these truths? How relevant are they to conditions in the world today? Think of all the situations existing today. East–West relations, Arab–Jew, domestic developments, sects, denominations, and churches. Think of all the different barriers and walls.

Everybody expresses concern about producing peace, having unity, and solving all the ills and problems of mankind and the world. A lot of ideas and information are generated, but that does not produce the desired results. Why? The Apostle provides the answer. The unity producing the desired results occurs only under certain conditions. It is demonstrated in the bringing together of the Jew and Gentile, the Greek and barbarian. The only way they can be brought together is by the Holy Spirit in Christ. It is the only way. All others lead to failure.

One of the real tragedies of our time is that so many church leaders talk about unity instead of expounding the Gospel of Jesus Christ. It is the Gospel alone that produces unity. It is a waste of breath to discuss any other way of achieving unity, whether it is in the church or the outside world.

Men have tried throughout recorded history to resolve their differences. They have expended considerable energy and time to negotiate, draft, and execute well intentioned agreements and treaties, but to no avail. Why? Because of the frailties of man succumbing to the lusts of the flesh and mind. Unfortunately, "(N)o treaty ever made or to be made can weld antipodal nations into peace. It may temporarily disarm a nation, but it can never destroy its will to war. The heart of peace is not an 'it', but a 'He.' 'He is our peace,' and there is peace in no other way. God works to unite men, not by the reconstruction of human society, but by the construction of a divine society on an altogether new basis, as Paul shows in (Ephesians) 2:11, 3:13, where he passes from the personal to the corporate aspect of salvation," as forthrightly stated by Ruth Paxson. Her assessment is valid at all levels of society from family units to international affairs.

The Apostle wanted the Ephesians to realize that there are several factors that must be considered before there is any real hope of unity in different situations and resolving existing problems or difficulties.

First, Paul wanted the believers to recognize the cause. This sounds very simple, and in many cases it is. Certainly, in this instance it is not difficult. People talk and write urging others to have unity and understanding. Yet they never seriously consider the cause of the problem. In writing to the Ephesians, Paul identifies the cause of the problem. The differences between the Jews and Gentiles had been turned into barriers. Then walls were erected between them. Yes, there are always going to be differences. You will have differences even when you have unity. My wife and I may have differences, but we still have unity.

Unfortunately, men exaggerate their differences and then they erect barriers. That is what the Jews were doing. However, let us remember God ordained that there should be Jews and Gentiles. God created the Jewish nation in order to speak to other people in the world. God made a nation of the Jews. Despite that God circumcised the Jews but not the Gentiles, circumcision was not intended to be a barrier. However, the Jews misunderstood and let their self-centeredness get in the way. As a result, the Jews erected a barrier between the *Circumcision*—the Jews, and the *Uncircumcision*—the Gentiles. The Jews were to be witnesses. Instead they erected a wall between themselves and others. We are to be witnesses to others, but at times we build a wall or partition instead of witnessing.

The Jews had forgotten that circumcision was the gift of God, and we forget that salvation is the gift of God. We forget what God has done through Christ Jesus. During His encounter with . . . *those Jews which believed on him,* (Jesus said) *If ye continue* (abide) *in my word, then are ye my disciples indeed; And ye shall know the truth* (Christ)*, and the truth* (Christ) *shall make you free* [John 8:31–32]. This teaching of our Lord is as relevant today as it was two thousand years ago. We are to focus on His teachings and the truths contained in them. We are not to misinterpret them and establish our own self-satisfying ideas.

What contributes to building a wall between others and ourselves? What are the ingredients in that brick and mortar? Pride, self-centeredness, and prejudice. Ultimately, these are the primary causes of every division, barrier, and obstacle. Pride, self-centeredness, and prejudice are basic ingredients that divide people. Unfortunately, when a person overcomes pride through the grace of God, then other people interpret it as a sign of weakness.

Pride, self-centeredness, and prejudice blind us and dominate us. They combine to make a powerful force within us. They make us prejudiced, which is a horrible curse. When we are prejudiced, our spiritual sight is lost, and we cannot see two sides or points of view to a question or discussion.

Paul wants us to acknowledge that we develop a false view of ourselves. Oh, the lusts of the mind that create a false view within our minds and hearts. They occlude our vision and insight thereby making it difficult to grasp, accept, and believe that whatever we become in our relationship with God is due to Him, His mercy, and grace, not our achievements or capabilities.

Note what the Jews said to Jesus in responding to Him and the following exchange:

> *They* (the Jews) *answered him, We be Abraham's seed* (descendants), *and were never in bondage* (enslaved) *to any man: how sayest thou, Ye shall be made free* [John 8:33]?

> *I know that ye are Abraham's seed* (descendants); *but ye seek to kill me, because my word hath no place in you* [John 8:37].

> *They answered and said unto him, Abraham is our father. Jesus saith unto them, If ye were Abraham's children, ye would do the works of Abraham* [John 8:39].

The Jews thought they were responsible for themselves, that they had done everything through their own works and had the ability to make themselves right with God. They had forgotten, or had chosen to ignore the fact, that God had bestowed His gifts and blessings upon them. That is what pride, self-centeredness, and prejudice will do.

The previously identified factors—the circumcision of the Jews and the uncircumcision of the Gentiles, the false views of ourselves, and the lusts of our minds—contribute to our development of or our acceptance of a false view of others. These factors exhibit themselves in our own lives. We exaggerate what we have and can do and detract from what others have and can do. We exaggerate our own goodness and importance, but by the same token, we malign the goodness, gifts, and contributions of others.

The Jew was convinced there was nothing of value in the Gentiles. They were dogs or worse; certainly they were not human beings. They were not people God loved or for whom He cared. The same can be said about others throughout the history of man.

There is a fourth factor that causes divisions: a wrong sense of values! What does a wrong sense of values have to do with building barriers?

Some think that circumcision in the flesh matters. Paul says what really is important is being circumcised in the spirit. *For we are the circumcision, which worship God in the Spirit, and rejoice in Christ Jesus, and have no confidence in the flesh* [Phil. 3:3]. The person who is right with God is the individual who has been circumcised in the spirit. This is available to the Jew and Gentile and to the Greek and Barbarian.

Note, Paul says, . . . *who are called Uncircumcision by that which is called the Circumcision in the flesh made by hands.* Paul is calling attention to the external signs, the physical signs and factors raised as barriers: nationality, culture, birth, blood, family, school, city, state, training, money, politics, vocation. All these things can cause divisions or erect barriers. They all contribute to pride, self-centeredness, prejudice, and the lusts of the mind.

Also, we can have ceremonies, rituals, dress, forms, orders of service and other items within the community of believers, which emphasize the physical, the flesh, and being made with hands.

We even carry it to the Lord's table. We allow differences of opinion to become the brick and mortar that build a partition that divides us. Some people become more devoted to tradition, or form, than they are to the Lord Jesus Christ.

What is it that can help us, change us, and cure us? Christ alone! The requirement under these circumstances and conditions is a change of heart and a change of mind.

Goodwill, kindness, friendliness, brotherliness, or applying the teachings of Christ will not do the job. These things will neither break down the barriers nor bring about desirable changes unless there is true conversion within those who hope and strive for a better world. The important truth to remember is that man's nature is basically corrupt. Therefore, it must be transformed.

How can this be done? Only one way: Jesus Christ! Why? Because He makes me face myself, see the truth, realize I have nothing about which to boast, understand what is true of others is also true of me, and that THERE IS NONE RIGHTEOUS, NO, NOT ONE [Rom. 3:10]. What else does He show me, if I will but open mine eyes? That we all need God's grace, mercy, and love; that we receive them through Jesus

Christ; and that every good and perfect gift comes through Him. It is all received: I receive, you receive, and they receive.

Since these things are true, we should get rid of the pride, self-centeredness, and prejudice which divide us. They are the lusts of the mind. When we overcome them, then we can get rid of the jealousy, envy, and quarrels that plague us.

That is Christ's way. It is putting the spirit of Christ into a person rather than trying to apply certain teachings. There is a very simple fact: an unregenerated person cannot apply the principle and spirit of Christ. He does not want to do so.

There is only one hope: God giving friend and foe a new nature, a new heart, and a new spirit. When this occurs they will worship Him, praise Him, and glory in Him. They will not glory in themselves. The only basis for unity is being Christ-centered, Christ-dominated, and Christ-obedient.

As stated earlier, we need to not only realize certain facts about ourselves, but we need to address them. We need to relegate pride, self-centeredness, prejudice, and the lusts of the mind to where they belong. We need to get rid of the mote in our own eyes.

Amen!

13

Aliens from the Commonwealth of Israel

> *That at that time ye were without Christ, being aliens from the commonwealth of Israel, and strangers from the covenants of promise, having no hope, and without God in the world:*
> *But now in Christ Jesus ye who sometimes were far off are made nigh by the blood of Christ* [Eph. 2:12–13].

How can things happen in our lives, which earlier under different conditions or circumstances might never have happened? What causes us to change or to act differently? What happened to cause the Jews and Gentiles—the Circumcision and the Uncircumcision—to worship together?

When considering these questions, we need to examine Scripture and inquire as to what God has been doing and is doing. Unfortunately, too many people think they are active and God is passive, instead of realizing and accepting the truth. Also, too many people are interested in Scripture as history, as to what has happened in the past, especially two thousand or five thousand years ago. They fail to realize God is active today, not just yesterday. His truths are as applicable today as they were when initially revealed to man in order to give him hope and understanding. Further, they will be just as applicable in another two to five thousand years, since man is man controlled by the lusts of the flesh and the mind. Individuals, like you and me, need to know God, His grace and peace, and the joy of walking with the Lord Jesus along life's pathway.

People have a strong tendency or determination to look for signs. Is he circumcised? Is he a member of a church? Is he a member of a good family? People look for the external signs. That was where the Jews had gone astray. To them the external signs meant everything. That is also true today. People look at the external signs, whereas God looks upon the heart.

The Jews completely misunderstood the purpose and the spirit of circumcision. Paul clarifies the question of circumcision concerning both the Jew and the Gentile, stating succinctly,

> *For circumcision verily profiteth, if thou keep the law: but if thou be a breaker of the law, thy circumcision is made* (has become) *uncircumcision.*
> *Therefore if the uncircumcision keep the righteousness* (righteous requirements) *of the law, shall not his uncircumcision be counted for circumcision?...*
> *And shall not uncircumcision which is by nature* (physical)*, if it (he) fulfill the law, judge thee, who by the letter* (even with your written code) *and circumcision dost transgress the law?*
> *For he is not a Jew, which is one outwardly; neither is that circumcision, which is outward in the flesh:*
> *But he is a Jew, which is one inwardly; and circumcision is that of the heart, in the spirit, and not in the letter; whose praise is not of men, but of God* [Rom. 2:25–29].

The Jews failed to realize that the purpose of the covenant with Abram was spiritual, a right relationship with God. This is equally true of people today. Since the Apostle is concerned about it, we should be too.

We fail to realize the full impact of the Lord's Supper. We do not realize what Christ has done for us. We think it is something we are doing, something we have done. We think of it as works on our part. Therefore, we do not realize the full impact of the *blood of Christ* and what He did for each of us.

We are *the children of the promise* and should realize we are not children of the flesh. The children of the promise are the spiritual descendents of Abraham and the people of faith. Paul clarifies this fact.

At first glance, it appears Paul is employing unusual language when he states five important truths regarding their status before Christ's incarnation and their acceptance of Him saying,

- *ye were without Christ,*
- *aliens from the commonwealth of Israel,*
- *strangers from the covenants of promise,* and
- *having no hope,*
- *without God in the world* [Eph. 2:12].

These are five tough, straightforward phrases.

Paul affirmed these truths when he wrote to the Romans,

> *For they are not all Israel, which are of Israel:*
> *Neither, because they are the seed of Abraham, are they all children: but, IN ISAAC SHALL THY SEED BE CALLED.*
> *That is, They which are the children of the flesh, these are not the children of God: but the children of the promise are counted for* (as) *the seed* [Rom. 9:6–8].

The Apostle states clearly an important truth that all descendents of Abraham are not his spiritual descendents, even though they may be of his seed. Today, there are descendents of believers in Christ who *are the children of the flesh,* while others are Christ's spiritual descendents and counted as *the children of the promise.* Paul affirmed these truths when he wrote to the Romans.

Why does the Apostle use these terms? What is he saying? Paul is making a general review of the Old Testament: *the commonwealth of Israel; covenants of promise;* and *no hope without God.* Yet he even goes further, saying *ye were without Christ,* ye were outside Christ.

Paul declares to the Ephesian Gentiles, who are now members of the community of believers, that they had been on the outside looking in. They did not even have the tokens with which to erect barriers. Paul is explaining to them that everything God did in the Old Testament, everything He did for the Jews, was because of Christ and in making preparations for His incarnation. Paul puts it in a special way, saying, *The law was our schoolmaster to bring us unto Christ* [Gal. 3:24]. The law did not and does not save. Paul wants the Ephesians to understand God's truths, that

- the foundation of all promises and hope is Christ;
- the commonwealth of Israel was founded on Christ;
- the unity of the people of God is in Christ;
- God called Abram, made a new nation, and set them apart;
- God made covenants regarding the coming of the Messiah, who is the great Deliverer, our Redeemer; and
- There is one great promise, as Calvin says in illuminating Scripture, and on it all the other promises depend: *In thy seed shall all nations of the earth be blessed* [Gen. 22:18].

Paul amplifies upon this saying, *For all the promises of God in him are yea, and in him Amen, unto the glory of God by us* [2 Cor. 1:20]. Paul expands upon this truth, saying,

> *Now he which stablisheth* (establishes) *us with you in Christ, and hath anointed us, is God;*
> *Who hath also sealed us, and given the earnest* (down payment) *of the Spirit in our hearts* [2 Cor. 1:21–22].

He reminds us that it all comes from God for the purpose of our salvation.

Glossing over Scripture can be detrimental to our understanding of God's grace, mercy, and love as well as our increasing in faith and knowing the contentment, joy, and peace provided to those who *do hunger and thirst after righteousness*. Paul chooses his words carefully and, at times, forcefully in writing to *the saints and faithful*. Unfortunately, today as well as 2000 years ago, people question their faith and what God has done for them in Christ. When this happens they should dwell on the assurance Paul, through the Holy Spirit, provides. If you have questions regarding your relationship with God, think on four concrete facts: (i) *who stablisheth* (establishes) *us with you in Christ,* (ii) *hath anointed us, is God;* (iii) *hath also seated us,* and (iv) *hath given the earnest* (down payment) *of the Spirit in our hearts.* This is confirmation of God's promises to the saints and faithful.

The renowned John Calvin provides additional insight and clarity saying, " . . . we should note first the relation that Paul requires between God's Gospel and our faith. Since all that God says is utterly certain, he wants us to receive it into our minds with a firm and unwavering assent. Secondly we should note that, since this degree of certainty is beyond the capacity of the human mind, it is the office of the Holy Spirit to confirm within us what God promises in His Word. Thirdly we should note that all who do not have the witness of the Holy Spirit, so that they answer Amen to God when He calls them to a sure hope of salvation, have no right to be called Christians." May we accept God's truths with unwavering faith and know that we are among *the saints . . . and . . . the faithful in Christ Jesus.*

Paul states that the Holy Spirit has sealed us. What is the significance of this? It is threefold: " (i) to indicate ownership; (ii) to indicate genuineness; and (iii) to preserve and to keep safe," (King James Study Bible). All this is of God who owns us, who is truly concerned for us, and who will keep us safe and secure through the Holy Spirit.

What happens if you take away the covenant of salvation? There is no hope! Paul describes the covenants of promise to the Ephesians: Calvin translates it as the tables of the promise, or the instruments; God made His covenant with Abram; God would be their God; the covenant was confirmed through Moses and the prophets; and the Jewish nation had a peculiar treasure.

Paul fully realized that no one could rejoice in Christ unless he or she recognized, in the cold light of day, their position and status before they became members of the community of believers. The reason people do not fully rejoice in Christ is that they do not realize their condition in sin before God called them, or they do not want to accept that fact.

Paul tells them in verse 12 the five things that were true of them. Then in verse 13 he says, *But now in Christ Jesus ye . . . are made nigh by the blood of Christ*. Oh, that we had the gift to see what we were before Christ, and what we are when we are in Christ.

What did God in Christ do? He formed a commonwealth, a community of believers. He forms a people; He sets them apart; and He has a particular and a peculiar relationship with them.

> *But ye are a chosen generation, a royal priesthood, a holy nation, a peculiar* (his own special) *people; that ye should show forth* (proclaim) *the praises of him who hath called you out of darkness into his marvellous light:*
> *Which in time past were not a people, but are now the people of God: which had not obtained mercy, but now have obtained mercy* [1 Pet. 2:9–10].

That is God's way of salvation. God made *the covenants of promise* as revealed in Hebrews:

> *God made (a) promise to Abraham . . . he sware by himself,*
> *Saying, . . . SURELY BLESSING I WILL BLESS THEE, AND . . . I WILL MULTIPLY THEE;*
> *Wherein God, . . . to show . . . the immutability* (unchangeableness) *of his counsel, confirmed it by an oath:*
> *[I]t was impossible for God to lie, we might have a strong consolation, . . . to lay hold upon the hope set before us;*
> *Whither the forerunner . . . entered, even Jesus, made* (having become) *a high priest for ever after the order of Melchizedek* [Selections from Heb. 6:13–20].

God pledged Himself, He made an oath, and He fulfilled it.

The Ephesian Gentiles were strangers to God's promises. Today, there are many strangers to God's promises. They know nothing about them and they are not interested in them. They are more interested in their own promises and works. They are strangers to the Word of God, even though they may read it or hear it, at times.

Then there is the phrase *without God in the world*. There are those who are without God even though they may appear to be or profess to be believers. Paul regarded all notions about false gods as nothing. Further, all idols must be nothing since they are nothing among the godly.

Also, those who do not worship the true God are without God. John is very specific in one of his letters, saying,

> *Whosoever transgresseth, and abideth not in the doctrine of Christ, hath not God. He that abideth in the doctrine of Christ, he hath both the Father and the Son.*
> *If there come any unto you, and bring not this doctrine, receive him not into your house, neither bid him* (give him a greeting) *God speed:*
> *For he that biddeth him* (greets him) *God speed is partaker of* (shares in) *his evil deeds* [2 John 1:9–11].

How do we come to God? John records Jesus saying very specifically *I am the way . . . unto the Father* [John 14:6]. Now consider that beautiful and glorious verse, *But now in Christ Jesus ye who sometimes* (once) *were far off are made nigh by the blood of Christ*. That is a wonderful, succinct statement about the whole Gospel! It is the very essence of God's message to us. The Ephesian Gentiles were far off, but now they are made nigh. How? *In Christ, not by works lest any man should boast*, not by going to church, or doing this or that, not by anything that man initiates or originates. It is only in Christ and by His shed blood.

What determines whether we are Christians or not? Certainly, it is not what we are, nor what we have done. It is not because we have been brought up in the church nor because we have joined the church and are active in it. What is it then? It is our relationship to God and His Son, Christ Jesus.

Scripture says *made nigh*. It does not say that we have improved, or our conduct is proper, or our morality is impeccable, or our attendance is 100 percent, or our giving has increased, or our behavior is better. No! It says, *made nigh by the blood of Christ*.

Unfortunately, peer pressure has a great influence and affects our thinking in many ways. Further, we do not seek to know the truth, because at times it is difficult to acquire, or incompatible with our thinking, our culture, and the secular world. Therefore, people think a Christian is one who displays goodness and the proper behavior, or has repented of past evil deeds and now performs good works.

However, it is really knowing God and rejoicing in Him. Being *made nigh by the blood of Christ*, praising Him, and giving thanks to Him. As Calvin says with appropriate insight, "when the Ephesians were far off from God and salvation, they were reconciled to God through Christ, they were *made nigh* in His shed blood." What happened? The blood of Christ removed the barrier that had existed between them and God. They were no longer outside. They were now sons and daughters, part of the family.

What happens when we are *made nigh*? We are able to go into the presence of God. How do we do this? Through Christ. We do this with all the other members of the community of believers. There are no barriers. We have been brought into the covenants of promise.

> *FOR THIS IS THE COVENANT THAT I WILL MAKE WITH THE HOUSE OF ISRAEL AFTER THOSE DAYS, SAITH THE LORD; I WILL PUT MY LAWS INTO THEIR MIND, AND WRITE THEM IN THEIR HEARTS: AND I WILL BE TO THEM A GOD, AND THEY SHALL BE TO ME A PEOPLE:*
>
> *AND THEY SHALL NOT TEACH EVERY MAN HIS NEIGHBOR, AND EVERY MAN HIS BROTHER, SAYING, KNOW THE LORD: FOR ALL SHALL KNOW ME, FROM THE LEAST TO THE GREATEST.*
>
> *FOR I WILL BE MERCIFUL TO THEIR UNRIGHTEOUSNESS, AND THEIR SINS AND THEIR INIQUITIES* (lawless deeds) *WILL I REMEMBER NO MORE [Heb. 8:10–12].*
>
> *BUT THIS SHALL BE THE COVENANT THAT I WILL MAKE WITH THE HOUSE OF ISRAEL; AFTER THOSE DAYS, SAITH THE LORD, I WILL PUT MY LAW IN THEIR INWARD PARTS (MIND),*
>
> *AND WRITE IT IN THEIR HEARTS; AND WILL BE THEIR GOD, AND THEY SHALL BE MY PEOPLE. AND THEY SHALL TEACH NO MORE EVERY MAN HIS NEIGHBOR, AND EVERY MAN HIS BROTHER, SAYING, KNOW THE LORD: FOR THEY SHALL ALL KNOW ME, FROM THE LEAST OF THEM UNTO THE GREATEST OF THEM, SAITH THE LORD: FOR I WILL FORGIVE THEIR INIQUITY, AND I WILL REMEMBER THEIR SIN NO MORE [Jer. 31:33–34].*

That is the new covenant.

Other things are true when we are *made nigh*. We know God, and we come into His presence with the full assurance of faith. We should always remember what John says,

> *But as many as received him, to them gave he power* (the right) *to become the sons* (children) *of God, even to them that believe on his name:*
> *Which were born, not of blood, nor of the will of the flesh, nor of the will of man, but of God* [John 1:12–13].

The Christian not only has access into the presence of God, he knows God as his Father and the Father of Jesus Christ. The believer knows he has been adopted. He knows he has been *made nigh*. *For ye have not received the spirit of bondage again to fear; but ye have received the Spirit of adoption, whereby we cry, Abba, Father* [Rom. 8:15].

The adopted ones go willingly, lovingly, and joyfully, knowing they will be received by God the Father in a willing, loving, and joyful Spirit. Why? Because we have been *made nigh* (near) *by the blood of Christ.*

Amen!

14

By the Blood of Christ

> *But now in Christ Jesus ye who sometimes* (once) *were far off are made nigh* (near) *by the blood of Christ* [Eph. 2:13].

The New Testament Epistles were written to those identified as the community of Christian believers. They were written to inform, support, and strengthen those who had accepted Christ's call. *The writers of the Epistles wanted the followers of Christ to realize the importance and greatness of their salvation.*

The apostles realized the followers had questions, doubts, and problems with respect to their daily lives and the encounters they had in the real world. Further, they recognized that many of the followers, when looking at themselves, failed to realize what was true of them in Christ and being part of Him. This is as true today as it was then.

Paul wants to divulge to the Ephesians how they can begin to understand the greatness of their salvation. Why does he want to do this? Because it will lead to joy, thanksgiving, and to a confidence in Christ that cannot be shaken. However, to reach this point they must realize what they were without Christ, what is true now that they are in the Lord Jesus Christ, and how this happens, how this change takes place.

When looking at this verse, note that it says *Ye who sometimes were far off are made nigh. Ye . . . were far off,* you were, as the saying goes, "out in left field," but now your position or place has changed, and you are near.

How were they *made nigh*? Paul states it clearly and explicitly, *by the blood of Christ*. If there is anything that should make us sit up and take notice, if there is anything that should grab hold of us, it is this thought, this truth *by the blood of Christ. Not by anything else.*

To get the full impact, go back to the eleventh and twelfth verses of the second chapter, which highlight

- *Gentiles in the flesh,*
- *Uncircumcision, Circumcision,*
- *Without Christ,*
- *Aliens from the commonwealth,*
- *Strangers from the covenants of promise,*
- *Having no hope,*
- *Without God in the world.*

All these things were true, yet all of them were changed by one single, monumental event: *by the blood of Christ*. Please note it does not say by faith, works, or piety. It was the love of God that sent Christ to the Cross. His blood was shed because the love of God required atonement. God's love is His justice.

Simply, yet forcefully, what has happened? We have been *made nigh by the blood of Christ*. Our whole condition has been changed. This is the very foundation of the Christian faith, yet many, many people choose to ignore it or to focus on other things. However, the New Testament is explicit. The different apostles are united in the truth in Christ, and by His blood.

Today people do not want to accept the fact that our Gospel is a Gospel of Blood. They removed The Old Rugged Cross from our hymnals. They gloss over the blood of the new covenant in our communion services. The seminaries stress social justice and the sins of industry and governments. People like to hear about what they can do, not what Christ has done. But there it is: we are in Christ, we are transformed *by the blood of Christ*. That is what gives us the privilege of realizing our true relationship to God.

What beliefs determine our relationship to God and the extent of it? Some say, or believe, it is because of what they are by nature, or due to some goodness or morality. However, the right to go to God, or to draw nigh to Him, is not based on trying to live a good life and even living one. We all realize there are moral people who are not really interested in God or in Christ.

After considering this verse and several previous ones, it is safe to say that if we think our works or morality bring us close to God, then we are denying the Gospel of our Lord Jesus Christ.

If a person thinks he has the right to go to God in prayer because he has been good, then he does not understand the Gospel. If a person could go to God in prayer for such reasons, then Christ did not have to come into the world, and He did not have to go to Calvary's Hill.

A prime example of people trying to go into the presence of God is depicted in the parable of the Pharisee and the publican. The Pharisee *prayed thus with himself* but was not heard by God, for he was not nigh unto God.

Think for a moment. There is a real sense in which the religious person who thinks his goodness has some value is in reality far from God. We are all sinners. We all fall short of keeping God's commandments. We all need God's grace and mercy. We all can relate to

> *And the publican* (tax collector), *standing afar off . . . smote* (beat) *upon his breast, saying, God be merciful to me a sinner.*
> *I tell you, this man went down to his house justified rather than the other: for every one that exalteth himself shall be abased; and he that humbleth himself shall be exalted* [Luke 18:13–14].

We are to learn from Christ Himself and emulate the publican. God always welcomes the sinner, the one who is dependent upon Him and in need of His grace and mercy.

Others think they can draw nigh to God because of the good deeds they may do. People in this category say, I may not be perfect, but I am making up for it by my actions, by my giving. They believe if someone has deficiencies or conducts himself in a reprehensible manner, but tries to compensate for it, then he or she will draw nigh to God.

People in this group include do-gooders, idealists, public benefactors, and others. They make sacrifices, and they exert great effort, but it does not admit them to God, it does not draw them nigh to Him.

And many people believe that we cannot draw nigh to God because we are religious, because we are interested in worship, because we are interested in God, or because we are interested in the church. However, a reliance upon religious practices will not draw us nigh to God. People may attend services, make sacrifices in order to participate, but that is not the way.

Paul was a very religious person before his conversion; Martin Luther was very religious before his conversion. Just because a person is religious does not mean he or she will draw nigh unto God.

The fact is that a person cannot draw nigh unto God without a Mediator. A person cannot go directly to God. Calvin explains this in a meaningful and humbling way, saying, "Men mock God and themselves by the fruits of their unbelief. They add to this their pride, because unbelievers despise or reject the Mediator's grace, and throw themselves into the presence of God."

Ponder the following thoughts that permeate the minds of many people. Cain's lack of acceptance was not because he defrauded God, but due to the impurity of his heart. People hold God under an obligation to them but they cannot escape His authority so they try to offer blandishments. They wish to bargain with God on their own terms. When this is denied, they want to retaliate and they want honor for their sacrifices. However, with Abel, faith and obedience were better than sacrifices. Therefore, he worshipped in the Spirit.

There was a popular idea several years ago embodied in the exhortation, "Let go and let God." Proponents of this idea felt if you were in trouble or if you did not know what to do, then the only thing to do was to just sit back, relax, and wait for God to send a post card. When asked, "Where does Christ come in?" they say that comes later. They say what you must do is get in contact with God; later you can learn how to come to Christ. When you desire you can come to Christ.

We have considered four rather popular erroneous beliefs as to how people are *made nigh* to God. But how does Scripture say we are *made nigh*? In Christ Jesus, by the blood of Christ.

The Apostle says we are *made nigh by the blood of Christ*. This brings to mind Jesus:

- Carrying the Cross,
- *Wearing a crown of thorns,*
- *Climbing Calvary's Hill,*
- *Uttering in pain, I Thirst,*
- *Praying, Father, forgive them; for they know not what they do,*
- *Asking from the depths of his heart, Why hast thou forsaken me?*
- Exclaiming, *It is finished.*

This is the death of Christ and the life poured out contained in the monumental phrase, *by the blood of Christ.*

The Apostle does not say we are *made nigh* by the teachings of Christ, by the Sermon on the Mount, by following His example, or by keeping the law.

The Pharisees believed that they would draw near by keeping the law. However, when Christ expounded the law, they began to realize they were far from God. It was a jolt to the Pharisees, and it is a jolt to us that God is just as interested in a desire as in a deed. He is just as interested in a motive as an action and He views a look or lust as bad as an act.

When we really and truly get down to the nitty-gritty of Jesus' teachings and honestly consider them, we cannot say that His teachings bring us nigh to God. Further, His wonderful living example does not bring us nigh to God, though it may inspire one. Who can follow Him? Who can do as He did? Please note: the Apostle does not say we are brought nigh to God because God is love.

There is a misconception that all Jesus did was to tell us God is love. Some say that if you just tell enough people God is a God of love that they will come rushing into His presence.

Would that really happen? No, those individuals would say since God is a God of love, I can do what I want to do, and He will forgive me. Jesus Christ does not bring us to God by stating God is a God of love, ready to forgive one and all.

How are we drawn nigh to God? *By the blood of Christ.* First is the expiation for our sins: to atone for and to pay the penalty for them. *Behold the Lamb of God, which taketh away the sin of the world* [John 1:29]. . . . *ye were not redeemed with corruptible* (perishable) *things, . . . But with the precious blood of Christ* [1 Pet. 1:18–19]. You are redeemed by the Lamb, the Lamb of sacrifice and the Lamb of God.

Why should there be a sacrifice? *The wages of sin is death* [Rom. 6:23]. Without the shedding of blood there is no remission of sins. God's punishment for sin is death, spiritual death, separation from God.

Why did Christ come into the world? The following New Testament descriptions provide the answer:

> *But we see Jesus, who was made a little* (for a little while) *lower than the angels for the suffering of death, crowned with glory and honor; that he by the grace of God should taste death for every man* [Heb. 2:9].

> Who his own self bare our sins in his own body on the tree, that we, being dead to sins, should live unto righteousness: BY WHOSE STRIPES (wounds) YE WERE HEALED [1 Pet. 2:24].
>
> For he hath made him to be sin for us, who knew no sin; that we might be made the righteousness of God in him [2 Cor. 5:21].

These statements affirm that it was necessary for Christ to obey His Father and to shed His blood.

Why did Christ die on the Cross? God laid on Him the iniquity of us all. He shed His blood that we may not be separated from God, that we might be drawn nigh to Him and become like His Son.

> Thinkest thou that I cannot now pray to my Father, and he shall presently give me (provide me with) more than twelve legions of angels?
> But how then shall the scriptures be fulfilled, that thus it must be [Matt. 26:53–54]?

Before I could draw nigh to God something had to be done about my sins and my sinful condition. That something was the shed blood of Christ.

There is a second way in which we are made nigh to God.

> BEHOLD THE DAYS COME, SAITH THE LORD, WHEN I WILL MAKE A NEW COVENANT WITH THE HOUSE OF ISRAEL AND WITH THE HOUSE OF JUDAH:
>
> ... I WILL PUT MY LAWS INTO THEIR MIND, AND WRITE THEM IN THEIR HEARTS: AND I WILL BE TO THEM A GOD, AND THEY SHALL BE TO ME A PEOPLE:
>
> ...FOR I WILL BE MERCIFUL TO THEIR UNRIGHTEOUSNESS, AND THEIR SINS AND THEIR INIQUITIES (lawless deeds) WILL I REMEMBER NO MORE.
> In that He saith, a new covenant, He hath made the first old (obsolete). Now that which decayeth (is becoming obsolete) and waxeth (growing) old is ready to vanish away [Heb. 8:8, 8:10, 8:12–13].

There is the new covenant. The new covenant is ratified *by the blood of Christ.* It is guaranteed. Christ is the Mediator. We are the beneficiaries of the New Covenant. How are we drawn nigh to God? The author of Hebrews says,

> ... and to the blood of sprinkling, that speaketh better things than that of Abel [Heb. 12:24].

> *And Cain talked with Abel his brother (and said let us go out to the field): and it came to pass, when they were in the field, that Cain rose up against Abel his brother, and slew him.*
>
> *And the Lord said unto Cain, Where is Abel thy brother? And he said, I know not: Am I my brother's keeper?*
>
> *And he said, What hast thou done? the voice of thy brother's blood crieth unto me from the ground.*
>
> *And now art thou cursed from the earth, which hath opened her mouth to receive thy brother's blood from thy hand* [Gen. 4:8–11].

The blood of Abel speaks of judgment, vengeance, and a curse.

That is far different than the blood of Christ, which speaks of nearness, pardon, expiation, and peace with God. The blood purges in order to serve the living God. Also, *Let us draw near with a true heart in full assurance of faith, having our hearts sprinkled from an evil conscience, and our bodies washed with pure water* [Heb. 10:22]. We are sprinkled with the blood of Christ and therefore should have the full assurance of faith, pardon, and redemption.

We come into the presence of God because the Mediator has dealt with our sins. We fall into a trap as we continue to commit acts or think thoughts that are sins of the flesh and the mind. *If we walk in the light, as he is in the light, we have fellowship one with another, and the blood of Jesus Christ his Son cleanseth us from all sin* [1 John 1:7]. Even though we fall when we walk in the light, the blood of Christ cleanses us from our sin.

How are we *made nigh* unto God? *By the Blood of Christ*. It is not by relying upon ourselves. It is not by being "good enough." It is by knowing that even though I am a sinner and have a sinful nature within me that I am *made nigh by the blood of Christ*.

Therefore, may we have boldness accompanied by reverence and godly fear knowing that we are drawn near to God *by the blood of Christ*. Our confidence is in Christ. Note the teachings of Christ in the four Gospels as he proceeds to Jerusalem. He describes why He is going to Jerusalem. *The person and work of Christ is the essence of all Scripture*.

Many look to or want to see God the creator, the power of creation, the material things available. However, they turn away from and do not want to accept and focus upon God in Christ creating, sustaining, reconciling, and redeeming us to Himself. Everything from God comes through and *in Christ*. Everyone going to God does so through and *in Christ*. It is all *by the blood of Christ*. For this we give thanks to God the Father.

Amen!

15

Making Peace

> *For he* (himself) *is our peace, who hath made both one, and hath broken down the middle wall of partition* (division) *between us;*
> *Having abolished in his flesh the enmity, even the law of commandments contained in ordinances; for to make* (create) *in himself of twain* (the two) *one new man, so making peace;*
> *And that he might reconcile both unto God in one body by the cross, having slain* (put to death) *the enmity thereby* [Eph. 2:14–16].

The Apostle presents new thoughts in verses 14–16 of chapter 2 regarding how Christ reconciles us to God. When considering these verses it is beneficial to examine the community of believers, especially Jesus Christ, who is the Head and the Lord of that community.

God's election calls a person to become a "living member" of the community. To be an elect person means to be a member of the community. How does this occur? It occurs in, through, and by Christ Jesus. The person in Christ is always in fellowship with the other members. "The person called is in the community with the other believers," according to the renowned theologian Otto Weber.

Our membership in the community of believers is not the result of our being in Christ, but is fully identical with our being in Christ in both act and fact. The individual who isolates himself or herself lives an existence contrary to his election into the community. A member of the community does not live a withdrawn or isolated existence.

Although our presence in the community is equivalent to being *in Christ* it does not mean that the community becomes the object of our faith, or that it attains a position next to Christ, or that Christ exists as the church. It does not mean that a person joining or affiliating with a church is also a member of the community.

The community belongs with the person and work of Jesus Christ. The New Testament describes it as His body, His flock, His bride, God's people, and God's building. However, the primary requirement is Jesus Christ as its Lord, Head, and Shepherd.

The community of believers can have unity with Jesus Christ only through its dependence upon Him and its obedience to Him. The community is a company of people under human direction. It does not have all the good or better people; it does not have all the activists or doers of good deeds; it does not have all the people who accomplish great things; but it contains people who have a relationship with the Lord Jesus Christ and are dependent upon Him.

It is important to remember that the community's being and activities do not receive their validity and importance due to the manner in which it exists or the state in which it finds itself. The community cannot legitimize itself by preaching the greatest sermons, by winning the world, or by accomplishing the most honorable achievements. The only way the community achieves legitimacy is through its Lord Jesus Christ who "has realized it" and who "has actualized it," as Dietrich Bonhoeffer proclaimed. Consider these thoughts expressed by the Apostle Paul,

> *For ye see* (consider) *your calling, brethren, how that not many wise men after the flesh, not many mighty, not many noble, are called* [1 Cor. 1:26].

> *... that your faith should not stand* (be) *in the wisdom of men, but in the power of God* [1 Cor. 2:5].

Concerning the question of legitimacy, the community must refer to its proclamation, that its being is empowered by the Spirit. "The community is legitimized only through the Christ proclaimed in the power of the Spirit," as specifically stated by Otto Weber. Therefore, it is important to grasp certain truths about the Lord Jesus Christ, His being, and the reason God sent Him into the world. Ponder the truths revealed to Paul by the Holy Spirit.

> *For this cause ... to desire that ye might be filled with the knowledge of his will in all wisdom and spiritual understanding:*

> *That ye might walk worthy of the Lord unto all pleasing, being fruitful in every good work, and increasing in the knowledge of God* [Col. 1:9–10].
>
> *In whom we have redemption through his blood, even the forgiveness of sins:*
> *Who is the image of the invisible God, the first-born of (first in rank over) every creature* [Col. 1:14–15].
>
> *For it pleased the Father that in him* (Christ) *should all fullness dwell;*
> *And, having made peace through the blood of his cross, by him to reconcile all things unto himself; by him, I say, whether they be things in* (on) *earth, or things in heaven* [Col. 1:19–20].

These affectionate words of Paul deserve further consideration. They are extremely important to becoming mature Christians and devoted followers of Christ. What does Paul want for them and us? "That they may know God more fully. By this he suggests that something is still wanting in them, that he may prepare the way for teaching them, and may win a hearing for a fuller statement of doctrine. For those who think that they have already attained everything worth knowing, despise and disdain anything more advanced. He removes this idea . . . , lest it should be a hindrance to their willing progress, and allowing what had been begun in them to be finished. But what knowledge does he desire for them? The knowledge of the *divine will*, by which expression he rejects all inventions of men and all speculations foreign to the Word of God. "For His will is not to be sought anywhere else than in His Word," as expressed by the heartfelt theologian John Calvin.

Unfortunately, too many people become complacent and self-centered instead of being vigorous in pursuing more and more knowledge of God's *divine will*. Dr. John McKay, a renowned theologian of the last century and President of the Princeton Theological Seminary was actively learning, researching, and writing in his mid-nineties.

Why is it important that we walk worthy of God? Calvin sheds light on this question saying, ". . . that it may appear in our life that we have not been taught by God in vain. . . . if we would walk worthy of God, we must above all things take heed to devote our whole course of life to the will of God, renouncing our own views, and bidding farewell to all the inclinations of our flesh.

"Hence, if it is asked what kind of life is worthy of God, let us always remember this definition of Paul, that it is one that, leaving what accords with men, and leaving, . . . all carnal inclination, is adjusted to obedience to God alone. From this follow good works, which are the fruits that God requires of us."

The most important factor in the life of the community of believers, more important than any so-called accomplishments or achievements that may be identified, is that the Christian community, in its speaking, acting, and serving, points beyond itself. It must always point to the centrality of Christ. It must continually point to Christ as its Lord, Head, and Shepherd, to the obedient servant with the crown of thorns going to Calvary's Hill and shedding His blood. All other activities, proclamations, and urgings pale in comparison to what Christ did. We are in Christ and we are members of the community. Therefore, our obedience is to be to God's will in accordance with Christ's teachings and His life.

Why consider these factors when examining verses 14–16 in chapter 2 of Ephesians? Because these verses begin with the phrase *For he is our peace*. We are members of the community, yet we live in the world. We are to improve continuously our understanding of Christ's teachings and our knowledge of what He has done. God is not a God of confusion, but of peace; therefore, everything should be done properly and in accord with His teachings.

What does *peace* mean in the New Testament? It does not mean the absence of conflict, but the presence of a whole, healthy condition in each of our lives. God is active. He wants us to have and to enjoy a healthy, active life in the midst of our daily living. This peace impacts all our relationships and the order of the community is to be seen in this context. The wall of partition is broken down between Jew and Gentile, freeborn and slaves, men and women, parents and children, and master and servant. The community is to manifest peace in its order.

What is the biblical message concerning peace? God is a God of peace. He produces peace and makes peace in and through His only begotten Son. *The scepter* (a symbol of kingship) *shall not depart from Judah, nor a lawgiver from between his feet, until Shiloh come; and unto him shall the gathering* (obedience) *of the people be* [Gen. 49:10].

What is the Shiloh about which Jacob speaks when blessing his sons? It is a description of the Messiah as the Prince of Peace, as the seed of Judah. Sin always leads to separation. Sin separates man from man as well as from God. It puts men at enmity with one another and with God. How can men be reconciled to one another and to God? There is only one way: Christ Jesus, who is our peace.

We hear many suggestions as to how peace can be attained. Unfortunately, such suggestions are the ways of the world. There are members and leaders of the church who ignore the teachings of Scripture and the centrality of Christ when proclaiming what must be done to achieve peace. It is difficult to be patient when reading and hearing about people in the Christian church completely misunderstanding and misinterpreting Scripture, saying, "You only have to do what we tell you, and the peace you desire will come to pass." It is tragic, and it is misleading!

Sin is the cause of man's trouble with man and with God. The root cause is the pride of man. Man is interested in himself. Man asks the question: Who is God to tell you what you may or may not do? Man, don't you realize how important or great you are?

Man becomes the victim of his own devices, pride, self-interest, and self-concern. He talks and thinks about his rights and his demands. He becomes overly consumed and protective about his self-interest, self-adulation, self-love, self-praise, and everything else about self. Unfortunately, practically everyone is doing this, and that is where the trouble comes in. People have enmity amongst themselves. They have enmity against God.

Our Lord and Master stated it clearly and succinctly when He was asked,

> *Master, (Teacher) which is the great commandment in the law?*
> *Jesus said unto him,* THOU SHALT LOVE THE LORD THY GOD WITH ALL THY HEART, AND WITH ALL THY SOUL, AND WITH ALL THY MIND.
> *This is the first and great commandment.*
> *And the second is like unto it, Thou shalt love thy neighbour as thyself.*
> *On these two commandments hang all the law and the prophets*
> [Matt. 22:36–40].

Our Lord put the commandments in their proper order. The tragedy today is that the first great commandment is ignored. People think they can start with the second commandment instead of the first, and they cannot. *It is impossible to do so.* Man must start with God and submit to God first and foremost. He cannot reconcile himself to his fellow man until he has reconciled himself to God.

The Scripture being considered says *For he is our peace*. What does this mean? He Himself is our peace. The Lord Jesus not only *makes* peace. He *is* peace. This is another way of saying that we must be in Christ before we can enjoy God's blessings as the God of Peace.

Christ makes peace. How? When examining Scripture we realize that God through Christ extends the blessings of reconciliation. He says that all are united to God through Christ. "For if Christ is our peace, it follows that all who are outside Him are at enmity with God," as artfully described by John Calvin.

Christ is the peace between man and God and between man and man. God shows His favor and bestows His blessings on those who remain in Christ. He does not withhold them. In this verse, Paul continues *who hath made both one*. The Jews had thought for generations that they were superior to the Gentiles. What does the Apostle tell them? That they have all been united into one body. When this thought is put into its proper perspective, one recognizes the following, as Calvin so clearly stated, "if the Jews wish to have peace with God, they must have Christ as their Mediator; Christ will not be their peace, except by making them and the Gentiles one body; and unless the Jews admit the Gentiles into fellowship, they have no connection with God."

Paul continues saying, *For he* (himself) *is our peace, who hath made both one, and hath broken down the middle wall of partition* (division) *between us*. What about *the middle wall of partition* (division)? Two things must be observed in order to understand this passage. First, the Jews were separated from the Gentiles for a period of time due to God's appointment. God chose a peculiar people for Himself. God set the boundaries for marking off one people for Himself. Consequently, an enmity arose between the Jews and Gentiles.

Second, says the Apostle, now that the enmity is removed the partition is broken down. It is smashed; it does not exist. How? *By the blood of Christ*. However, breaking down the partition does not produce peace by itself.

According to Scripture, *peace* does not mean the cessation of hostilities or preventing combat in its various forms. God is not content with preventing the visible and aggressive acts of enmity. He wants to make peace inwardly. God's idea of peace is that men should not only love one another, but they should embrace one another.

God's idea of peace is that there should be unity and oneness. We are to love one another as we love ourselves. He wants us to have and to enjoy the second great commandment, but in order to do that, we must obey the first great commandment.

Peace must be thought of in terms of heartfelt attitudes, inward unity, and love. Paul says that Christ and Christ alone produces that peace. He is the One producing a complete, healthy condition in a person. *The middle wall of partition* prevented God from bringing together the Jews and Gentiles, so Christ broke it down through the Cross. Paul continues, saying *Having abolished in his flesh the enmity, even the law of commandments contained in ordinances.* Paul expressly states what was meant by the word *wall*, saying that the ceremonies establishing distinctions between the two have been abolished through Christ. He amplifies upon this, saying the ceremonies such as circumcision, sacrifices, fasting, washings, and abstination that were supposed to be signs of sanctification were abolished because they were misused. They were intended to be tools for witnessing, but were used to establish barriers.

Paul informs the community of believers that the Gentiles were admitted into the fellowship and that the differences between Jews and Gentiles, such as ceremonies and circumcision, were abolished. Therefore, the Gentiles no longer differed from the Jews.

Calvin states that some people mistakenly connect the phrase *in ordinances* with *having abolished*. Scripture says *the law of commandments contained in ordinances*. What does Paul mean? He speaks of the ceremonial law through which God provides the Israelites with a simple rule of life that also binds them to various statutes. We may deduce from this that Paul is speaking exclusively of the ceremonial law.

Scripture continues by saying *for to make* (create) *in himself of twain* (the two) *one new man*. The word *make* in this verse means *found*, and it is the only place it is used in Scripture. Calvin interprets it as saying that he "might create," or "for he might create in himself."

Paul, guided by the Holy Spirit, focuses the believers' attention on the words *in himself* so that they will realize that the unity is *in Christ*, not in man, or men, or the things of men. The two, who had been so different in their former condition, have become one *in Christ*. Spiritual regeneration in the Holy Spirit joined them together.

Paul means that nothing external is of any value. The only thing of value is the new creature. This is first and foremost, as well as the last and only thing. It is spiritual regeneration in the Holy Spirit that joins us together. Since we are renewed by Christ, there is nothing to boast about in and of ourselves. Paul continues, . . . *and that he might reconcile both unto God in one body by the cross, having slain* (put to death) *the enmity thereby* [Eph. 2:16]. He asserts that we are at peace among ourselves and back in favor with God only through the Mediator. Further, both the Jews and Gentiles have need of the Mediator. Without Him, the Law, the ceremonies, the lineage is of no avail; it means nothing.

All are sinners. The forgiveness of sins is obtained only through the Mediator. *By the Cross* denotes the sacrifice of Christ, the expiation for our sinful condition.

Sin is the cause of the enmity between God and ourselves, between man and man. We can never be in God's favor until our sinful condition has been abolished. This was done on the Cross *by the blood of Christ* where He and He alone was able to achieve the ultimate victory in *having slain* (put to death) *the enmity thereby.*

This phrase should be connected to the Cross, because it means by His death on the Cross, Christ has reconciled us to God and has taken away the Father's wrath; and by redeeming both the Jews and Gentiles alike, He has brought them into one flock. He has brought them into the community of believers. He has brought them unto Himself. We are *in Christ* and should rejoice in this knowledge.

Amen!

16

Reconcile Both Unto God

> *Having abolished in his flesh the enmity, even the law of commandments contained in ordinances; for to make (create)in himself of twain (the two) one new man, so making peace;*
>
> *And that he might reconcile both unto God in one body by the cross, having slain the enmity thereby* [Eph. 2:15–16].

Paul makes a profound statement, one that should focus our attention, when he says under the influence of the Holy Spirit *for to make* (create) *in himself of twain* (the two) *one new man.*

What does he mean by *in himself?*

- Christ is the Mediator between Jew and Gentile as well as all opposing factions;
- Christ is the Eradicator of all barriers between the Jew and Gentile and all other opposing groups;
- Christ is the Reconciler of Jew and Gentile unto God and all differing groups;
- Christ is the Conciliator of Jew and Gentile with each other and family to family; and
- Christ is the Center of the new man, composed of both Jews and Gentiles who are members of the community of believers.

Paul wants us to focus attention upon the one and only Mediator, saying, *And that he might reconcile both unto God in one body by the cross, having slain* (put to death) *the enmity thereby.*

The teaching being examined is fundamental and vital to the whole question of peace and unity. These factors relate to all people. All the divisions, quarrels, and separations among people are ultimately due to the fact that these people are separated from God.

The world, countries, communities, and even families are full of divisions. Scripture teaches that the significant thing about these situations is that these people are separated from God and in a wrong relationship to Him. Therefore, unity among people, groups, or nations is possible only after the people involved are reconciled together in Christ to God.

This is where the secular world and the natural man have real difficulty. They think the teachings of Christ can be applied to problems, and that everything will work out. That will not happen! The people who make up the groups must first be reconciled to God. Christian behavior cannot be obtained from people who are not Christians.

The Apostle says *And that he might reconcile both unto God*. What does the word *reconcile* mean in this instance? The word *reconcile*, or a form of it, is used twenty-three times in the Bible. However, this particular word in the Greek is used only three times, here and in Colossians 1:20-21. The actual translation from the Greek means *to change thoroughly from*.

> *And, having made peace through the blood of his cross, by him to reconcile all things unto himself; by him, I say, whether they be things in (on) earth, or things in heaven.*
> *And you, that were sometime alienated and enemies in your mind by wicked works, yet now hath he reconciled* [Col. 1:20-21].

What does it mean or not mean *to change thoroughly from*? It does not mean merely bringing people together after an estrangement and saying that everything is all right; or that two parties have decided, on their own, to get together and lay aside their differences.

However, it does mean there is an action from God bringing two antagonistic parties together into a relationship of complete amity and harmony. There has been a restoration of something positive that had existed previously. It is a bringing together again, reuniting, reconnecting, and re-establishing a mutually beneficial relationship by eliminating the causes of the separation. And there is a total completeness to the action. Enmity is totally and completely replaced by amity and togetherness. It is not a compromise, it is not temporary, it is not patchwork. It is perfect!

After considering these meanings, what is the Apostle teaching? First and foremost, sin separates us from God. Go back to where it says,

That at that time ye were without Christ, being aliens from the commonwealth of Israel, and strangers from the covenants of promise, having no hope, and without God in the world [Eph. 2:12].

The opposite of being aliens or strangers is being *made nigh* or being drawn nigh. What is so bad about sin is something that is not normally thought about. It is not the mere transgression of the law, though it is that; it is not only missing the mark, though it is that. The worst thing about sin is that it separates us from God and breaks our fellowship with Him. It results in not being in a right relationship with God, and not only separates one from God, but it also produces enmity between man and God, and between man and man.

Man was made for God. He was to have fellowship with God, and he was to walk with God. In Genesis, the third chapter, man disobeyed and broke his relationship with God. The basic question is, how can our fellowship with God be restored?

When this question is asked, many people go astray. They begin to look inwardly. That is neither the place to start nor the direction to go. We need to remind ourselves that God is the one who acts. If our thinking is wrong, then we do not understand the death of Christ, the blood of the Cross, nor the real meaning of the Communion Service.

People want to believe that there is no problem. Further, they want to believe that if they do something wrong or commit some act, God will forgive them, and as a result everything is A-OK in their lives. However, the New Testament teaching is not that simple. If it were, then the Lord Jesus Christ would never have come into the world, and gone to Calvary's Hill.

What is the problem? It is one of fellowship. How can the fellowship be restored? This fellowship is essential when we start our Christian life, and is vitally important during all the stages of our Christian growth. Therefore, it is important to begin thinking of our sins in terms of our relationship to God. We need to ask the question: How can we proceed through the process of sanctification without having a positive relationship with God and His Son Jesus Christ? The sooner we begin to think this way, the sooner we shall become more committed Christians.

It is important to understand these truths. However, as we go through this process, we need to remind ourselves "We are only able to understand the knowledge of God as we (do), did (or will) because God Himself discloses and has disclosed Himself as a person: In Jesus

Christ through the Holy Spirit," as positively proclaimed by Otto Weber. Further, Weber says in terms of substance and being "revelation unconditionally precedes knowledge."

God reveals Himself through His Word and His Son. It is through them by the power of the Holy Spirit that we acquire knowledge and understanding. If we do not have fellowship with Him, then those things cannot happen. What do we need to know regarding our fellowship with God? The Apostle John says, *Our fellowship is with the Father, and with his Son Jesus Christ* [1 John 1:3].

How is this fellowship possible? John advises that there is an important condition to satisfy if we are to experience this fellowship throughout life and states it succinctly, saying,

> *If we say that we have fellowship with him, and walk in darkness, we lie, and do not* (practice) *the truth:*
> *But if we walk in the light, as he is in the light, we have fellowship one with another, and the blood of Jesus Christ his Son cleanseth us from all sin* [1 John 1:6–7].

Calvin provides appropriate illumination to the Apostle John's statement saying "For it is not a naked command that he (John) gives, demanding holiness of life from us, but rather he shows that the grace of Christ serves to scatter darkness and to kindle in us the light of God. It is as if he said, 'God does not communicate to us an empty fiction. For the power and effect of this fellowship must needs shine forth in our life; otherwise our profession of the Gospel is false.'

"He walks in darkness who is not ruled by the fear of God and does not aim with a pure conscience at devoting himself wholly to God nor seek to promote His glory. On the other hand, he who in sincerity of heart spends every part of his life in God's fear and service and worships Him faithfully, may be regarded as walking in the light, for he keeps to the right way, even though in many things he may err and groan under the burden of the flesh. Therefore, it is integrity of conscience alone that distinguishes light from darkness."

How can we walk in fellowship with Him? We need to pray and think positively regarding our fellowship with God. This comes first. We should not think only in terms of our acts and practices. We need to realize we are in the presence of God and a companion of Christ's. What a difference that makes! When I realize I am with them, it is difficult to do or think the things that they dislike or that will hurt them. To a degree this is true of our relationships with others.

We are to think positively about our relationship with God and our fellowship with Christ. We are to be ever mindful of the fact that the most damaging thing about sin is that it separates us from God; it breaks the fellowship. Therefore, reconciliation is necessary.

Remember, it was God who called Abram and formed the nation of Israel. It was God who took the action. All men need to be reconciled to God. Therefore, God singled out Abram and established a nation to be His witnesses. Why did He do it? He did this in order to have fellowship with Abraham, Israel, and their descendents, and that they might have fellowship with Him. The Gentiles and others were not in fellowship with Him at that time. This is an important truth to grasp in order to understand the Old Testament. God formed a peculiar people for Himself and for the relationship between them.

However, that was not sufficient. As the Apostle says, the Jews as well as the Gentiles needed to be reconciled, and all the ceremonies, sacrifices, burnt offerings, paschal lambs, blood of bulls and goats were not enough to deal with the problem. *For all have sinned, and come* (fall) *short of the glory of God* [Rom. 3:23].

Therefore, we need to be justified. How can this be accomplished?

> *Being justified freely* (without any cost) *by his grace through the redemption that is in Christ Jesus:*
> *Whom God hath set forth to be a propitiation* (a mercy seat) *through faith in his blood, to declare* (demonstrate) *his righteousness for the remission* (passing over) *of sins that are past, through the forbearance of God;*
> *. . . that he might be just, and the justifier of him which believeth in Jesus* [Rom. 3:24–26].

The Jews misunderstood it completely. They thought (and many still do) that because they were Jews, they were right with God. However, they needed to be reconciled. Both the Jew and the Gentile needed to be reconciled to God, and they were both reconciled in exactly the same way.

There is only one way of being reconciled to God. *For there is one God, and one mediator between God and men, the man Christ Jesus* [1 Tim. 2:5]. There are no separate ways into the kingdom of God. There is only one way, and that is through the one Mediator. The Old Testament figures, the New Testament people, the individuals up to the present

Reconcile Both Unto God

time, and the ones in the future are all reconciled in and through Christ. There is no other way.

How is this reconciliation achieved? By the Lord Jesus Christ. God sent Him. God initiated the action. Scripture explicitly states *that he might reconcile both unto God in one body by the Cross* [Eph. 2:16]. It is by the Cross. There is no reconciliation apart from the Cross. *And, having made peace through the blood of his cross, by him to reconcile all things unto himself; by him, I say, whether they be things in* (on) *earth, or things in heaven* [Col. 1:20]. There is no way reconciliation can be achieved apart from the death of our Lord Jesus Christ on the Cross.

The Apostle continues, saying *Having slain the enmity thereby*. This leads to a specific point. Some people say that cruel men put our Lord to death, and God forgives them for doing what they did. They even expand the definition of "cruel men" to include all of us. They continue by saying God forgives all of us for crucifying Christ, and as a result there is peace.

However, that is endeavoring to make peace in spite of the Cross. Another explanation people make is that God produces good out of evil. They will refer to Joseph and the action of his brothers. They will say that men meant it for evil, but God meant it for good.

The true teaching about reconciliation is that before it is possible, something has to happen on God's side. Sin has brought enmity. God hates sin. The enmity has to be removed. When it is removed, then God can bless man and individuals. Then there can be reconciliation. The enmity has been removed by the blood of the Cross.

Why does Paul emphasize the Cross and the blood? Because one cannot think of the Cross without thinking of the blood. That is the explanation of the Old Testament teachings about sacrifices. That was God's own method. He had ordained it.

In the Old Testament (see Lev. 16:7–22) they took the animal and put their hands on the head: what did this mean? That they were taking their sins and transferring them to the animal. Then the animal was killed, its blood was presented as an offering, and the animal was offered as a sacrifice. That is the Old Testament teaching, and that is precisely the teaching about Christ's death on the Cross.

God imputed their trespasses unto Him. God took their sins (yours and mine) and put them on the head of Christ, and then, as the Lamb of God He slew Him. That is how we are reconciled to God.

> *Moreover the law entered, that the offense* (sin) *might abound. But where sin abounded, grace did much more abound* [Rom. 5:20].

> *For he hath made him to be sin for us, who knew no sin; that we might be made the righteousness of God in him* [2 Cor. 5:21].

Man's enmity against God was put on Christ. God slew that enmity by Christ's blood of the Cross. That is what did it. Not by any action on our part. The enmity has been removed. The reconciliation can take place. God knew the Jews needed it, the Gentiles needed it, all others needed it, and we need it.

It is important to know these truths and for them to be revealed to us. As noted earlier, "Revelation unconditionally precedes knowledge," as noted by Otto Weber.

We are reconciled to God; we are reconciled to one another, but only by one way: in Christ on the Cross by His shed blood!

Paul states, in this magnificent letter, a significant truth: *And that he might reconcile both unto God in one body by the cross, having slain* (put to death) *the enmity thereby.*

In conclusion, may we remind ourselves that Paul commanded the elders at Ephesus *To feed* (shepherd) *the church of God, which he hath purchased with his own blood* [Acts 20:28]. The only way to reconcile God and man, man and God, man and man, is by the blood and death of Christ on the Cross.

May we close by remembering those memorable words from the beautiful hymn "In the Cross of Christ I Glory", by John Bowring:

> *In the Cross of Christ I glory,*
> *Towering o'er the wrecks of time;*
> *All the light of sacred story*
> *Gathers round its head sublime.*
>
> *When the woes of life o'er-take me,*
> *Hopes deceive, and fears annoy,*
> *Never shall the cross forsake me:*
> *Lo! It glows with peace and joy.*
>
> *When the sun of bliss is beaming*
> *Light and love upon my way,*
> *From the cross radiance streaming*
> *Adds more luster to the day.*

Bane and blessing, pain and pleasure,
By the cross are sanctified;
Peace is there that knows no measure,
Joys that through all time abide. Amen.

May we always glory in the Cross of Christ and His shed blood.
Amen!

17

He Came and Preached Peace

> *And came and preached peace to you which were afar off, and to them that were nigh* [Eph. 2:17].

This verse provides additional insight into the Apostle Paul's great statement concerning salvation. The Apostle tells us what has been accomplished through Christ and what He has prepared for us.

The Lord Himself comes to us and tells us what He has done, and heralds the good news that peace between God and man is available.

When considering this verse, please note there are two interpretations. One refers to the incarnation of our Lord and His earthly ministry as described in the four Gospels, which was primarily to the lost sheep of Israel; while the other refers to the evangelism of the Gospel by the apostles and disciples. The latter refers also to Christ's preaching through the church and the apostles' ministry after His death, resurrection, ascension, and sending the Holy Ghost.

When reviewing the four Gospels in light of the first interpretation, it is interesting to note that our Lord's ministry was primarily to the Jews during His incarnation. Calvin provides additional insight. He says that peace was preached through the apostles to the Gentiles because "It was necessary that Christ should rise from the dead before calling the Gentiles to the fellowship of grace." Christ says, *I am not sent but unto the lost sheep of the house of Israel* [Matt. 15:24].

Matthew records that during His earthly ministry,

> *These twelve Jesus sent forth, and commanded them, saying, Go not into the way of the Gentiles, and into any city of the Samaritans enter ye not:*
> *But go rather to the lost sheep of the house of Israel* [Matt. 10:5–6].

"Christ proclaimed the Gospel to the Gentiles through His Apostles, as by trumpets," as John Calvin eloquently describes Christ proclaiming the Gospel. However, what the apostles did in the name of Christ and at the command of Christ is rightly ascribed to Christ as if He were doing it in His own person. It is Christ through the Holy Spirit that gave them the capability and instructed them.

May we realize that the Gospel would be weak if it depended upon the strength of men. The authority of the Gospel comes from realizing that the men proclaiming it are the instruments of God and Christ speaks through them. Through it God declares that He is favorably disposed to us and reveals His fatherly love.

When you take away the Gospel or do not apply it, then there is war and enmity between God and man, and between man and man. On the other hand, when you have the proper effect of the Gospel, you give peace and calmness to the conscience, which otherwise would be tormented and disquieted.

Although our Lord appears to confine His ministry to the Jews and his disciples, He gave clear instructions that there was a wider and greater ministry, especially after what He accomplished on the Cross.

> THE SPIRIT OF THE LORD IS UPON ME, BECAUSE HE HATH ANOINTED ME TO PREACH THE GOSPEL TO THE POOR; HE HATH SENT ME TO HEAL THE BROKENHEARTED, TO PREACH DELIVERANCE TO THE CAPTIVES, AND RECOVERING OF SIGHT TO THE BLIND, TO SET AT LIBERTY THEM THAT ARE BRUISED (OPPRESSED), . . . [Luke 4:18].
>
> Go ye therefore, and teach (make disciples of) all nations, baptizing them in the name of the Father, and of the Son, and of the Holy Ghost:
> Teaching them to observe all the things whatsoever I have commanded you: and, lo, I am with you alway, even unto the end of the world. Amen [Matt. 28:19–20].

After the resurrection, Jesus clearly commanded His apostles and disciples that a wider and broader ministry was to be undertaken and accomplished.

Paul elaborates on this when he says that Jesus *came and preached peace to you which were afar off, and to them that were nigh*. The inimitable Ruth Paxson adds understanding with the following perceptive words: "Having become peace and having made it, Christ now preaches peace. It was His personal message after His resurrection [Luke 24:36; John 20:19–21, 20:26]. He preached it later through His apostles, and continues to preach peace through His Word faithfully given by His ministers.

"It is God's clearly declared purpose to heal the schism made by sin in humanity; otherwise His plan of salvation would be incomplete. In this present age He would do it through grace. Peace has not been established on earth because men will not follow God's way. But in the age to come, *through government* the Lord Jesus Christ shall rule over the earth as King of Kings and Lord of Lords. Then righteousness shall prevail and peace shall be its fruit."

The second interpretation is for Gentile Christians more personal, since Christ through His apostles, disciples, evangelists, and servants preached the gospel of peace with God plus fellowship with Himself. This ministry was made possible by the Cross. After His resurrection, after having become peace and having made peace, He preached peace through the apostles and others.

> *Then the same day at evening, being the first day of the week, when the doors were shut where the disciples were assembled for fear of the Jews, came Jesus and stood in the midst, and saith unto them, Peace be unto you* [John 20:19].
>
> *Then said Jesus to them again, Peace be unto you: as my Father hath sent me, even so send I you* [John 20:21].
>
> *And after eight days again his disciples were within, and Thomas with them: then came Jesus, the doors being shut, and stood in the midst, and said, Peace be unto you* [John 20:26].

It was God's plan to heal the schism between God and man, and man and man, through the Cross. This peace between man and man is achieved through the Cross. This is God's way. This is the way we are reconciled to God. If we are not reconciled to God, we cannot be reconciled to one another.

What teachings do we find in Paul's words, *And came and preached peace to you which were afar off, and to them that were nigh?*

One teaching we find is that an individual's basic need is peace with God. This peace is needed first and foremost. Then you can have peace within groups, between man and man, and with yourself.

Every person has thought or talked about their conscience. Certainly, all of us have expressed the idea at one time or another that we wished we did not have one! The reason man has a conscience is that he knows in his heart that he was really meant for something better than what he does or what he thinks. Man has a sense of right or wrong somewhere inside of himself, a sense of good and evil, and of justice and injustice.

A person has a sense of God. However, he may not like it, or may want to bottle it up or put it away. That is one side. Then there is the other side within man, his fallen nature, lust, passion, jealousy, envy, and self-centeredness. The Apostle clearly states that this conflict dwells within a person and at times boils over into conduct that is less than desirable. Paul describes it as only he can, saying,

> *For that which I do I allow (understand) not: for what I would (want to do), that do I not; but what I hate, that do I* [Rom. 7:15].
>
> *For I delight in the law of God after (according to) the inward man:*
> *But I see another law in my members, warring against the law of my mind, and bringing me into captivity to the law of sin which is in my members.*
> *O wretched man that I am! . . .*
> *I thank God through Jesus Christ our Lord. So then with the mind I myself serve the law of God; but with the flesh the law of sin* [Rom. 7:22–25].

The two factions warring within me make me antagonistic, restless, and fractious. These opposing forces cause me to do that which I would not do because I am weak. When I succumb, what do I do? I fail to understand the real reason and place the blame for my sinfulness on circumstances or other people or the environment, but not on myself. I try to find peace and forget the only way to find it is in Christ and to have fellowship with God. There is no other way.

We must realize in order to have peace that the first thing is to have peace with God. People try everything else, but that is the one that works.

Another teaching we find in Paul's words is that all men need peace, not just some, or 99 percent. He *came and preached peace to you which were afar off, and to them that were nigh.*

> *And suddenly there was with the angel a multitude of the heavenly host praising God, and saying,*
> *Glory to God in the highest, and on earth peace, good will toward me* [Luke 2:13–14].

The *peace* stated herein is God's peace, not man's fabrication or interpretation of the Word. It is God's peace that is needed.

Calvin amplifies on man's need for God's peace by reminding us that the Lord Jesus said, *I am not sent but to the lost sheep of the house of Israel* [Matt. 15:24]. Then he provided clarification as revealed to him by the Holy Spirit saying that, "He forbade the apostles to carry their first embassy to the Gentiles while He was still in the world [Matt. 10:15]. Therefore He proclaimed the Gospel to the Gentiles through His apostles as by trumpets. What they did, not only in His name, and by His command, but as it were in His own person, is justly ascribed to Him alone.... The faith of the Gospel would be weak indeed, were we to look only to men. Its whole authority comes from recognizing men as God's instruments, and hearing Christ speak to us by their mouth. Observe also, that the Gospel is the message of peace, by which God declares Himself favourable to us, and brings down to us His fatherly love.... and, on the other hand, the proper effect of the Gospel is to give peace and calmness to the conscience."

The Jews thought because they had the law, that somehow they could keep it. Therefore, they were right with God and had fellowship with Him. This is no different from those who think because they go to church, or make a profession of faith, that they are right with God and have fellowship with Him. The Israelites of the Old Testament relied upon their privileges and their possessions in believing that because of them they had achieved salvation. However, it was because of these very privileges that they were outside the kingdom of God.

There are people today in congregations throughout the land who think that evangelism needs to be preached to certain people only, but not to everyone. Certainly, not to people who have been brought up in Sunday School, who have joined the church, who work in the church, and who regularly attend the services of the church. Remember, Christ preached to and taught the Pharisees and scribes.

Christ preached to them *that were afar off and to them that were nigh*. This is important. Those who *are nigh* need the very same message as those who are *afar off*. Isn't that a blow to some of us? Imagine that we who attend, who worship, who have made a profession of faith need the very same message as those who never darken the doors of a sanctuary.

What does this do to your mindset? What are your thoughts, what is your reaction when you think about those who are *afar off*? The drunkards, the adulterers, the women of the street, the idolaters, the murderers, the thieves, the blasphemers and all the others we put in this category. It makes one stop and think, does it not?

Luke records in Acts the occasion when Paul and Silas were in prison. The jailer was charged with keeping them there and not allowing them to escape. To make sure they could not get away, the jailer *made* (fastened) *their feet fast in the stocks* [Acts 16:24]. That night there was an earthquake. The jailer feared for his life and would have killed himself if the prisoners had fled. When he saw that Paul and Silas were still there, he . . . *brought them out, and said, Sirs, what must I do to be saved? And they said, Believe on the Lord Jesus Christ, and thou shalt be saved, and thy house* (household) [Acts 16:30–31]. The jailer and his family had been far off; now they were nigh.

In this portion of Scripture, we have Paul, who was nigh to God, and we have the jailor, who was afar off. Yet Paul tells us that both he and the jailor had the very same need. They both needed the Gospel of Peace. Christ came into the world to save sinners. Paul says, THERE IS NONE RIGHTEOUS, NO, NOT ONE [Rom. 3:10].

Does it sound odd that Paul in the midst of his ministry is in the same position as the Philippian jailor? How about today? We are all in the same position. We need the Gospel, we need the shed blood, we need the Cross, and we need the peace of God. We need to hear the Word frequently in order to receive the nourishment and strength it provides.

Consider the nice, quiet, respectable people who never do anything outwardly evil, who perform good works, who support worthy causes, who pursue intellectual interests, who espouse high moral standards, who attend church and participate in its affairs. Compare them with those who are guilty of succumbing daily to the lusts of the flesh and mind, who do not attend church on a regular basis, who either ignore God or do not accept His teachings and are self-centered, not Christ-centered. They both need the peace of God. Those who are nigh and those who are far off. They both yearn for it. However, it is available only one way: through Christ Jesus and His shed blood.

The individuals in both groups are plagued by restlessness until they find peace with God. That is why the angels heralded His birth by proclaiming *And on earth peace, good will toward men* [Luke 2:14]. That is why our Saviour preached peace.

The real question is: are you in the kingdom of God or are you outside it? If you are outside, it does not matter if you are far off or if you are nigh. The following story of the game of golf illustrates this point. Two men are putting on the green of the last hole of an important championship round. Their scores are exactly the same. The first one putts, and he misses the hole by several feet; the second one putts, and the ball stops on the very edge of the cup. It is not more than one-sixteenth or one-eighth of an inch out of the hole. One is nigh, the other is far off. They are both in the same relative position. They are outside the hole. Both men are restless; both men are anxious. They both need to be in the cup to have the peace for which they yearn. One is nigh; the other is far off.

Where does this lead? Christ and Christ alone not only offers but is able to provide the peace which every person seeks. No one can reconcile himself or herself to God. It is only God who can reconcile us. He is the active one. Reconciliation is achieved *by the blood of Christ* shed on the Cross.

He did this for those who were nigh and those who were far off. He did it for Peter, Andrew, James, and John, for the Pharisees, for Barrabas, for the one on His right hand and the one on His left hand, and for Judas Iscariot.

Near the end of His earthly ministry Jesus said to the other Judas, not Iscariot, *Peace I leave with you, my peace I give unto you: not as the world giveth, give I unto you. Let not your heart be troubled, neither let it be afraid* [John 14:27]. It is God through Christ who reconciles us unto Himself and provides the peace that passes all understanding. He provides His peace, and He provides His fellowship.

Oh, that we could carry in our hearts and minds forever those four beautiful verses from Philippians:

> *Rejoice in the Lord always: and again I say, Rejoice.*
> *Let your moderation be known unto all men. The Lord is at hand.*
> *Be careful (anxious) for nothing; but in every thing by prayer and supplication with thanksgiving let your requests be made known unto God.*
> *And the peace of God, which passeth all understanding, shall keep your hearts and minds through Christ Jesus* [Phil. 4:4–7].

Oh, that we had the faith to take everything to Him and to leave it there. What is this faith that enables one to take all fears and anxieties to God knowing that He will *keep your hearts and minds through Christ Jesus?* It is a living, active, positive faith based upon God's promises, Christ's shed blood, and the Holy Spirit's revelations. May we remember this and live accordingly.

The beautiful hymn, What a Friend We Have in Jesus, by Joseph Scriven provides additional understanding to taking everything to Him and leaving it there:

> *What a Friend we have in Jesus, All our sins and griefs to bear!*
> *What a privilege to carry Everything to God in prayer!*
> *O what peace we often forfeit, O what needless pain we bear,*
> *All because we do not carry Everything to God in prayer!*
>
> *Have we trials and temptations? Is there trouble anywhere?*
> *We should never be discouraged: Take it to the Lord in prayer!*
> *Can we find a friend so faithful, Who will all sorrows share?*
> *Jesus knows our every weakness—Take it to the Lord in prayer!*
>
> *Are we weak and heavy laden, cumbered with a load of care?*
> *Precious Saviour, still our Refuge—Take it to the Lord in prayer!*
> *Do thy friends despise, forsake thee? Take it to the Lord in prayer!*
> *In His arms He'll take and shield thee, thou wilt find a solace there.*
> *Amen*

May we find the faith to take everything, I mean everything little and big to Him in prayer. May we know from the depths of our hearts and minds that *in His arms He'll take and shield thee,* then we *wilt find a solace there.*

Amen!

18

Through Him By One Spirit

> *For through him we both have access by one Spirit unto the Father* [Eph. 2:18].

This verse is the apex of what the Apostle began to describe in verse eleven. Look at the words, the meaning, and the context of what should be a stimulating, thought-provoking statement: *For through him; We have access; By one Spirit; Unto the Father.* The trouble today, with both individuals and the so-called church as a body, is that the people involved do not realize the significance of this statement. *Prosagoge,* the Greek word for *access,* means "a leading unto." The same word is also used in Romans 5:2 and Ephesians 3:12. If people realized the meaning of this statement it would probably revolutionize the Christian church. It would transform the church as we identify it today.

Consider how many people believe or think of Christianity and the Christian church as a place where they attend or participate:

- maybe in a perfunctory manner;
- maybe hesitatingly;
- maybe doubtfully;
- maybe as a duty;
- maybe as a place to exercise certain gifts;
- maybe to be busy;
- maybe as a club, institution, or social activity.

What a contrast to the reconciliation that has taken place between God and the individual members of the human race, and the reconciliation that has been accomplished on the Cross through the shed blood of our Lord Jesus Christ. The reconciliation God initiated has resulted in the realization that two separate parties, the Jew and the Gentile, *have access by one Spirit unto the Father*. The Restoration has begun. This is Christianity; this is what makes a person a member of the community of believers. The Christian realizes that the whole object and purpose of everything is *access by one Spirit unto the Father*. This truth must be considered, examined, and accepted.

When you read this eighteenth verse slowly, one of the great doctrines of Christianity hits you right between the eyes: *Through Him . . . by one Spirit unto the Father*. Father, Son, and Holy Ghost. The Doctrine of the Trinity. Consider not only this Scripture, but also what precedes it and what follows it.

The reconciliation is followed by:

- *Fellowcitizens with the saints, and of the household of God,*
- *Foundation of the apostles and prophets, Jesus Christ himself being the chief corner stone,*
- *Fitly framed (Being joined) together, groweth unto a holy temple in the Lord:*
- *A habitation* (dwelling place) *of God, through the Spirit* [Eph. 2:19–22].

The Doctrine of the Trinity differentiates the Christian faith from every other religious entity. It is a great and inscrutable mystery. We do not understand it fully. We merely assert it and affirm it. But Scripture very definitely teaches that Jesus Christ is truly God, that the Holy Spirit is truly God, and that there is but one God the Father.

You cannot begin to understand either the Bible or Christianity until you believe it, accept it, and bow down before it. It is a vital doctrine. We should continually remind ourselves of it and not be afraid if we do not completely understand it. Another important observation is that the Holy Trinity is definitely interested in us as individuals and acts within us for our salvation and sanctification. Have you ever thought of it that way? It is an imposing thought that the three Persons of the Trinity are interested in each of us:

> The Father thought of salvation and initiated it. He conceived of it and planned it. He purposed it. He sent His Son. Jesus says in His high priestly prayer, *I have finished the work which thou gavest me to do* [John 17:4].

> The Son volunteered to do the work. *Father, I will* (desire) *that they also, whom thou hast given me, be with me where I am; that they may behold my glory, which thou hast given me: for thou lovedst me before the foundation of the world* [John 17:24].

Foundation in this verse means, "casting or laying down, founding."

The Father conceived the plan, the Son volunteered to execute it. We need to remember this. The Son humbled Himself and made Himself of no reputation. He went to the Cross to bear our sins, and to shed His blood. He did this for us, not for Himself.

The Holy Spirit works out our salvation and sanctification one by one. The Son subordinates Himself to the Father, and the Holy Spirit subordinates Himself to the Father and the Son. The Spirit enables us to see our need and to accept the redemption worked out by the Son.

The Holy Spirit works in the individual and in the church, and fills the church with His presence. The Holy Spirit speaks of Christ,

> *Howbeit when he, the Spirit of truth, is come, he will guide you into all truth: for he shall not speak of* (on his own authority) *himself; but whatsoever he shall hear, that shall he speak: and he will show you things to come.*
> *He shall glorify me: for he shall receive of* (what is) *mine, and shall shew* (declare) *it unto you* [John 16:13–14].

These words of the Lord Jesus are important and revealing. He tells us what *the spirit of truth* will do when He comes. John Calvin sheds additional light on Jesus' words saying, "He (Jesus) therefore does not promise them predictions of things that would happen after their death, but only means that His kingdom would be of a different nature and its glory far greater than their minds could now conceive. Paul, in the Epistle to the Ephesians from the first to the end of the fourth chapter, explains the treasures of this hidden wisdom which even the angels in heaven learn with amazement through the church [Eph. 3:10]."

The Lord Jesus further states that He, the Holy Spirit, will take what is mine and declare it unto you. What is it that He will declare? "To be cleansed by Christ's blood; sin to be blotted out in us by His death; our old man to be crucified; His resurrection to be efficacious in reforming us to newness of life; and, in short to become partakers of His blessing. Therefore, the Spirit bestows on us nothing apart from Christ; but He takes from Christ what He sheds on us," as proclaimed by Calvin. The Spirit has glorified Christ, and He continues to glorify Him.

Our initial consideration of this verse reveals two important facts: first, the doctrine of the Trinity, and second, the Trinity's concern about us individually and our salvation. The Trinity works to bring about our salvation and sanctification.

When considering these facts you must relate them to another important doctrine, the Doctrine of Sin. Why? Because individual sin is such a problem, and the magnitude of the problem has resulted in the three Persons of the Trinity dealing with it, the Father, the Son, and the Holy Ghost. Salvation is not a matter of God being a God of love and providing forgiveness. It is more than that. It involves the three Persons of the Trinity and their respective activities.

When thinking about it, the amazing, staggering fact is that the Holy Trinity so loves us that They did this for us. God the Father knows you and is interested in you. Jesus Christ the Son loves you and gave Himself for you. The three Persons of the Trinity love you and do for you.

What is the chief object of salvation? To know God as our Father and to have fellowship with Him. The Apostle wants us to know that we have access unto the Father, by the Spirit.

Please note that Paul wants us to know that we have access to the Father. He wants us to know there is something very wonderful beyond the amazing grace of reconciliation. Reconciliation is not the end. We have access to the Father, and we have fellowship with Him, which will continue on and on. This particular verse points out three significant truths. First, we *have access by one Spirit unto the Father*. How? Through Him! The relationship is restored through Him. The Lord Jesus Christ actually implements and brings about access to the Father. He introduces us to the Father and brings us into His presence.

Remember, the primary objective of salvation is to bring us into the presence of God, to know Him, and to glorify Him. *And this is life eternal, that they might know thee the only true God, and Jesus Christ, whom thou hast sent* [John 17:3]. *Having therefore, brethren, boldness* (confidence) *to enter into the holiest by the blood of Jesus* [Heb. 10:19].

The people of the Old Testament knew it was a significant holy moment for the high priest to enter into the holiest of holies. They were always concerned about him and greatly relieved when he came out alive.

What does Peter say about access to the Father? *For Christ also hath once suffered for sins, the just for the unjust, that he might bring us to God, being put to death in the flesh, but quickened* (made alive) *by the*

Spirit [1 Pet. 3:18]. The renowned theologian, Otto Weber, says clearly and distinctly, "In contrast to the Old Testament, the 'sacrifice' of Jesus Christ is final and once for all. To be sure, God has 'given' the blood for atonement, that He might bring us to God."

What does John say? *That which we have seen and heard declare we unto you, that ye also may have fellowship with us: and truly our fellowship is with the Father, and with his Son Jesus Christ* [1 John 1:3]. Second, the Apostle emphasizes *unto the Father*. Please note the difference from verse 16 to verse 18. The Apostle deliberately changes the term from God to *Father*. Why? Because God in Christ by the Holy Spirit becomes our Father. The Lord Jesus in His model prayer says *Our Father*.

The Lord Jesus when talking to the woman from Samaria says *The Father seeketh such to worship him* [John 4:23]. Jesus also says, *I am the way, the truth, and the life: no man cometh unto the Father, but by me* [John 14:6].

The New Testament explicitly teaches that although people may believe in God they will never know Him as their Father except through Jesus Christ and by the Holy Spirit. *And if ye call on the Father, who without respect* (partiality) *of persons judgeth according to every man's work, pass the time of your sojourning* (stay) *here in fear* [1 Pet. 1:17]. The Christian is one who is brought into the same relationship with God as is the Lord Jesus Christ. Therefore, "(t)he fear which he (Paul) mentions, stands in opposition to the carelessness that is wont to creep in when there is a hope of deceiving with impunity. As God's eye is so keen as to penetrate into the hidden recesses of the heart, we ought to walk with Him carefully and not negligently," as appropriately clarified by John Calvin.

Third, *we both have* access. Note, the author of the letter to the Hebrews says, *Let us therefore come boldly* (confidently) *unto the throne of grace, that we may obtain mercy, and find grace to help in time of need* [Heb. 4:16].

The following questions deserve our attention and consideration as we walk with Jesus: Do we go to God instinctively as the Father of our Lord Jesus Christ and as our Father? Do we take all our cares, anxieties, and worries to Him? Do we leave them with Him confidently? Are we certain that He can deal with them?

Have you noticed how this one verse, *For through Him we both have access by one Spirit unto the Father*, contains and presents the truth of the Doctrine of the Holy Trinity? Through Him, one Spirit, and the Father.

The blessed Trinity is concerned about our salvation. They work to bring us into a right relationship with the Father in order that we might have fellowship with Him. That is the purpose of our salvation, not just our eternal existence.

The eighteenth verse says *we both have access*. Naturally, this leads to the question: How do we have access? The word *access* means "a leading unto." It is through Him, Jesus Christ, that we are led unto the Father. *By whom also we have access by faith into this grace wherein we stand, and rejoice in hope of the glory of God* [Rom. 5:2]. To have access unto the Father we are led by the one Spirit through Him, Christ Jesus.

This leads to other questions: How are we led? How are we drawn nigh? Certainly it is God who acts; but one way we have access unto the Father is through prayer. We should have confidence in our prayers. If we do not, then our prayers will not be effective and even may be useless.

There are many who fail to enjoy the benefits of salvation, who do not take advantage of access to the Father, who do not grasp the essence of prayer because they do not understand the teaching of this verse. Yet this short statement provides clear insight to true prayer. However, let me add rather quickly, prayer is not a simple matter.

Many people have a very definite mindset about prayer. They say that it is not important what you believe, or that doctrine is not essential to one's faith. They believe that the only thing that matters is praying to God. That belief contradicts the teaching in this verse. Prayer is based upon the teachings of Scripture and having a true understanding of them.

Luke reveals that the disciples went to Jesus and said, *Lord, teach us to pray, as John also taught his disciples* [Luke 11:1]. Have not each and every one of us felt at one time or another that we needed to learn how to pray, that we needed instruction, that we needed someone to care for us and to show us how to pray? The disciples came to Jesus after observing Him in prayer, and as a result of their question He gave them (and us) the Lord's Prayer.

Jesus' encounter with the Samaritan woman, at the well, is revealing. She had said to Jesus that people needed to worship in certain places. But,

> *Jesus saith unto her, Woman, believe me, the hour cometh, when ye shall neither in this mountain, nor yet at Jerusalem, worship the Father* [John 4:21].

> *But the hour cometh, and now is, when the true worshipers shall worship the Father in spirit and in truth: for the Father seeketh such to worship him* [John 4:23].

Jesus pointed out that the Samaritans' idea of God was erroneous. They wanted to localize Him and put Him in a specific place. Jesus is saying you cannot worship with wrong ideas. Before we can worship God we must know the One to whom we are praying. Therefore, teaching is essential to prayer. We should know to whom we are praying, and we should know how to enter into His Holy presence.

Two things are absolutely essential to prayer and being led unto the Father: Christ the Son and the Holy Spirit.

Amen!

19

Christ's Righteousness

For through him we both have access by one Spirit unto the Father [Eph. 2:18].

Praying to God is based upon two principles *through him . . . by one Spirit*. Both are essential. They go together. This needs to be emphasized because there is confusion about it.

Some teach that the whole matter of approaching God in prayer is really very simple and easy. All you need to do is go immediately into the presence of God, regardless of your situation, whether it is trouble, difficulties in your future, the need for guidance, having desires, or interceding for others. They continue by saying that all you need to do is sit back and wait for God to speak. Further, you have immediate contact with Him and nothing else is needed. This is one approach.

Another school of thought emphasizes the Doctrine of our Lord Jesus Christ and His atonement but neglects the Holy Spirit and its impact. They do not realize the importance of the Holy Spirit in prayer and their prayer life. On the other hand, there are those who place their whole emphasis on the Holy Spirit and ignore the Lord Jesus Christ and His work.

Then there is the group that wants to add something. They say something else is necessary in addition to the Lord Jesus Christ and the Holy Spirit. For example, the Roman Catholics want to add the Virgin Mary and put her alongside the Lord Jesus Christ and the Holy Spirit. However, to add anyone, or anything, to the Lord Jesus Christ and the Holy Spirit is to both deny Scripture and to go astray in this most vital matter of prayer. Remember, . . . *through him we both have access by one Spirit unto the Father.*

When looking at this statement by itself, we are to note what precedes it and what follows it as we focus our attention on the words, *through him*. Why? Because there is not access to the Father except through the Lord Jesus Christ and by one Spirit.

> *There is . . . one mediator between God and men, the man Christ Jesus* [1 Tim. 2:5-6].

> *Having therefore, brethren, boldness* (confidence) *to enter into the holiest by the blood of Jesus* [Heb. 10:19].

The only way to enter and gain access is by the Lord Jesus and the one Spirit. It is not by the blood of bulls and goats. Is that teaching not plain? Yet people talk about having contact with God, about knowing God, being blessed by God, and being led by God without ever mentioning the Lord Jesus Christ. When praying to God, remember that apart from the Lord Jesus there is no access at all.

It is through Christ, in Christ, and by Christ that we have access to the Father. He is our great sin-bearer and this admits us into God's presence. Remember,

> *Who was delivered for* (because of) *our offenses, and was raised again for our justification* [Rom. 4:25].

> *But now in Christ Jesus ye who sometimes* (once) *were far off are made nigh by the blood of Christ* [Eph. 2:13].

Have you noted Paul's statements in this portion of the Epistle? He stresses Jesus' Cross, body, flesh, and blood. These things come first. The great preacher of the nineteenth century Charles Spurgeon used to say, "the ultimate way to test whether a man is truly preaching the gospel or not, is to notice the emphasis which he places on the blood." It is not enough to talk about the Cross and the death; *the test is the blood*. Some people do not like that explanation. Paul says *by the blood of Christ* and so does the author of the letter to the Hebrews. *Having therefore, brethren, boldness* (confidence) *to enter into the holiest by the blood of Jesus* [Heb. 10:19].

The blood makes one think of sacrifice and the atonement. It is by the sacrifice, which God provided, that reconciliation is made. He is our peace, and the truth is that the atonement is a "covering" of our sins. As a result, they are considered non-existent, and the individual is looked upon as having never committed them.

It is not that our sins are condoned or forgotten because we have been baptized and are united with Christ; our sins are erased *only* because of what Christ did for us on the Cross by shedding *His* blood.

Thus the roots of sin, pride, and self-love are extracted, and the process of healing is initiated. We share in the righteousness of Christ only because of what He has done, not because of anything we have done. Without the shedding of blood, there is no remission of sins. It is that which enables us to become new creatures in Christ.

Let us not forget that a just and holy God had to punish sin, the great stumbling block to reconciliation. He punished it on Calvary's Hill. Therefore, we must consider the righteousness and justice of God, as well as the absolute necessity for punishing sin. Otherwise, we are misrepresenting the Doctrine of Christ's death. It is Christ who is our sin-bearer, our only sin-bearer.

Christ is our great High Priest.

> *Seeing then that we have a great high priest, that is passed into* (through) *the heavens, Jesus the Son of God, let us hold fast our profession.*
>
> *For we have not a high priest which cannot be touched* (sympathize) *with the feeling of our infirmities; but was in all points tempted like as we are, yet without sin.*
>
> *Let us therefore come boldly* (confidently) *unto the throne of grace, that we may obtain mercy, and find grace to help in time of need* [Heb. 4:14–16].

Why are we able to *come boldly* (confidently) *unto the throne of grace*? Calvin provides appropriate understanding stating that: "The basis of this confidence is that the throne of God is not marked by a naked majesty which overpowers us, but is adorned with a new name, that of grace. . . . Therefore in order to help our lack of confidence, and to free our minds of all fears, the apostle clothes it with grace and gives it a name which will encourage us by its sweetness. It is as he were saying, since God has fixed on His throne as it were a banner of grace and of fatherly love towards us, there is no reason why His majesty should ward us off from approaching Him.

"The sum of all this is that we may safely call on God, since we know He is propitious to us. This happens because of the mercy of Christ, as stated in Eph. 3:12 (*In whom we have boldness and access with confidence by the faith of him*) because when Christ accepts us into His faith and discipleship, He covers with His goodness the majesty of God which could otherwise be fearful, so that nothing appears except grace and fatherly goodwill."

Jesus Christ died upon the Cross. His blood was shed, He went through the veil into the holiest of holies, atonement was finally made, and He has gone into the presence of God.

What happened as a result? God pronounces that the death of Christ is sufficient. Therefore, His justice is satisfied. He admits the High Priest into His presence and has Him sit down at His right hand.

What does this mean? The throne of judgment becomes a throne of grace. How do I know this? Because the Lord Jesus Christ is seated by the side of God, and He is my representative. He makes my access to the Father not only possible, but feasible.

Christ is our righteousness. *For he hath made him to be sin for us, who knew no sin; that we might be made the righteousness of God in him* [2 Cor. 5:21]. We are clothed with the righteousness of Christ. That is what Scripture teaches. There is a change made. My sins and your sins are imputed to Him. His life, His holiness are imputed to you and me. Therefore, we are clothed with the righteousness of Christ. When you realize you are covered by the righteousness of Christ then you can go into the presence of God with confidence and assurance. Then you can pray boldly.

We have access through Him because we are new creatures in Him. *Even when we were dead in sins, hath quickened us* (made us alive) *together with Christ, (by grace ye are* (have been) *saved); And hath raised us up together, and made us sit together in heavenly places in Christ Jesus* [Eph. 2:5–6]. Christ finished His work, He is seated at the right hand of God, and since I am in Christ, I am there with Him. There is a beautiful verse by Charles Wesley which expresses this thought so clearly:

> *There was no other good enough*
> *to pay the price of sin*
> *He only could unlock the gates*
> *of heaven and let us in.*

How do we get in? Through Christ. We are dependent upon Him. He shed His blood for each of us. Christ is our sin-bearer, our High Priest, our righteousness, and He makes us new creatures.

When considering these facts remember;

> *For in that he died, he died unto sin once* (for all): *but in that he liveth, he liveth unto God.*
> *Likewise reckon* (consider) *ye also yourselves to be dead indeed unto sin, but alive unto God through* (in) *Jesus Christ our Lord* [Rom. 6:10–11].

Why does Paul say consider yourselves *to be dead indeed unto sin, but alive unto God through* (in) *Jesus Christ our Lord*? "This is the view you are to take of your case—as Christ died once to destroy sin, so you have died once in order that in (the) future you may cease from sin. Indeed, you must make daily progress in the mortification of your flesh which has been begun in you, until sin is wholly destroyed. As Christ was raised to an incorruptible life, so you are regenerated by the grace of God, in order that you may lead the whole of your life in holiness and righteousness, since the power of the Holy Spirit, by which you have been renewed, is eternal, and will flourish forever," according to John Calvin.

When we realize our dependence upon Him, we can have a prayer life filled with assurance by what He has done and boldly approach His throne of grace.

Amen!

20

Making Intercession According to the Will of God

> *Likewise the Spirit also helpeth our infirmities: for we know not what we should pray for as we ought: but the Spirit itself maketh intercession for us with groanings which cannot be uttered.*
>
> *And he that searcheth the hearts knoweth what is the mind of the Spirit, because he maketh intercession for the saints according to the will of God* [Rom. 8:26–27].

The blessed Holy Trinity is concerned with our salvation and plays an important part in it. Probably the greatest benefit of our salvation is that we have access to the Father. Who has provided this access? God through His Son, Christ Jesus. When having access to the Father, what is the most difficult thing to do? Probably the most difficult thing for us to do is to pray. And at the same time it is probably the greatest thing we do.

Why is it so difficult to pray? First, because we have difficulty recognizing the presence of God. Further, God is Spirit and is unseen. *No man hath seen God at any time* [John 1:18]. Often, individuals have a sense of unreality in their prayer life.

Second, there is a problem of concentration. At times we have difficulty concentrating on the books we are reading, or the people with whom we are conversing. When beginning to pray, our minds often start wandering in many different directions. It is difficult to gather one's thoughts and to concentrate exclusively on praying to God the Father.

Third, there is a sense of unworthiness. This is another way of recognizing or reminding ourselves of our sinfulness. Remember during times of prayer that it is really the supreme activity of the human soul, because prayer is communion with God. Do not be discouraged by the fact that you find it difficult to pray. The one thing to fear regarding prayer is thinking or acting that it is too easy.

Paul's words to the Romans regarding prayer and praying as we ought are comforting and heartwarming. They change our focus from negative, subjective thoughts to the glory of God and how *the spirit itself maketh intercession for us with groanings which cannot be uttered*. What comfort and joy this should be to us when we go to God in adoration and awe, but cannot properly express ourselves to Him.

"Paul concludes that the presence of heavenly grace already shines forth in the very zeal for prayer, because no one of his own accord conceives devout and godly prayers.... The Spirit, therefore, must prescribe the manner of our praying. Paul calls the groans into which we break forth by the impulse of the Spirit *unutterable*, because they far exceed the capacity of our intellect. The Spirit of God is said to *intercede*,... because He stirs up in our hearts the prayers which it is proper for us to address to God. In the second place He affects our hearts in such a way that these prayers penetrate into heaven itself by their fervency. Paul has spoken in this way for the purpose of attributing the whole of prayer more significantly to the grace of the Spirit.

"The fact that we are heard by God while we pray through His Spirit is a notable reason for confirming our confidence, for He Himself is intimately acquainted with our prayers, as being the thoughts of His own Spirit.... As, therefore, Paul had recently declared that God aids us while He leads us into His bosom, so now he adds another consolation. Our prayers which He regulates, will by no means be disappointed.... Let us also learn from this that the first part of prayer is consent to the will of the Lord, who is by no means bound to follow our desires. We must, therefore, pray to God to regulate our prayers according to His will, if we would have them accepted by Him," according to Calvin's insight into our prayer life and the Holy Spirit's role in presenting them to God according to His will.

Once these factors are recognized, we should begin to learn how to pray. There are certain fundamental truths regarding prayer. When preparing, we should collect our thoughts and realize what we are doing before rushing into the presence of God. We should sincerely remind ourselves of the essence of prayer and give forethought as to why and how we are going into the presence of God, and know that we are going to have communion with Him.

As mentioned previously, there are two things about which we should be certain when we consider praying. They are the Lord Jesus Christ and the Holy Spirit. The Apostle teaches that the Holy Spirit is essential to prayer, and so is the Lord Jesus Christ. The two go together and are inseparably intertwined.

We cannot truly pray without the Holy Spirit, and true prayer is always by the Holy Spirit through the Lord Jesus Christ.

> *Praying always with all prayer and supplication in the Spirit, and watching thereunto with all perseverance and supplication for all saints* [Eph. 6:18].

> *For we are the circumcision, which worship God in the Spirit, and rejoice in Christ Jesus, and have no confidence in the flesh* [Phil. 3:3].

> *But ye, beloved, building up yourselves on your most holy faith, praying in the Holy Ghost* [Jude 1:20].

To the New Testament writers, the term *in the Spirit* or *in the Holy Ghost* was the very essence of prayer.

You will recall that during Jesus' encounter with the Samaritan woman, He said to her *God is a Spirit: and they that worship Him must worship Him in spirit and in truth* [John 4:24]. What do we learn from this portion of Scripture?

Obviously, prayer is neither a matter of place nor a matter of ceremony. We do not worship on a certain mountain or in a certain place. True prayer is not confined to any specific space or to a particular type of ceremony.

Second, prayer is not a question of posture. You can pray standing with arms outstretched as the prophets of the Old Testament did, or you can pray while you are kneeling, or while you are seated. It is not the posture that matters. The important factors are praying *through Him* by the *one Spirit*.

Third, there is the question about the forms of prayer. This one question generates numerous sub-questions:

- Should we have set prayers?
- Should we have formal prayers?
- Should we have liturgies?
- Should we have freedom in prayer?
- Should the emphasis be on beautiful phrases or on diction?

Please do not misunderstand. I am not saying that a written or read prayer cannot be effective and meaningful. I remember reading about a great preacher who always wrote out his pastoral prayers for the Sunday Worship Service. When asked why, he responded by saying that he "spent time preparing his sermon for men; therefore it was more important that he spend time preparing his prayer to God Almighty."

In the matter of prayer, it is important to keep the proper balance between the Spirit and the form. These two things are important, but clearly the teaching of our Lord Jesus is that the Spirit is the vital element. The control and the inspiration of the Holy Spirit is essential. The real emphasis in true prayer should be placed upon the Spirit, not upon beautiful words or phrases. The Spirit through Him.

While members of the First Presbyterian Church in Pittsburgh we were truly blessed due to the prayer life of the Fellowship Class. Some wonderful and amazing things happened during that ten-year period. Our teacher was a lady named Helen Wilson. She was a retired schoolteacher and must have been an excellent one according to her former students. Her major was English.

On one occasion she told us about her father, who had been an uneducated person, especially by today's standards. She related how he used horrible grammar when he spoke, yet he was a man of prayer. He believed in prayer. He practiced prayer. Helen told us she never once heard him make a grammatical error when he was praying. Such is the power of the Holy Spirit.

Fourth, there is the question about prayer at specific times of the day. Some people stress the importance of praying at certain times. Unfortunately, saying prayers at certain times is stressed more than having communion with God.

Fifth and last, there is another important point regarding "saying a prayer." Frankly, we should not think, or talk, about just "saying a prayer." Why? Because you cannot just say a prayer when you are talking with, going into the presence of, or having communion with God the Father. Saying a prayer should include awe, humility, reverence, respect, thankfulness, and joy.

Where is the Holy Spirit? Where is the living, active element? Prayer is a matter of the Spirit. God is a spirit, and they that worship Him, worship Him in Spirit and in truth. It is *through Him* that we have access unto the Father by *one Spirit*.

When you get down to basics, prayer means that my spirit is communing with God. It is personal; it is an immediate fellowship with Him. However, you cannot really communicate with God who is a spirit without the activity of the Holy Ghost.

Without the Holy Spirit, prayer is mechanical, lifeless, and difficult. However, with the Holy Spirit it becomes free, delightful, glorious, refreshing, and supreme enjoyment. *But the hour cometh, and now is, when the true worshippers shall worship the Father in spirit and in truth: for the Father seeketh such to worship him. God is a Spirit: and they that worship him must worship him in spirit and in truth* [John 4:23–24].

What about prayer in the Old Testament? Prayer in its most primitive forms was akin to magic and charming. However, prayer in the Old Testament is definitely far removed from magic. It involves a personal God and a personal relationship with Him. We see it in the lives of Abraham and Moses. Abraham had a personal relationship with God and went to Him in prayer. This is seen vividly as Abraham proceeded toward Sodom and . . . *stood yet before the Lord . . . And said, Wilt thou also destroy the righteous with the wicked* [Gen. 18:22–23]?

At first, Abraham asked the Lord if He would destroy Sodom if fifty righteous people could be found therein. *And the Lord said, If I find in Sodom fifty righteous within the city, then I will spare all the place for their sakes* [Gen. 18:26]. The dialogue continued between Abraham and God, with Abraham asking, probably beseeching, God to spare Sodom if there could be found forty righteous, then thirty righteous, then twenty righteous, and finally ten righteous. This is revealing about the status of Sodom at that time. And then God *said, I will not destroy it for ten's sake. And the Lord went his way, as soon as he had left* (finished speaking) *communing with Abraham: and Abraham returned unto his place* [Gen. 18:32–33].

The second incident of intercessory prayer involves Moses, when God expressed His wrath against the Israelites for making a molten calf and worshipping it. God called them *a stiffnecked* (stubborn) *people*. When this occurred *Moses besought* (the face of) *the Lord . . . and said . . . why doth thy wrath wax hot against thy people, which thou hast brought forth out of the land of Egypt with great power, and with a mighty hand* [Exod. 32:11]? After asking God this question, Moses asked God what might the Egyptians say regarding His reason for bringing His people out of Egypt: was it for mischief, or to slay them, or to consume them?

Moses also asked God to *Remember Abraham, Isaac, and Israel . . . to whom thou swarest by thine own self . . . I will multiply your seed as the stars of heaven, and all this land that I have spoken of will I give unto your seed, and they shall inherit it for ever* [Exod. 32:13].

Moses reveals how we may go to God through intercessory prayer and bring items to His attention in a manner exhibiting a deep, respectful love for Him, as well as compassion and concern for others. Also, it bears witness to the fact that God listens and responds. Scripture tells us that after hearing Moses' petition . . . *the Lord repented of the evil* (relented from the harm) *which he thought to do unto his people* [Exod. 32:14]. May we learn from Moses and go boldly to God in prayer.

We know that Abraham and Moses had conversations and discussions with God. Further, the patriarchs exercised a ministry of intercession as a result of their covenant relationship with God. And their prayers found favor in God's sight.

During the time of the prophets there was a definite conception that the prophet possessed the Spirit of God, and was a channel for communications between God and man. In reality, the belief was God speaks to man, through the Spirit, by the prophet; and man may speak to God, by the Spirit, through the prophet. The intercessory prayers were not restricted to the prophets. The kings could and did pray for their people.

The period of the exile was a landmark time for the Israelites regarding prayer. It was during this time that they could not perform their sacrificial offerings in the Temple. Therefore, prayer became the sole effective means of worship.

The prominence of prayer is seen in Daniel, Nehemiah and Isaiah, as recorded in the following:

> *Now when Daniel knew that the writing was signed, he went into his house; and his windows being open in his chamber toward Jerusalem, he kneeled upon his knees three times a* (that) *day, and prayed, and gave thanks before his God, as he did* (had been doing before this) *aforetime* [Dan. 6:10].

> *Then the king said unto me, For what dost thou make request? So I prayed to the God of heaven* [Neh. 2:4].

> *Hear, O our God for we are despised: and turn their reproach upon their own head, and give them for a prey* (plunder) *in the land of captivity* [Neh. 4:4].

> *Nevertheless we made our prayer unto our God, and set a watch against them day and night, because of them* [Neh. 4:9]

> *Even them will I bring to my holy mountain, and make them joyful in my house of prayer: their burnt offerings and their sacrifices shall be accepted upon mine altar; for mine house shall be called a house of prayer for all people* [Isaiah 56:7].

May we learn to pray, and may we pray often and confidently, because our Father in heaven wants to have communion with each of us day by day. May we give thanks that we have access to the Father through Christ and the Holy Spirit.

Amen!

21

Having Faith in Prayer

For through him we both have access by one Spirit unto the Father [Eph. 2:18].

The Psalms were collected between the Exile and the Maccabean periods for use in the Temple liturgy. They abound with all types of prayer, primarily representing corporate instead of individual worship. It was during this period that the Israelites expected to see the goodness of the Lord in the land and among the people, therefore the prayers tended to be for temporal rather than spiritual blessings.

This period was followed by the time when the synagogue played a vital role in fostering prayer in the hearts and homes of the people. Probably the initial function conducted in the synagogue was instruction in the law. Gradually prayer was added, and the synagogue became a place of worship. Prayer became the substitute for the sacrifices offered in the temple. As a result, prayer began to deeply influence the daily life of the people.

When considering prayer in the New Testament, we must begin with the Lord's Prayer, which was the result of a request by Christ's disciples. The significance of this prayer is in the choice and arrangement of the petitions, with only one of them for a material blessing. It should be noted and emphasized that the petitions for God's glory and kingdom come first. They precede all other requests. The reason is simple. All requests and petitions must be subordinated to God's eternal purpose to establish His kingdom among men. Jesus stated it clearly and forcefully, saying, *But seek ye first the kingdom of God, and his righteousness; and all these things shall be added unto you* [Matt. 6:33].

John's Gospel records the instructions given by Jesus that all prayers were to be offered in His name.

> *And whatsoever ye shall ask in my name, that will I do, that the Father may be glorified in the Son* [John 14:13].
>
> *Ye have not chosen me, but I have chosen you, and ordained (appointed) you, that ye should go and bring forth fruit, and that your fruit should remain: that whatsoever ye shall ask of the Father in my name, he may give it you* [John 15:16].
>
> *And in that day ye shall ask me nothing. Verily, verily, I say unto you, Whatsoever ye shall ask the Father in my name, he will give it you.*
> *Hitherto have ye asked nothing in my name: ask, and ye shall receive, that your joy may be full.*
> *These things have I spoken unto you in proverbs (figurative language): but the time cometh, when I shall no more speak unto you in proverbs (figurative language), but I shall show (tell) you plainly of the Father.*
> *At that day ye shall ask in my name: and I say not unto you, that I will pray the Father for you* [John 16:23–26].

Jesus makes it abundantly clear that we are to go through Him when we go to the Father in prayer, and that God the Father will give to us whatsoever we ask in His name. Therefore, to pray with true understanding requires praying *through Him* and by the *one Spirit*.

Calvin provides additional clarity to Christ's words saying ". . . when Christ is said to intercede with the Father for us, let us not imagine anything fleshly about Him, as if He were on His knees before the Father offering humble supplications. But the power of His sacrifice, by which He once pacified God toward us, is always powerful and efficacious. The blood by which He atoned for our sins, the obedience which He rendered is a continual intercession for us. This is a remarkable passage, by which we are taught that we have the heart of God as soon as we place before Him the name of His Son."

In addition, there is the need for importunity in prayer. Little emphasis is placed on the significance of importunity in prayer today. Too often the perception is that we merely have to ask God for something without exerting any further effort, and He will provide it. That is not what the Lord teaches. He tells us in no uncertain terms that we are to go to God the Father with a sense of urgency and persistently seek His favor. This is revealed to us in the parable of the widow who besought a judge who feared neither God nor man. She persisted in asking the judge to *Avenge me of* (vindicate me against) *mine adversary* [Luke 18:3]. The woman continued to incessantly make her request known to the judge. Finally, the judge relented and said *I will avenge* (vindicate) *her, lest by her continual coming she weary me* [Luke 18:5].

The Lord Jesus summed up His parable beautifully, saying, *And shall not God avenge* (vindicate) *his own elect, which cry day and night unto him, though he bear long with them* [Luke 18:7]? Jesus acknowledges and encourages importunity in prayer. We are to exhibit these qualities in our prayer life. The reason for exercising persistence in prayer is not that God is unwilling, but faith needs resistance before it can exercise real strength and develop according to God's will.

There is also a need for unquestioning faith in prayer. We find this in the following Scripture:

> *And the Lord said, If ye had faith as a grain of mustard seed, ye might say unto this sycamine* (mulberry) *tree, Be thou plucked up by the root, and be thou planted in the sea; and it should obey you* [Luke 17:6].
>
> *If ye abide in me, and my words abide in you, ye shall ask what ye will, and it shall be done unto* (for) *you* [John 15:7].
>
> *And this is the confidence that we have in him, that, if we ask any thing according to his will, he heareth us* [1 John 5:14].

An important point is this: Answer to prayer is certain if it is in the name and spirit of Christ and in line with God's will.

What about intercession in the New Testament? The primary examples are given in the Lord's Prayer and in the High Priestly Prayer of Jesus in John 17. Another excellent example is *Bless them that curse you, and pray for them which despitefully* (spitefully) *use you* [Luke 6:28].

In his Epistles, Paul stresses interceding for others and asking the members of the community to pray for him.

> *Now I beseech you, brethren, for* (through) *the Lord Jesus Christ's sake, and for* (through) *the love of the Spirit, that ye strive together with me in your prayers to God for me* [Rom. 15:30].
>
> *Finally, brethren, pray for us, that the word of the Lord may have* (run) *free course, and be glorified, even as it is with you* [2 Thess. 3:1].

We have the Doctrine of Heavenly Intercession which is so magnificently stated by Paul and confirmed by the Apostle John,

> *Who is he that condemneth? It is Christ that died, yea rather, that is risen again, who is even at the right hand of God, who also maketh intercession for us* [Rom. 8:34].

> *MY little children, these things write I unto you, that ye (may not) sin not. And if any man sin, we have an advocate (intercessor) with the Father, Jesus Christ the righteous* [1 John 2:1].

What about the intercession of the Holy Spirit? Paul tells the Romans,

> *Likewise the Spirit also helpeth our infirmities* (weaknesses): *for we know not what we should pray for as we ought: but the Spirit itself maketh intercession for us with groanings which cannot be uttered.*
>
> *And he that searcheth the hearts knoweth what is the mind of the Spirit, because he maketh intercession for the saints according to the will of God* [Rom. 8:26–27].

Paul's revelation provides us with special insight.

In the Old Testament, the prayers of the patriarchs and the prophets had special power and capabilities because they were spirit-filled men. Paul says that the community of believers, the Christian followers, have the same Spirit and the same power of prayer. This indwelling Spirit is distinct from man's spirit and is able to interpret groanings we are not able to utter or articulate.

Prior to the War Between the States, Stonewall Jackson was a member of the First Presbyterian Church in Lexington, Virginia. One Wednesday evening he approached Dr. White, the minister, and asked if he could give the prayer the next Wednesday at the midweek service. Dr. White said he could. The next Wednesday, Dr. White called on Thomas Jackson to give the prayer. He stood up, he groaned, and he groaned; but he could not utter any audible words, and then he sat down. After the service, Jackson apologized to Dr. White and asked if he could offer the prayer next Wednesday. Dr. White said he could. The results were the same. The third Wednesday, Thomas Jackson offered a beautiful, meaningful prayer that everyone understood, and they were uplifted by it. Dr. White said from that time forth people came on Wednesday night to hear Thomas Jackson pray.

"The inarticulate groanings suggest the difficulty of shaping or forming prayers in the sinful human mind," is a revealing and comforting statement by a knowledgeable unknown person. Intercession by the Spirit is necessary due to our ignorance. We may not know what is required; therefore, we may pray contrary to God's will. The Spirit knows not only our minds but also the mind and will of God. Therefore, He is able to frame and form our prayers and provide the proper content for them.

Every human prayer offered with the right intention is supported by a double intercession. Think of that! Supported by the indwelling Spirit and the glorified Christ. If you have not had difficulties in your prayer life, then you have not begun to realize what is involved. Please note the New Testament does not suggest that either of these ministries is available except to believing Christians in the community of believers.

What contributions does the Holy Spirit make regarding prayer?

He creates within us the realization that we worship God in spirit and in truth. God, through the Spirit, develops within us a mind in the Spirit, an outlook in the Spirit, or as we are wont to say, a spiritual mind, a spiritual outlook.

> *Blessed be the God and Father of our Lord Jesus Christ, who hath blessed us with all spiritual blessings in heavenly places in Christ*
> [Eph. 1:3].

The Holy Spirit enlivens us, quickens us, disturbs us, moves us, and stimulates us in the Spirit.

The Holy Spirit reveals our need for God, His mercy, and His blessings. The Holy Spirit brings us to a point where we realize that God has given us the special gifts of the soul and the spirit. As a result, we begin to desire to know Him, and we begin to pray to Him. Then we begin to hunger and to thirst after righteousness. The Holy Spirit produces the felt need of God.

The Holy Spirit also reveals God in His glory to us. This is vital and essential. We want to rush in, to see if God conforms to our image of Him, and will do as we ask. When we go to God in prayer, we need to remember we are on holy ground. We are going into the presence of God.

Yes, the Holy Spirit reveals God in His glory, but He also reveals Him as our Father and the Father of Jesus Christ. He creates within us a desire to know the living God, to have communion with Him, and to have an intimate knowledge of Him.

Fourth, He keeps our eyes on the Lord Jesus Christ. The Holy Spirit enables us to see Him in all His glory, and to see what He has done and is doing. "The Holy Spirit reveals and unfolds the Lord Jesus Christ. He enables us to see and understand the exalted views and meanings of the work and person of Jesus Christ. He enables us to see realistically our relationship to Christ. Charles Wesley expresses it so eloquently in the hymn Jesus, Lover of My Soul:

> *Just and holy is thy name,*
> *I am all unrighteousness,*
> *Vile and full of sin I am,*
> *Thou art full of truth and grace.*

"Last, the Holy Spirit leads us to an understanding of all the promises of God. We are beset by our own little worlds, our trials and tribulations, and our own weaknesses. The Holy Spirit reveals to us the exceeding great and precious promises of God in Christ. As He does, we begin to realize that God is the Father of Jesus Christ and He is our Father. And we begin to feel the presence of God," as proclaimed by Martyn Lloyd-Jones.

It is the Holy Spirit that does all these things, enabling us to grow in our relationship to Christ and to increase in faith. As Paul says, *For ye have not received the spirit of bondage again to fear; but ye have received the Spirit of adoption, whereby we cry, Abba, Father* [Rom. 8:15]. Therefore, we are not in bondage; we have sonship and freedom!

Amen!

22

Unity In Christ

> *Now therefore ye are no more strangers and foreigners, but fellow citizens with the saints, and of the household of God;*
> *And are built upon the foundation of the apostles and prophets, Jesus Christ himself being the chief corner stone;*
> *In whom all the building fitly framed (being joined) together groweth unto an holy temple in the Lord:*
> *In whom ye also are builded* (being built) *together for a habitation* (dwelling place) *of God through the Spirit* [Eph. 2:19–22].

Two seemingly innocuous words, *strangers and foreigners*, are used by Paul to inform members of the community of believers that, *Now therefore ye are no more strangers and foreigners, but fellow citizens with the saints, and of the household of God.*

With Paul you must always think of what he has said previously and be prepared for what he is going to present. He does not leave you dangling. He reveals God's Word and Christ's message to you and for you. He reminds the Ephesians that they were formerly strangers regarding the covenant. However, their condition has changed, not by anything they may have done, but by God's action in making them citizens of His household. They have become *fellow citizens with the saints.*

In these closing verses of the second chapter, "Paul now summarizes the results of God's workmanship and shows the benefit of His work to God as well as to the saints. Connecting two verses [Eph. 2:18–19], . . . show that the Jew and Gentile have equal access to the Father through the Son by the Spirit," as aptly described by Ruth Paxson. Think about it! Those who were previously unworthy to be partners with the godly now have rights with Abraham, Moses, the patriarchs, the prophets, the apostles, and even the angels. They have been admitted into the household of God; they are members of the family. They have unity with the family of God through Christ by one Spirit.

Note what Paul is saying, *Ye Gentiles ye knew God. However, ye did not glorify Him, but gave yourselves up to idolatry.* Paul says to the Romans,

> *When they knew God, they glorified him not as God, neither were thankful; but became vain* (futile) *in their imaginations* (thoughts), *and their foolish heart was darkened.*
> *Professing themselves to be wise, they became fools* [Rom. 1:21–22],
>
> *Wherefore God also gave them up to uncleanness through the lusts of their own hearts, to dishonor their own bodies between themselves:*
> *Who changed* (exchanged) *the truth of God into* (for) *a lie, and worshipped and served the creature more* (rather) *than the Creator, who is blessed forever* [Rom. 1:24–25].

These words of Paul deserve further consideration and should not be glossed over. Let us begin by focusing attention on *When they knew God, they glorified him not as god, . . .* This truth is as true today as it was when Paul wrote them. Therefore, it is appropriate to embrace the wisdom of Paul as amplified upon by the renowned John Calvin who said, "No conception of God can be formed without including His eternity, power, wisdom, goodness, truth, righteousness, and mercy. His eternity is evidenced by the fact that He holds all things in His hands and makes all things to consist in Himself. His wisdom is seen, because He has arranged all things in perfect order; His goodness, because there is no other cause for His creation of all things, nor can any other reason than His goodness itself induce Him to preserve them. His justice is evident in His governing of the world, because He punishes the guilty and defends the innocent; His mercy, because He bears the perversity of men with so much patience; and His truth, because He is unchangeable. . . . Since men have not recognized these attributes in God, but have conjured up an imaginary picture of Him . . . , they are justly said to have wickedly robbed Him of His glory."

Paul continues his discourse with a note of sarcasm in expressing an ancient truth. *Professing themselves to be wise, they became fools, . . .* once again, Calvin guided by the Holy Spirit expounds upon Paul's words with perspicacity saying, "All men have sought to form some conception of the majesty of God, and to make Him such a God as their reason could conceive Him to be. . . . It is evident that this evil has flourished in all ages, so that men have allowed themselves every liberty in devising superstitious practices. The arrogance, therefore, which is here condemned is that, when men ought in humility to have given glory to God, they sought to be wise among themselves, and to reduce God to the level of their own low condition. Paul maintains this principle, that if a man is estranged from the worship of God, it is his own fault, as though he said, 'Because they have exalted themselves in pride, they have been made foolish by the righteousness vengeance of God.' Paul concludes these few verses with a statement that has been true through the ages, *For that they exchanged the truth of God for a lie.* . . . When they exchange the truth of God for a lie, His glory is obliterated. It is right that those who have tried not only to deprive God of His honour, but also to blaspheme His name should be covered with every kind of ignominy. . . . It is an empty excuse to pretend that the images are worshipped for God's sake, since God does not acknowledge such worship, nor regard it as acceptable. It is not the true God at all who is then worshipped, but a false God whom the flesh has devised for itself. . . . 'We ought to honour and adore God alone, and we are not permitted to take anything from Him, however small' as explicitly stated by the renowned John Calvin. May we thank God for illuminating our hearts and minds.

Paul of Tarsus says, *Ye are . . . fellow citizens with the saints, and of the household of God.* How did this happen? By the Cross of Christ and His shed blood. All racial prejudices and enmities were abolished. Now you are fellow citizens and fellow members of the body of Christ. Both have the same access to the Father.

It is imperative to consider what God has done through Christ. He has broken down the middle wall of partition, not only between the Jew and Gentile, but also between all others where a partition had been erected. People may build walls, but once they are in Christ, the walls disappear. Therefore, if there is not a wall and if there is not a division, then there must be unity.

When studying the scriptures, when going back to Genesis and methodically proceeding through the Old and New Testaments, we realize that nothing can ever bring people together except the Gospel of our Lord Jesus Christ. This is true of the church, families, businesses, and certainly international affairs. Without being *in Christ*, there can be no unity. Do not confuse this with situations where people appear to have unity for a period of time due to peculiar circumstances or expedient situations. Those developments are completely different.

True unity exists among the community of believers. Note what I said. Since the term Christian has become used in general terms, it has lost much of its original meaning and definition. Unity among true believers is inevitable and cannot be avoided. Why? Because it is not man's creation. It is the work of the Holy Spirit. It comes back to this key point: the sinful nature of each individual. Before there can be unity among men or between different individuals, groups, and nations, there must be a radical change in them. This is brought about only by the Holy Spirit.

There is a question to consider: Why are all those who are truly Christians, or members of the community of believers, one? First, we are all sinners, each and every one of us. What determines this? It is not determined by the number of individual acts we have committed, but it is determined by our total attitude toward God and our relationship, or lack of it, with Him. How is our fellowship with Him? As Scripture says, THERE IS NONE RIGHTEOUS, NO, NOT ONE [Rom. 3:10]. In addition, *All have sinned and have come* (fall) *short of the glory of God* [Rom. 3:23]. Remember, each one of us must come face to face before God, because we are like sheep who have gone astray.

Second, we are all equally helpless before God. Martyn Lloyd-Jones amplifies on this stating clearly and emphatically that: "No one can stand in judgment before God simply on his own moral code, his own works, or his own efforts. His moral strivings or accomplishments cannot satisfy God and God's demands. The following verse aptly states the situation:

- Not the labours of my hands
- Can fulfill thy laws and demands;
- Could my zeal no respite know,
- Could my tears forever flow,
- All for sin could not atone..."

We have nothing of which to boast. It is all of God.

With whom do we have unity? The person who says and knows that he is a vile, condemned, and hopeless sinner; who relies only on the most important fact of history that Christ shed His blood for me; who trusts only in the reconciling work of God in Christ; and who realizes he has become a new creation. That is a person who is *in Christ*.

We also have unity with the person who has been raised in a Christian home and as the saying goes "grew up in the church." This person not only sincerely and truly worships God, but has a strong, personal relationship with the Lord Jesus Christ. They do not attend church in a perfunctory manner, but to continue maturing in the faith.

There is also the profligate or atheist who wanders and wanders until one day he or she hears a call and responds in faith. Then they continue to grow as they walk with the Lord Jesus. It is with all different types that we have unity.

Once we have this unity, it should lead us to realize the privileges of being a member of the community of believers. You may remember your past and your sinful condition at that time, but now, *Ye are no more strangers and foreigners, but fellow citizens with the saints, and of the household of God.*

Why does Paul allude back to their condition as expressed previously?

> *Wherefore remember, that ye being in time past Gentiles in the flesh, who are called Uncircumcision by that which is called the Circumcision in the flesh made by hands;*
> *That at that time ye were without Christ, being aliens from the commonwealth of Israel, and strangers from the covenants of promise, having no hope, and without God in the world* [Eph. 2:11–12].

Why did he do this? Because he wanted them to remember where they had been, be certain of the position they had achieved, and know what God had wrought in them. They had lived a different type of life. Now they had been changed.

They were first-generation Christians. They had been in darkness and paganism; therefore, the change was noticeable. It is the same today with the foreign missions that present and preach the Word to nonbelievers. It is the same today with the people in this land who have not had the Word proclaimed to them and been called. Then after being called, they were converted by the Holy Spirit. However, it is not as simple when you come to the second, tenth, or twentieth generation of professing Christians, or to an area where it is tacitly assumed everyone is a Christian, or as we all have heard on occasion, "we are a Christian nation" or "this is a Christian community."

Why does the Apostle make this point? What is he talking about? He is not referring to the fact that they were now attending services, or that they were enrolled as communing members. He is talking about the principle of life, the quality of life, and the commitment of life. That is what he has been expressing and dwelling upon in this paragraph.

The Apostle points out at the beginning of this second paragraph that we have been quickened. He says to the Ephesians, *Even when we were dead in sins, hath quickened* (made alive) *us together with Christ, (by grace ye are* (have been) *saved;)* [Eph. 2:5]. This word *quickened* is important and forceful. It means *to give or to preserve life together*. In this instance, it is given in Christ and preserved with Him.

In some instances, the word is used merely to signify the living as in contrast to the dead. For example, Paul writes to Timothy saying, *I charge thee therefore before God, and the Lord Jesus Christ, who shall judge the quick* (living) *and the dead at his appearing* [2 Tim. 4:1]. The magnitude of the meaning of *quickened* in this instance is much greater and much deeper than in the other verses that were noted.

In Ephesians, the believers are described as *quickened* or raised from spiritual death by the life-giving power of the Father. This is the same power that the Father exercised in raising Christ from death in the tomb to endless living in eternal life.

The principle of life the Apostle is talking about is stated no less than five times in this paragraph: with Christ, in Christ, and through Christ. These phrases are used after saying they have been *quickened* or *to give or to preserve life together*.

The Apostle also uses in the nineteenth verse the two words *strangers* and *foreigners*. When you are a *stranger* you are among people who are not your own. We have all had that type of experience. They belong, but you do not. The word *foreigner* is sometimes translated *sojourner*. Originally it meant someone who lived near a community but not in it. Now it usually means someone who finds himself in another country.

Why does the Apostle use the words, *strangers* and *foreigners*? The former term denotes someone who is not known in a specific area, whereas the latter identifies a person from another country.

Then there are people who may live in a place for years. They may adopt the customs, the dress, and the attitudes of that place, yet they are living there on a passport and are not citizens. They are still considered strangers, or foreigners.

> *Who are Israelites; to whom pertained the adoption, and the glory, and the covenants, and the giving of the law, and the service of God, and the promises;*
>
> *Whose are the fathers, and of whom as concerning the flesh Christ came, who is over all, God blessed (the eternal blessed God) for ever. A'-men.*
>
> *Not as though the word of God hath taken none effect. For they are not all Israel, which are of Israel:*
>
> *Neither, because they are the seed of Abraham, are they all children: but, IN ISAAC SHALL THY SEED BE CALLED.*
>
> *That is, They which are the children of the flesh, these are not the children of God: but the children of the promise are counted for* (as) *the seed.* [Rom. 9:4–8]

Please note especially the words in the sixth verse: *Not as though the word of God hath taken none effect. For they are not all Israel, which are of Israel* [Rom. 9:6].

What a verse! You may look at the total and say they are all of Israel, but that is not what the Apostle is saying. There is an Israel and there is an "Israel." There is an Israel of the flesh as well as an Israel of the Spirit. There is a remnant. You can be a part of a group, but in reality you are apart from the group. That is the apostolic teaching in the New Testament and it is a most vital and important doctrine.

The Apostle John says, *They went out from us, but they were not of us; for if they had been of us, they would no doubt have continued with us: but they went out, that they might be made manifest that they were not* (none of them were) *all of us* [1 John 2:19]. They had been in the church and they appeared to be Christians, but they never really belonged.

How can we amplify upon this doctrine? *Beware of false prophets, which come to you in sheep's clothing, but inwardly they are ravening* (ravenous) *wolves* [Matt 7:15]. You cannot enter by both the narrow and the broad gate. There is the

- True prophet–False prophet;
- Good tree–Bad tree;
- Good fruit–Bad fruit; and
- House on rock–House on sand.

As Aristotle said, "There is no mean between opposites."

The Christian position is neither vague, nor is it superficial. Whether or not a person is *in Christ* does not depend upon the individual's general appearance. Further, there is no intermediate position. We are either *in Christ* or we are not. This should lead us to the point of knowing whether or not we are *in Christ*. Why is it important?

Ask someone who has gone through real tests and trials, perhaps even more than their share. It does not take long to know whether or not a person is a Christian. Some turn their backs on Christ, while others grab hold and grasp Him with all their strength. Is it any wonder when you go through the test of fire that you know how well and how true the iron of your faith has been forged in the furnace? Is it any wonder that Christ closes the Sermon on the Mount the way He does with the parable of the two men who built houses? One built on solid rock, while the other built on sand. When the challenges, storms, and tests came, the one withstood and remained standing, while the other fell and great was the fall of it.

This leads to an important question: how do we know if we are in Christ? Consider whether or not we are at ease. Are we comfortable with, and do we want to be among, Christian people? Is our fellowship in Christ, or is it in something else? Is it in each other? Is it in certain activities?

Once we consider these questions, we have other ones to ponder. Is there a real living interest in Christ? In fellowship with God? When you have an active interest in something, be it music, art, drama, sports, or whatever, then you are alive in your interest. A person who truly delights in something finds that it is not an effort to participate. As a matter of fact, he or she enjoys doing so. Certainly, it is not a matter of duty.

Do you know and understand what is being discussed? We have all been exposed to situations where we were uncomfortable. We have been on the fringes of the conversation, but not really welcomed as participants. We may listen to the conversation, but we are not really expected to enter into it and to enjoy it. Do you really understand the language of God's people and have knowledge of the terms being discussed? Do you wish to know more about them? Or do you become impatient with the topic of discussion and show your anxiety for it to end? If you answer in the affirmative, then you are exhibiting how you really feel.

Are you in on the secrets? Of course there are secrets. It is possible for someone to be interested in religion, philosophy, and theology, and to willingly discuss abstract questions but when you begin to get more specific and start talking about being in Christ, about the Holy Spirit functioning within a person, about being members of the community of believers, then there are some who are on the outside looking in.

There are times when we need to come to grips with the great truths of the Christian faith involving our personal response and commitment. It requires our grabbing hold and not letting go. Are you conforming to the laws of God and His Commandments? *For this is the love of God, that we keep his commandments; and his commandments are not grievous* (burdensome) [1 John 5:3]. They may be grievous to others, but they are not to the community of believers. The true followers exclaim, *O how love I thy law* [Ps. 119:97]! However, there are many who neither know nor honor the laws and commandments of the heavenly kingdom.

A final question: Do you have a passport or a birth certificate? Which is it? What is the Christian's birth certificate?

> *For ye have not received the spirit of bondage again to fear; but ye have received the Spirit of adoption, whereby we cry, Abba* (Daddy), *Father.*
> *The Spirit itself beareth witness with our spirit, that we are the children of God:*
> *And if children, then heirs; heirs of God, and joint-heirs with Christ; if so be that we suffer with him, that we may be also glorified together* [Rom. 8:15–17].

What a magnificent, powerful, and revealing truth describing our relationship to the Father through Christ!

Note what Paul reveals under the influence of the Holy Spirit:

- *Received the Spirit of adoption;*
- *We cry, Abba* (Daddy), *Father;*
- *The Spirit itself beareth witness;*
- *We are the children of God;*
- *Heirs of God;*
- *Joint-heirs with Christ;*
- *That we may be also glorified together* [Rom. 8:15–17].

This is the assurance that our Christian birth certificate is valid and has the seal of Christ's blood upon it.

The Christian's birth certificate is the assurance that can be given only by the Holy Spirit. We are no longer *strangers* or *foreigners*, but we are *fellow citizens with the saints* in *the household of God.*

Thanks be to God that we are!

Amen!

23

Fellow Citizens with the Saints

> *Now therefore ye are no more strangers and foreigners, but fellow citizens with the saints, and of the household of God* [Eph. 2:19].

After saying *Ye are no more strangers and foreigners*, Paul tells them, *Ye are . . . fellow citizens with the saints, and of the household of God*. What does it mean to be *fellow citizens with the saints*? What privileges and benefits come to those who follow in the way, or in the current vernacular are Christians? The Greek term for saint most frequently used is *hagios*, which means "set apart," "separate," "holy."

It is used throughout the New Testament to define the quality of things, men, angels, and God. It is applied to the following in the New Testament:

- Holy Scriptures,
- Holy Calling,
- Holy Faith,
- saints before Christ in the flesh,
- followers of Christ as Holy Brethren,
- Holy Child Jesus,
- members of the community of believers,
- helping fellow saints,
- ministering to the believers,
- greeting the believers in Christ,
- Christ glorified and admired in the followers,
- patience and faith of the believers, and
- keeping the commandments of God.

Also, it is used to describe the Lord Jesus, God the Father, and their followers.

Peter uses another Greek word *Theios* that is translated into our word *divine*. It means "Godly," "God-like."

> *According as his divine power hath given unto us all things that pertain unto life and godliness, through the knowledge of him that hath called us to* (by) *glory and virtue:*
> *Whereby are given unto us exceeding great and precious promises: that by these ye might be partakers of the divine nature, having escaped the corruption that is in the world through lust* [2 Pet. 1:3–4].

Peter speaks of Christ's divine power and having granted to the followers of Christ *all things that pertain unto life and godliness* and to escape from *the corruption that is in the world* and to become *partakers of the divine nature*.

Note the change regarding the individuals who become *partakers of the divine nature*. He or she, by the divine power of the Lord Jesus, is changed from *corruption* to *life and godliness*. This immortal nature begins and partakes of it in this present life.

It is illuminated and illustrated by both Paul and John.

> *But we all, with open* (unveiled) *face beholding as in a glass* (mirror) *the glory of the Lord, are changed* (being transformed) *into the same image from glory to glory, even as by the Spirit of the Lord* [2 Cor. 3:18].
>
> *Who shall change our vile body, that it may be fashioned like unto his glorious body, according to the working whereby he is able even to subdue all things unto himself* [Phil. 3:21].
>
> *Beloved, now are we the sons* (children) *of God, and it doth not yet appear what we shall be: but we know that, when he shall appear, we shall be like him; for we shall see him as he is* [1 John 3:2].

Another important factor to consider in these words is not only their application, but their revelation.

> *That they should seek the Lord, if haply* (in the hope that) *they might feel after* (grope for) *him, and find him, though he be not far from every one of us:*
> *For in him we live, and move, and have our being; as certain also of your own poets have said, For we are also his offspring.*

> *Forasmuch then as we are the offspring of God, we ought not to think that the Godhead* (Divine Nature) *is like unto gold, or silver, or stone, graven* (shaped) *by art and man's device* (devising) [Acts 17:27–29].

Please note the term *Godhead*. In this instance, it means "that which is divine," or the "Divine Nature." The spelling of the Greek words in 2 Peter and Acts is slightly different. However, they are both designated *Theios*.

Therefore, the God of whom we are offspring is not like unto gold, silver, stone, graven art, or man's devices. *For the invisible things of him from the creation of the world are clearly seen, being understood by the things that are made, even his eternal power and Godhead* (Divine Nature); *so that they are without excuse* [Rom. 1:20]. The Apostle uses the word *Godhead* to reveal that God's everlasting power and divinity are understood by the things that are made.

Scripture ties together God, the Lord Jesus Christ, the Holy Spirit, the saints, you and me, and those who have gone before us. It does not separate them.

After considering this background we can proceed to examine the privileges and benefits of being joint citizens in the community of believers or as we say today, in the Christian church. It is really the advantages and glories of being *in Christ*. We should always think of it as being *in Christ* not just being members of some organization.

Why did Paul want *the eyes of your understanding being enlightened* [Eph. 1:18]? The church is merely an institution to those people whose eyes and spirit are not enlightened by the Holy Spirit. There may be people who like the church as an institution, who take comfort or pride in it, or who even glory in it. But that is not what the Apostle wanted the Ephesians to do, nor what he wants us to do.

The Apostle and the Holy Spirit want us to know that we are joint citizens with Him; we are followers in the way; we are true Christians; and we are *joint-heirs* with Him.

What messages do the Epistles present? They are written to the members of the various churches. They all begin by describing our position as members of the community of believers, and then show how in light of this association we are to live. It is important for each person to realize these things, and by the power of the Holy Spirit to implement and practice them. Think what an impact this would have on our trials, tests, tribulations, and problems. Think what an impact it would have on those organizations we identify as churches if they knew what the writers were really saying and knew how to apply these truths.

What are the peculiarities of these fellow citizens with the saints? Probably, the first thing it indicates is a comparison to a city, a state, or a kingdom.

It is not surprising that the Apostle would use a comparison. Probably he was in Rome when writing this letter and knew the Ephesians could relate to this description. Therefore, he used it to convey precious truths to them.

The approach Paul uses is similar to what is used in other sections of Scripture. There are important portions of Scripture that we do not grasp or understand unless we see the broad perspective, or digest certain ideas.

The call of Abram certainly is one of the great turning points in history. During the first eleven chapters of Genesis, God was dealing with the whole world and all the people.

> NOW the Lord had said unto Abram, Get thee out of thy country, and from thy kindred, and from thy father's house, unto a land that I will shew thee:
> And I will make of thee a great nation, and I will bless thee, and make thy name great; and thou shalt be a blessing:
> And I will bless them that bless thee, and curse him that curseth thee: and in thee shall all families of the earth be blessed [Gen. 12:1–3].
>
> And the Lord appeared unto Abram, and said, Unto thy seed will I give this land: and there builded he an altar unto the Lord, who appeared unto him [Gen. 12:7].

God calls Abram at the beginning of chapter 12. This begins the record of dealing specifically with one nation and one people. It is here that we are introduced to the concept that God's people are God's kingdom, they are God's nation.

Then we proceed to Exodus. All of us are familiar with the twentieth chapter, which contains the Ten Commandments, but we are not as familiar with the nineteenth chapter. There we have

- The house of Jacob (V3)
- The children of Israel (V3)
- The Egyptians (V4)

- Obey my voice . . . and keep my covenant (V5)
- A kingdom of priests, and a holy nation (V6)
- The people answered . . . and said, All that the Lord hath spoken we will do. (V8) [Selections from Exod. 19:3–8]

The people were citizens of God's kingdom, they belonged to Him, He was their King, and they were His people. This was done to control the children of Israel and their outlook. God wanted them to understand these things before they journeyed into the promised land.

However, the Israelites never realized this, and that was the crux of their tragedy. They never realized they were God's kingdom and that they were to be a kingdom of priests, a holy nation unto God. As a result of their failure, tragedy descended upon them. We see this tragedy throughout the Old Testament.

The book of Daniel expounds upon this concept in a most amazing manner. In it we read about different kingdoms, fights between them, and the relationship between the kingdom of God and other kingdoms. The beasts represent Babylon, Medo-Persia, Greece, and Rome, and their kingdoms, as compared to Israel.

The message of the prophet was an attempt to impress upon Israel their peculiar relationship to God, and that they are citizens of His kingdom. *And the kingdom and dominion, and the greatness of the kingdom under the whole heaven, shall be given to the people of the saints of the most High, whose kingdom is an everlasting kingdom, and all dominions shall serve and obey him* [Dan. 7:27]. Daniel talks about the saints, and that there shall be an everlasting kingdom.

The New Testament presents parables about the kingdom. The Lord Jesus Christ is revealed as our Lord, Saviour, and King. Nathanael said to Jesus, *Rabbi, thou art the Son of God; thou art the King of Israel* [John 1:49]. Jesus taught about the kingdom and the people entering it. What did he say to Nicodemus? *Jesus answered and said unto him, Verily, verily, I say unto thee, Except a man be born again* (from above), *he cannot see the kingdom of God* [John 3:3]. We are to see the kingdom of God.

There are three verses in Matthew which are seldom used in teaching or preaching. They are:

> *Jesus saith unto them, Did ye never read in the scriptures,* THE STONE WHICH THE BUILDERS REJECTED, THE SAME IS BECOME THE HEAD (CHIEF CORNERSTONE)

OF THE CORNER: THIS IS THE LORD'S DOING, AND IT IS MARVELLOUS IN OUR EYES?

Therefore say I unto you, The kingdom of God shall be taken from you, and given to a nation bringing forth the fruits thereof.

And whosoever shall fall on this stone shall be broken: but on whomsoever it shall fall, it will grind him to powder [Matt. 21:42–44].

Especially note what Jesus says to the chief priests, the elders of the people, and the Pharisees when they encountered Him: *Therefore say I unto you, the kingdom of God shall be taken from you, and given to a nation bringing forth the fruits thereof* [Matt. 21:43]. He foretold what was going to happen, and it has happened.

Calvin points out that "Christ directed His message to the leaders as well as to the people. All of them had contributed to hindering the grace of God as it is to be revealed, and evidenced in the people.

"The evil started with the priests, but the people, due to their own sins, deserved to have corrupt and degraded pastors. Therefore, they all contributed to infecting one another and to turning against God." Woe unto those who do not teach and preach God's Word, who focus on works, but not on the Gospel of Christ, His shed blood, and having a personal relationship with Him. It is as true today as it was then. Nothing has really changed.

Calvin also says: "This explains why God's dreadful vengeance is proclaimed by Christ on all without distinction." The priests were both puffed-up and narrow-minded due to their own self-importance and the offices they occupied, while the people had pride only in themselves, their belongings, and participation in the formal organizations. These were the same people who supposedly prided themselves on their adoption by God as His people.

Calvin continues saying, "Christ's threat to remove the Kingdom of God from those who have profaned it must strike our heart with terror: yet there is consolation for all godly men in the mark of its perpetuity. By these words Christ means that although the ungodly extinguish among themselves God's worship, they shall not succeed in abolishing the name of Christ or destroying true religion, for God (in whose hand are all the ends of the earth) will find elsewhere a dwelling place for His Kingdom. We must learn besides from this passage that the Gospel is not preached in order that it may lie barren and idle, but that it may bear fruit.

"Christ confirms the last sentence more fully; that is, that He suffers no loss or diminution by the rejection of wicked men: though their obstinacy be like stone or iron He will shatter them with His own hardness and will gain glory all the more from their destruction. He was amazed at the stubborn temper He saw in the Jews, and so He had to draw out their judgment in these severe terms, to stop their heedless rush. (What does Jesus see in professing Christians today?) We learn two lessons: first to be content to yield ourselves to Christ's command with a mild, flexible disposition, and then to be strong in the face of the wicked when they are infatuated and madly aggressive, for a dreadful end awaits them. . . . All they will achieve from this, Christ teaches, is to be broken by their own assault. He foretells a very different end for their lofty ambition: the stone they dared to attack will run them into the ground."

Paul, in his letter to the Romans, amplifies upon the Lord Jesus' teaching in Matthew. He describes both the root and the branches.

> *For if the firstfruit be holy, the lump is also holy: and if the root be holy, so are the branches.*
>
> *And if some of the branches be broken off, and thou, being a wild olive tree, wert (were) grafted in among them, and with them partakest of the root and fatness of the olive tree;*
>
> *Boast not against the branches. But if thou boast, thou bearest not (remember that you do not support) the root, but the root thee.*
>
> *Thou wilt say then, The branches were broken off, that I might be grafted in.*
>
> *Well; because of unbelief they were broken off, and thou standest by faith. Be not high-minded (haughty), but fear:*
>
> *For if God spared not the natural branches, take heed lest he also spare not thee.*
>
> *Behold therefore the goodness and severity of God: on them which fell, severity; but toward thee, goodness, if thou continue in his goodness: otherwise thou also shalt be cut off* [Rom. 11:16–22].

If God chooses us to be His people, then we should not revel in vain confidence or the flesh, but we should endeavor to behave as He not only asks His children to do, but commands them.

If He does not spare the natural branches, then He will not spare the grafts. The Jews thought that God's kingdom was theirs and theirs alone and that they had a hereditary right to it. They believed they could do as they pleased and not do the will of God. Consequently, Christ said to them, *Therefore, . . . The kingdom of God shall be taken from you, and given to a nation bringing forth the fruits thereof* [Matt. 21:43]. Christ will remove the *kingdom of God* from all who profane it. This should cause fear or terror in the hearts of many.

Christ is saying that although the ungodly within or without the church may extinguish the worship of God among themselves, they shall not succeed in abolishing the name of Christ, or destroying true faith in Him. God will find a dwelling place for His kingdom. The nation He refers to in this verse is His church, His community. This is the positive interpretation. We should learn from this that the Gospel does not lie barren and idle when it is proclaimed, but bears fruit, much fruit.

Amen!

24

Abraham's Seed

> *But ye are a chosen generation, a royal priesthood, a holy nation, a peculiar* (his own special) *people; that ye should show* (proclaim) *forth the praises of him who hath called you out of darkness into his marvellous light:*
>
> *Which in time past were not a people, but are now the people of God: which had not obtained mercy, but now have obtained mercy* [1 Pet. 2:9–10].

Note the significant phrases in this Scripture and what they convey: *Ye are a chosen generation, A royal priesthood, A holy nation, A peculiar* (his own special) *people, Are now the people of God, . . . but now have obtained mercy.*

Contemplate two thought-provoking verses that should command our attention:

> *Dearly beloved, I beseech you as strangers and pilgrims, abstain from fleshly lusts, which war against the soul;*
>
> *Having your conversation* (conduct) *honest* (honorable) *among the Gentiles: that, whereas they speak against you as evildoers, they may by your good works, which they shall behold, glorify God in the day of visitation* [1 Pet. 2:11–12].

After considering these powerful truths, one question comes to mind. How do we define the church and its membership?

First, we are a people distinct from all others. However, we do not have the normal boundaries that people think of when they talk about people, nations, or kingdoms.

The importance of this doctrine should reveal that we cannot be Christians, or in Christ, without being separated. You cannot be in the kingdom of God and in the kingdom of the world at the same time.

This whole concept is beautifully stated by Paul when he says,

> *Who hath delivered us from the power of darkness, and hath translated* (transferred) *us into the kingdom of his dear Son* (the Son of his love) [Col. 1:13]?

> *And he is the head of the body, the church: who is the beginning, the first-born from the dead; that in all things he might have the pre-eminence.*
> *For it pleased the Father that in him should all fullness dwell;*
> *And, having made peace through the blood of his cross, by him to reconcile all things unto himself; by him, I say, whether they be things in* (on) *earth, or things in heaven* [Col. 1:18–20].

The Pharisee separated himself in the wrong way, by the wrong spirit. He had an attitude that he was better than others. We are to separate ourselves, as Christ would have us to do.

Second, we are bound together by a common allegiance to a ruler, to an authority, to a law, and to a way of life. We are separated for specific purposes and objectives.

When presenting these truths, the Apostle is talking in the Spirit about the mystical union with Christ. He is not simply speaking about the external, visible church. He is not talking about the church as an organization. It is entirely possible to be a member of the visible, external church and at the same time to be ignorant of Christ, not to know Him, not to have fellowship with Him, not to be a member of the community, and not to be related to Him. There have always been such people, and there always will be.

Third, what Paul means is that as followers of Christ we are citizens of Christ's kingdom. Where is His kingdom? Wherever He reigns and rules. It is in the heart of the individual members of the community of believers. It is real, it is vital. It is in people not over them, it is internal, not external.

Unfortunately, one of the greatest tragedies since Christ walked on earth was the fact that Christianity became the official religion of the Roman Empire. Ever since then the actual role of Christianity has been confusing and foggy. Countries and other political entities have been given the tag "Christian."

Therefore, people have thought since they lived within those boundaries that they must be Christians. Simply stated, that is not true. We may be Christians, but we are not in Christ merely by association or by living in a certain country. However, we are Christians by the Spirit dwelling within us, reigning and ruling over us, and by faith accepting Jesus Christ as our Lord and Saviour.

When defining the church and its membership, what do we say about the privileges of our citizenship? As you know everyone wants and loves privileges. What is the first and greatest privilege? It is to recognize and proclaim that Christ is our Lord and King. The Son of God Himself is our King. Think about that!

A second privilege to realize is that we are members of Christ's kingdom. Our Lord Jesus said, *My kingdom is not of this world* [John 18:36]. Paul says *For our conversation* (citizenship) *is in heaven; from whence also we look for the Savior, the Lord Jesus Christ* [Phil. 3:20].

Another privilege is to keep the commandments of God. Jesus said, *For this is the love of God, that we keep his commandments: and his commandments are not grievous* (burdensome) [1 John 5:3].

Fourth, who are our fellow citizens? Each country, each nation has its heroes, whether they are statesmen, generals, artists, athletes, or whatever. Each country has its own attractions, which give pride to its citizens and attract travelers. Usually, these are natural phenomena, but they may be buildings, restaurants, theatres, coliseums, or whatever a person can boast about.

But we are fellow citizens with Abraham, Moses, Joshua, David, Isaiah, Jeremiah, Daniel, Amos, Hosea, and the other mighty people of the Old Testament. We are fellow citizens with Paul, John, Peter, James, Matthew, Mark, Luke, Augustine, Luther, Calvin, Knox, the great theologians and preachers of the sixteenth, seventeenth, eighteenth, nineteenth, and twentieth centuries, and the dedicated missionaries of the last one hundred plus years.

We are fellow citizens with an illustrious group. No nation can match it. What about this kingdom? It is where we belong. It is where we will have fellowship with our fellow citizens.

The fifth and last point in defining the church or the community of believers is the future glory of God's kingdom. At the present time the church, or community of believers, may seem weak, feeble, or disorganized. However, God said to Abraham, *In thy seed shall all the nations of the earth be blessed* [Gen. 26:4]. Count the stars, count the sand, and your posterity will be greater.

Consider what Daniel said about the great juggernaut that was going to dominate the world and crush God's people,

> *This image's head was of fine gold, his breast and his arms of silver, his belly and his thighs* (loins) *of brass,*
> *His legs of iron, his feet part of iron and part of* (baked) *clay.*
> *Thou sawest till that a stone was cut out without hands, which smote the image upon his feet that were of iron and clay, and brake them to pieces.*
> *Then was the iron, the clay, the brass, the silver, and the gold, broken* (crushed) *to pieces together, and became like the chaff of the summer threshing floors; and the wind carried them away, that no place* (trace) *was found for them: and the stone that smote the image became a great mountain, and filled the whole earth* [Dan. 2:32–35].
>
> *And in the days of these kings shall the God of heaven set up a kingdom, which shall never be destroyed: and the kingdom shall not be left to other people, but it shall break in pieces* (put an end to) *and consume all these kingdoms, and it shall stand for ever.*
> *Forasmuch as thou sawest that the stone was cut out of the mountain without hands, and that it brake in pieces the iron, the brass, the clay, the silver, and the gold; the great God hath made known to the king what shall come to pass hereafter* (after this): *and the dream is certain, and the interpretation thereof sure* (trustworthy).
> *Then the king Nebuchadnezzar fell upon his face* (prostrate before), *and worshipped Daniel, and commanded that they should offer* (present an offering) *an oblation and sweet odors* (incense) *unto him.*
> *The king answered unto Daniel, and said, Of a truth it is, that your God is a God of gods, and a Lord of kings, and a revealer of secrets, seeing thou couldst reveal this secret* [Dan. 2:44–47].

That is the kingdom of God. It starts as a despised stone and is as nothing compared to a colossus. But God smites it, smashes it, and crushes it so that it becomes as dust and disappears. That is what happens.

There is something else that is going to happen.

> *Wherefore God also hath highly exalted him, and given him a name which is above every name:*
>
> *That at the name of Jesus every knee should bow, of things (those) in heaven, and things (those) in earth, and things (those) under the earth;*
>
> *And that every tongue should confess that Jesus Christ is Lord, to the glory of God the Father* [Phil. 2:9–11].

There is a day coming when at the name of Jesus every knee shall bow and every tongue shall confess that Jesus Christ is Lord, and we are citizens in that kingdom.

> *Do ye not know that the saints shall judge the world? . . . .*
> *Know ye not that we shall judge angels? how much more things that pertain to this life* [1 Cor. 6:2–3]?

God's kingdom cannot be shaken—it shall have no end—and we are fellow citizens in it, along with all the other saints. Praise God for His grace, mercy, and love.

Amen!

25

God's Dwelling Place

> *And are built upon the foundation of the apostles and prophets, Jesus Christ himself being the chief corner stone;*
> *In whom all the building fitly framed (being joined) together groweth unto a holy temple in the Lord:*
> *In whom ye also are builded (being built) together for a habitation (dwelling place) of God through the Spirit* [Eph. 2:20-22].

The last three verses of this second chapter bring to a close certain thoughts Paul has been presenting. He said earlier, *Now therefore ye are no more strangers and foreigners, but fellow citizens with the saints, and of the household of God* [Eph. 2:19].

There is a progression Paul uses to describe membership in the community of believers. Why is he using these descriptions? What is he saying to the Ephesians and to us?

First, Paul states we are citizens with the saints, then he says we are members of the household, or the family of God. Now he says, *In whom ye also are builded (being built) together for a habitiation (dwelling place) of God through the Spirit*. Before examining the details of these last three verses, consider certain words and phrases the Apostle uses:

- *Built upon the foundation of apostles and prophets,*
- *Jesus Christ himself being the chief corner stone;*
- *Building fitly framed (being joined) together groweth unto a holy temple in the Lord:*
- *Builded (being built) together for a habitation (dwelling place) of God through the Spirit* [Selections from Eph. 2:20-22].

When considering the details of these verses, realize that the Apostle clearly and concisely presents, and then ties together the Holy Trinity, the Triune God.

This should guide us when considering the honors bestowed upon the Ephesians to be fellow citizens with the holy patriarchs, apostles, prophets, and all the saints; a member of God's house, a member of His family; and to become members of the household of God.

Calvin states that "these honors are founded on the doctrine of the Apostles and Prophets." Thus, we are able to distinguish between a true and false church when we know the different doctrines. This is the first necessity.

The word *foundation*, as used by Paul in Ephesians 2:20, undoubtedly refers to doctrine. The Greek word is *themelios*, and it means "anything laid." It is used sixteen times in the New Testament. One of those times is in Paul's letter to Timothy when he says, *Nevertheless the foundation of God standeth sure, having this seal, The Lord knoweth them that are his* [2 Tim. 2:19]. Why do we say Paul is referring to doctrine in this instance? Because he does not mention the patriarchs or the godly kings but only those who held the teaching office. Those who God appointed to build His church.

Quite properly, Paul teaches that the faith of the members ought to be founded and built upon doctrine. Christ is the only foundation. He alone is sovereign over the church, which is paradoxically both His bride and His body on earth. Christ alone is the rule and standard of faith. It is in Christ that the church is founded by the preaching and teaching of doctrine. Therefore, the prophets and apostles are called master builders.

Paul says that both the prophets and apostles never proclaimed anything other than the church being founded upon Christ and Him alone. This is true even when we begin with Moses and the law and proceed through Scripture. Everything is directed to Him.

We are to seek the Word of God in the prophets and apostles because they have a common foundation and labor together in building the temple of God. The prophets have not been replaced by the apostles.

Why does the Apostle Paul use this particular description and teaching? The Apostle is trying to complete the picture of the relationship that exists among the members in the community of believers, those who are *in Christ*. He is bringing out and emphasizing the great fact of unity. You will recall earlier discussing unity and breaking down the middle wall of partition. This illustration of the building completes the picture the Apostle Paul is painting. The fellow-citizens, in many respects, are tied together in a free and loose association.

The members of a family have a close bond, but they are still individuals. The family is a collection of individuals. Even though they may be separated by a few miles or many, they are still members of the same family, and they retain their individual identity.

A building is different. It is composed of many different items that are joined together, whether they be stones, bricks, or lumber. These items lose their individual identity when they become part of the building, which ties everything together. An essential point in the structure of a building is that the individual items lose their identity.

As mentioned previously, we are always looking for privileges, and there are privileges in our relationship to Christ as members of the household of God. Consider:

- a citizen has privileges in his state or country;
- *a child in a family has privileges, just as the other members of the family do; the relationship within the family is more intimate;*
- *the idea presented in the building is one of God dwelling within us and taking up residence;*
- *not only are we members of His kingdom, not only do we have access to Him, but God dwells within the community of believers;*
- *the Ephesians (and we) are parts of that great building, God's temple; and*
- *. . . ye who sometimes* (once) *were far off are made nigh by the blood of Christ* [Eph. 2:13].

The temple of God is given prominence in the New Testament. Unfortunately, in current times too much emphasis has been placed upon the church as a building or as an organization. The Apostle states clearly and concisely to the Corinthians,

- *We are laborers* (God's fellow workers) *together with God,*
- *Ye are God's husbandry (field), ye are God's building,*
- *As a wise master builder,*

- For other foundation can no man lay . . . which is Jesus Christ,
- Every man's work shall be made manifest (become evident):
- Know ye not that ye are the temple of God, and . . . the Spirit of God dwelleth in you?
- The temple of God is holy, which temple ye are [Selections from 1 Cor. 3:9–17].

The Apostle is talking to the followers in the Way, to the community of believers. He is not addressing everyone. He is not addressing the people who live in a particular area or who attend services occasionally and do not have a believing faith in Christ.

The Apostle deals with doctrine. The people were forgetting what they were; they were forgetting that they were members in Christ. They thought they belonged to something else. We have the same situation today.

We must realize the community of believers is in Christ. They are the bricks or stones in a great building, and the temple of God is holy.

> What? know ye not that your body is the temple of the Holy Ghost which is in you, which ye have of God, and ye are not your own [1 Cor. 6:19]?

> And what agreement hath the temple of God with idols? for ye are the temple of the living God; as God hath said, I WILL DWELL IN THEM, AND WALK IN THEM; AND I WILL BE THEIR GOD, AND THEY SHALL BE MY PEOPLE [2 Cor. 6:16].

Keeping these passages in mind, focus on what the Apostle is teaching at this point. There is the general concept of the church as a building. What about this building? It is in the process of being built. What is God doing at this time? What has God been doing since the fall of man? God is continually building, and this building is the community of believers. It *groweth unto a holy temple in the Lord* [Eph. 2:21].

When examining it from the biblical point of view you can see what is happening. God is the One who is building. He is the One selecting the materials and putting them into place.

In some generations and in some places there are revivals, some mighty ones, and some not so mighty. There are some great additions, and there are some not so great. Yet the building groweth stone by stone, piece by piece.

This edifice is a vital process. Did you notice the Apostle's statement and selection of words? *The building fitly framed* (being joined) *together groweth unto a holy temple in the Lord.*

Who has ever heard of a building growing? Paul is almost guilty of mixing his metaphors. You will recall Paul told the Corinthians, *Ye are God's Husbandry, Ye are God's Building.* Again he puts the two ideas together. The building groweth; it is a vital process! Paul conveys to us that it is a vital building, a living building.

This leads to considering an important truth: there is a significant difference between adding to the membership rolls of the church and the growth of God's holy temple. As mentioned many times, we bring our own mindsets with us. We are conditioned to numbers, to statistics, and to adding to the rolls. However, it does not necessarily follow that each and every one is being built into the holy temple of the Lord.

Peter said, *Ye also, as lively* (living) *stones, are* (being) *built up a spiritual house, a holy priesthood, to offer up spiritual sacrifices, acceptable to God by Jesus Christ* [1 Pet. 2:5]. The increase of the community of believers is vital; it is not mechanical. Men can add to the church rolls, but God alone can build through the Holy Spirit.

Contrast that with some of the things you hear today: mergers, campaigns, and programs. That is not Paul's concept of unity, growth, or increase. That is different from Paul saying *groweth unto a holy temple.* The church today emphasizes things that are mechanical or statistical such as increases in membership or contributions. Paul emphasizes growing *unto a holy temple.*

Paul is not saying anything about the size, the structure, and the beauty of the church, but he does say that it is to be holy. He assigns to it that one great characteristic. Unfortunately, this characteristic is often overlooked. Today people, including the leaders, want to emphasize other points or develop other characteristics. The church should first and foremost be holy. Then it will be attractive and influential.

There is an interesting anecdote to share with you: a man once said when discussing miracles that when the church could say "silver and gold have I none, it could say in the name of Jesus Christ of Nazareth, rise up and walk." Today the church has silver and gold. It has become large and powerful, it has lobbyists, but it seems to have forgotten holiness.

What about holiness? It is a characteristic of the temple; it is a place proper and meet for God to dwell therein. *In whom all the building fitly framed* (being joined) *together groweth unto a holy temple in the Lord: In whom ye also are builded* (being built) *together for a habitation* (dwelling place) *of God through the Spirit.*

The guarantee of true unity in the church of believers is the unity of the Holy Spirit. The outpouring of the Holy Spirit is essential; it is a prerequisite. It alone can bring about the unity of holiness, the unity of a holy people. When holiness is the main characteristic, then the unity takes care of itself. When you start with holiness, the numbers will increase in the temple of the Lord.

On the other hand, you can have organizations, you can have programs, you can have entertainment, you can have activity, and all that can be emphasized, but it does not mean it will be a building that *groweth unto a holy temple in the Lord*. The first priority is holiness, and that is to be its main characteristic.

As noted earlier, these three verses bring us face to face with the blessed Holy Trinity. Paul constantly refers to the Lord Jesus Christ. There is no church, no community of believers, apart from Him. There is no unity apart from Him.

A right relationship to God is dependent upon Christ being the center, the beginning, the end, the foundation, the everything. If it is not in Christ fully and completely, then it is not, in the common terminology, Christian. It is in Him, in Christ, that *Ye also are builded* (being built) *together for a habitation* (dwelling place) *of God through the Spirit.*

We are a dwelling place for God through the Spirit. Think of that. Think seriously of it. It should cause us to have different thoughts about our neighbors, the strangers, the foreigners, and ourselves. It should cause us to have a new perspective when realizing we are the ones that *groweth unto a Holy Temple* as others can and do.

The way is clear: *Jesus Christ*, and Him alone, *being the Chief Cornerstone. A habitation* (dwelling place) *of God through the holy Spirit.* This should cause us to look anew at the Sermon on the Mount. This should cause us to look anew at our privileges and responsibilities.

"Revelation unconditionally precedes knowledge," as wisely stated by Otto Weber. These revelations should cause us to hunger and thirst for more and more revelations and knowledge regarding Scripture.

Do you see the importance of this doctrine we have been considering? God dwells with the community of believers. He dwells with us. He is our Father. He dwells in the building that *groweth unto a holy temple* and *a habitiation* (dwelling place) *of God.*

This occurs through us. Therefore, it is important: it cannot be overstated that we are to know what Scripture is saying, and we are to be controlled by it. We are not to let human ideas, or the thoughts and trends of the secular world, replace biblical teaching and doctrine. It is up to each of us to be informed and prepared. Each of us is to know what God requires and to act accordingly in every facet of our lives, knowing that the power and might of Christ Jesus will strengthen us in our hour of need.

Amen!

26

The Foundation of the Apostles and Prophets

> *And are built upon the foundation of the apostles and prophets, Jesus Christ himself being the chief corner stone;*
> *In whom all the building fitly framed* (being joined) *together groweth unto a holy temple in the Lord:*
> *In whom ye also are builded* (being built) *together for a habitation* (dwelling place) *of God through the Spirit* [Eph. 2:20–22].

There are two great principles to grasp and retain as we continue examining Ephesians. First, unity is essential to the community of believers. God produces this unity in Christ.

> *AND you he quickened* (made alive), *who were dead in trespasses and sins* [Eph. 2:1].

> *Dead in sins, hath quickened us* (made us alive) *together with Christ* [Eph. 2:5].

> *For we are his workmanship* (creation), *created in Christ Jesus unto* (for) *good works, which God hath before ordained* (prepared) *that we should walk in them.*
> *Wherefore remember, that ye being in time past Gentiles in the flesh, who are called Uncircumcision by that which is called the Circumcision in the flesh made by hands;*
> *That at that time ye were without Christ, being aliens from the commonwealth of Israel, and strangers from the covenants of promise, having no hope, and without God in the world* [Eph. 2:10–12].

> *For he* (himself) *is our peace, who hath made both one, and hath broken down the middle wall of partition* (division) *between us;*
>
> *Having abolished in his flesh the enmity, even the law of commandments contained in ordinances; for to make* (create) *in himself of twain* (the two) *one new man, so making peace;*
>
> *And that he might reconcile both unto God in one body by the cross, having slain* (put to death) *the enmity thereby:*
>
> *And came and preached peace to you which were afar off, and to them that were nigh* [Eph. 2:14–17].
>
> *Now therefore ye are no more strangers and foreigners, but fellow citizens with the saints, and of the household of God* [Eph. 2:19].

Second, there is the privilege of being members of the household of God. The Apostle wishes to describe these two truths in a clear manner. An informed understanding requires revelation and a detailed examination of the Apostle's teaching as inspired by the Holy Spirit.

The Apostle teaches that the building is constantly developing through an active, living process. It is something that grows. Paul is not interested in size, but in quality, in holiness, and in the holy temple of the Lord.

Much of what is called unity today really means the joining together of separate physical entities. We are prone to think of it in the same light as two companies merging into one.

What does this have to do with us? We cannot live in isolation. If we are to have fellowship, which we are called to do, then we must examine our position with respect to what Scripture is saying. Unfortunately, disinterest and indolence in the local affairs of the community of believers results in allowing certain positions to go by default. This prevents people from being exposed to meaningful facts, truths, and ideas.

These truths are provided because it is our responsibility to understand Paul's teaching about unity. There are different types of unity. In this instance, unity is defined as oneness, accord, solidarity, and union. Words not being considered at this time are uniform, similar, alike, akin, or analogous.

For example, the Roman Catholic Church believes in unity, and no church preaches it more than they do. They mean uniformity, becoming absorbed, returning to Rome.

If we all call ourselves Christians, why be separate? Why not join together and all be one? These are important questions to ponder. You do not start with unity; you cannot start with unity. Why? Because you cannot create unity. It results from something else. Unity results from certain fundamental principles existing and developing. Consider the unity between members of a family. It is not artificially created. It is the result of their relationship.

What about unity between different religious organizations? Consider what Paul says, *But though we, or an angel from heaven, preach any other gospel unto you than that which we have preached unto you, let him be accursed* (an anathema) [Gal. 1:8].

That is strong language! However, we must observe, consider, and know what Scripture says and what God says through the apostles and prophets. It is not enough to talk about unity or say there should be unity. The important item is God's truth. It takes precedence. A unity not based upon that foundation which has Jesus Christ as the chief corner stone is false and not according to God's plan.

Why does Paul use the term *the chief corner stone*? He wants to mold the Jews and Gentiles into one spiritual building, one in Christ, those far off and those nigh, the foreigners and sojourners, and have them become fellow citizens with the saints.

It is Christ that joins them together. There were separating walls, but Christ joins the two together and brings about unity. There can be no true building without the proper foundation. You must start with the foundation. What is the foundation? *And are built upon the foundation of the apostles and prophets, Jesus Christ himself being the chief corner stone.* Note the limitation; note the fullness of Paul's statement.

John Calvin casts additional light on the *foundation* proclaiming that the "*Foundation* unquestionably here refers to doctrine: for he does not mention patriarchs or godly kings, but only those who held the teaching office, and whom God hath appointed to build His Church. And so Paul teaches that the faith of the Church ought to be founded on this doctrine. What, then must we think of those who rest entirely on the inventions of men, and yet accuse us of desertion because we embrace the pure doctrine of God? But the manner in which it is founded must be noted; for strictly, Christ is the only foundation, since He alone supports the whole Church. He alone is the standard rule of faith. But it is in Christ that the Church is founded by the preaching of doctrine. Hence, the prophets and apostles are called master-builders. It is there as if Paul said that the prophets and apostles never meant to do anything but found the Church on Christ.

When amplifying upon this truth presented by Paul, there are several essential points. What is an apostle? First, he has seen the risen Lord, and is a witness to the resurrection because he beheld Jesus Christ after His crucifixion, death, and burial.

When traveling on the road to Damascus, Paul was confronted by the Lord Jesus. Later, he says to the Corinthians regarding this encounter: *Am I not an apostle? am I not free? have I not seen Jesus Christ our Lord* [1 Cor. 9:1]?

Second, an apostle was specifically called, designated, and sent as a preacher of the Gospel by Jesus himself. He was called to preach the message of redemption and to glorify God.

Third, the apostles were given special authority. They were given the power to work miracles and to found churches.

Each of these requirements was found in the apostles. Without these three qualities a person could not be an apostle. Therefore, these inherent characteristics make apostolic succession an impossibility.

Next, what is a prophet? He is one who receives a direct message from God and to whom the truth is revealed directly by the Holy Spirit. It is not as a result of reading or studying Scripture. It is a direct message from God that is to be given unto others. Paul says,

> *But he that prophesieth speaketh unto men to edification, and exhortation, and comfort.*
> *He that speaketh in an unknown tongue edifieth himself; but he that prophesieth edifieth the church.*
> *I would that ye all spake with tongues, but rather* (even more) *that ye prophesied: for greater is he that prophesieth than he that speaketh with tongues, except he interpret, that the church may receive edifying* (building up) [1 Cor. 14:3–5].

In the early days after the resurrection of our Lord and before the Gospels and Epistles were available, there were those called prophets. They were given spiritual truths and understanding by direct revelation, which they were to impart to others.

It was the same with the prophets of the Old Testament. God revealed His truth to the prophets and enabled them to proclaim it, which was characteristic of the prophets.

Paul places the apostles first in the sentence because of their distinct uniqueness. John does the same: *And the wall of the city had twelve foundations, and in* (on) *them the names of the twelve apostles of the Lamb* [Rev. 21:14].

There is another question to consider: what does Paul mean when he says that the community of believers is built and established on the foundation of the apostles and prophets? It is because they were the first believers; they were the first stones to be laid in this great foundation. They were believers, and they exercised their faith in the Lord Jesus Christ.

This leads to a second point, that the teaching of the apostles and prophets is the real foundation. We cannot become real members of the community of believers without believing. This results in enjoying God's blessings and living as His disciples no matter what trials, tribulations, and tests may befall us.

The difference between believers and non-believers is the same as the difference between the Christians and non-Christians, or the members and non-members of the community.

What is the foundation—not the corner stone—but the foundation? It is the teaching of the apostles and prophets. It is their doctrine as revealed unto them. They proclaimed what had been revealed unto them and what they believed. In addition, they expressed through their conduct the faith by which they lived. So these three factors, revelation, belief, and conduct, become unified into one.

What makes us members of the community of believers, of this building that *groweth unto a holy temple*? It is our faith, but it is more. It includes believing and conducting ourselves in accord with the teachings and doctrine of the apostles and prophets. Accepting these truths is basic to growing in our relationship with Christ and living as He would have us live. It is graphically described by Paul in his letter to the Galatians:

- *I marvel that ye are so soon removed* (turning away) *from him that called you . . . unto another* (a different) *gospel:*
- *There be some that . . . would* (want to) *pervert the gospel of Christ.*
- *Though we* (or another) *. . . preach any other gospel unto you . . . let him be accursed* (an anathema).
- *If any man preach any other gospel unto you than that ye have received, let him be accursed.*
- *For do I now persuade men, or God? . . . for if I yet pleased men, I should not be the servant of Christ.*

- *The gospel which was preached of me is not after (according to) man.*
- *For I neither received it of man, neither was I taught it (of man), but by the revelation of Jesus Christ* [Selections from Gal. 1:6–12].

These are Paul's words, under the influence of the Holy Spirit. We should be aware of this revealing description regarding the hearing of the Gospel, and how those who pervert it are to be received. Whether we like it or not, our faith is a most intolerant one. It says that this and this alone is right and true.

We may be called many different things, but we must take our stand with Paul, this man of God, and with Scripture. What does the Word teach? What do the apostles teach? That is what matters and what we are called to understand. What is contained and revealed in Scripture is the only Gospel.

The apostles taught that the Gospel could be defined and that the Epistles were written in order to know what we are to believe, and why. The early followers *in the way* were aware of what was being taught and of the foundation of their faith. The first century members were not mesmerized by some vague idea one could not define or a wonderful feeling that might encompass them which could not be explained. Expressions such as these are a denial of New Testament teachings.

What is this foundation? What are its ingredients? The second chapter of Ephesians addresses these questions and reveals that:

- Man by nature *is dead in trespasses and sins, and under the wrath of God, because he is subject to the lusts of the flesh, and lusts of the mind.*
- *But God, who is rich in mercy, quickened (made alive) us together with Christ, that he might show the exceeding riches of his grace.*
- *They (we) had been aliens, strangers, having no hope, without God but were made nigh by the blood of Christ, which abolished the enmity, and reconciled both unto God.*
- Therefore, *through him* (Christ) *we both have access by one Spirit unto the Father, and we are no more strangers and foreigners, but fellow citizens with the saints, and of the household of God* [Selections from Chapter 2 of Ephesians].

Does that sound like something you cannot define, something illusory, something transient? These are essential ingredients of the foundation.

If a person does not accept and believe in the grace of God, the person and work of the Lord Jesus Christ, and the power of the Holy Spirit, then that person is not in Christ. That may sound intolerant. However, it is based upon the foundation of the apostles and prophets. Therefore, we cannot compromise it.

Remember, it is by the blood of Christ that we are made nigh, that we are saved, not by anything more or less than that, and not by anything else! There are people who scoff at that, who do not accept it, who say they must do something, some work or works. How can we have true fellowship in Christ with them? It cannot be; it is impossible.

How do we have unity with Christ? How are we delivered? By God's power of regeneration, by the gift of the Spirit, and by the blood of the Cross. That is how we have union with Christ. That is a wonderful doctrine! That is the foundation of the apostles and prophets. It is rather simple. We either accept their teaching and their message, or we do not.

We have been considering important and basic truths concerning the community of believers, the members in Christ. What truths may be drawn from this material?

First the church, as it is identified or called today, is founded on the confession of the Apostle Peter. *When Jesus came into the coasts* (region) *of Caesarea Philippi, he asked his disciples, saying, Whom do men say that I the Son of man am? But whom say ye that I am* [Matt. 16:13, 16:15]? The answer that Peter gave is the basis of our faith in Christ Jesus! He said *Thou art the Christ, the Son of the living God* [Matt. 16:16].

Jesus responds to Peter with these revealing truths

> *... flesh and blood hath not revealed it unto thee, but my Father which is in heaven; ...*
>
> *... upon this (large) rock I will build my church; and the gates of hell shall not prevail against it;*
>
> *And I will give unto thee the keys of the kingdom of heaven: and whatsoever thou shalt bind on earth shall be bound in heaven: and whatsoever thou shalt loose on earth shall be loosed in heaven* [Matt. 16:17–19].

We are to remember these truths and rejoice in them.

What does Christ say in Matthew 16:17–19? The Roman Catholics interpret it one way, but the Reformers another. Peter having seen, or more appropriately having had this truth revealed unto him, confesses it. What do we see in Peter? The confession, the belief, the faith in Christ.

The Apostle Paul does not contradict the teaching of our Lord Jesus Christ. There is no contradiction. The foundation is the apostles and prophets, all of them, not just one. This confession was first made by the apostles and prophets. They are the only foundation. Therefore, we cannot be one with those who say it is all founded on Peter alone and everything depends on him.

Second, there can be no repetition of the apostles and prophets. There is only one foundation, and they are it. God does not repeat the foundation. It is laid once and forever.

There are no successors to the apostles. Remember the definition of an apostle. Yet we hear from time to time talk about apostolic succession. There is no such thing as apostolic succession. When considering these points it is important to study and know the scriptures. You can have a priestly succession, but not an apostolic succession.

A third deduction is that there can be no addition to this foundation. You cannot add to it, nor can you take away from it. The foundation has been laid. It cannot be repeated. God is the builder, and He builds *upon the foundation of the apostles and prophets*, with Jesus Christ *being the chief corner stone*.

These deductions plus the truths we have been examining lead us to consider an important question. Before asking it, I must say that it is not sufficient to state I am a Christian, or I want to become one, and that nothing else is needed. The question is: What do you believe?

You cannot be *in Christ* without knowing what you believe. It is not possible. What brings us to God? It is the truth, *I am the way, the truth and the life* [John 14:6].

We are sanctified by the truth, and that truth is the Lord Jesus Christ. It is only as we know the truth concerning our Lord and Saviour; ourselves and our needs, and what God has done, that we can be *fitly joined together* and *a habitation* (dwelling place) *of God* [Eph. 4:16, 2:22].

The unity of the individual members of the community of believers is created through purity of doctrine and purity of life. When these exist, the community becomes the Lord's holy and visible temple.

What is a *chief corner stone*? A very apt definition is, "a corner stone is a primary foundation stone at the angle of the structure by which the architect fixes a standard for the bearings of the walls and the cross walls throughout."

The corner stone not only holds together all the subsidiary foundation stones, it also binds them together, and all the walls. Everything is supported by it and welded together by it.

Isaiah prophesied *Behold, I lay in Zion for a foundation a stone, a tried stone, a precious corner stone, a sure foundation* [Isa. 28:16]. Peter quotes from Isaiah and adds to it saying,

> BEHOLD, I LAY IN ZION A CHIEF CORNER STONE, ELECT (CHOSEN), *PRECIOUS: AND HE THAT BELIEVETH ON HIM SHALL NOT BE CONFOUNDED* (PUT TO SHAME) [1 Pet 2:6].

He said they are rejecting Him, but that He will become the headstone, the basis of the whole building, binding it together, and supporting the entire superstructure.

Further, did ye never read in the scriptures, THE STONE WHICH THE BUILDERS RJECTED, THE SAME IS TO BECOME THE HEAD (chief corner-stone) OF THE CORNER: THIS IS THE LORD'S DOING, AND IT IS MARVELOUS IN OUR EYES [Matt. 21:42]? He is central, He is vital, and it is in Him that the whole building is fitly framed (being joined) together and groweth unto a holy temple in the Lord.

Is your faith based solidly on the foundation of the apostles and prophets, or are you interested in some vague, nebulous Christianity that says you do not need to be concerned about doctrine, the exposition of Scripture, instruction to improve spiritually, and being *in Christ*? We must know in whom we believe and what we believe.

What is to be considered next? Obviously, it should be, where do we fit? What is our part, place, and position in this building that groweth and is *a habitation* (dwelling place) *of God through the Spirit*? We are being built into it; therefore, we should know about it. There are three things to keep in mind as we examine this *building fitly framed* (being joined) *together*. Certainly there is a relationship between the various parts used in this building. You cannot put shoddy or substandard material into a building and expect it to be perfect.

Therefore, the first thing to remember is that the individual parts (you and me) in this great temple must correspond to the foundation and be properly related to it.

> *For other foundation can no man lay than that is laid, which is Jesus Christ.*
> *Now if any man build upon this foundation gold, silver, precious stones, wood, hay, stubble (straw);*
> *Every man's work shall be made manifest* (become evident)*: for the day shall declare it, because it shall be revealed by fire; and the fire shall try* (test) *every man's work of what sort it is* [1 Cor. 3:11–13].

You choose to build with worthy or unworthy materials, and they will be tested. Some will last; some will not. They must stand the test of fire and the test of time.

Therefore, let every man take heed as to how he builds on this foundation. Each person, especially preachers and teachers, is to exercise great care and make sure that everything going into the building corresponds to the foundation. It is an awesome responsibility! There must be a definite and positive relationship to the one and only foundation.

We must be related to *the chief corner stone*. We must recognize, remember, and acknowledge the fact that we have a personal relationship with the Lord Jesus Christ Himself. We are joined to Christ; we are in Christ. We have been quickened, we have been raised, and we are seated with Christ.

There is also our relationship to one another. When we do this we should think not only of the buildings, but the other stones in the building. What about the other stones and materials? The Apostle says they are *fitly framed together*. The Greek word used by Paul occurs only twice in the Bible. It appears in Ephesians 2:21 and 4:16.

In Ephesians 2:21, it is translated *fitly framed together*. That is a little misleading. The Greek word Paul uses in Ephesians actually means, "harmoniously fitted together." He took three words and put them together in order to convey the truth he had in mind. He wanted the Ephesians to grasp and hold onto it.

The words he used to make the one word mean "binding, bringing together, to collect, gather, or pick out." So we have binding, bringing together, and choosing (or picking out). It is translated in the King James version *fitly framed together*.

As we digest this word it is helpful to think of a stone building and the stonemason doing the construction. What thoughts come to mind?

First, the stonemason chooses each stone to be placed into the wall, and decides where he will place it. It is not a mass-production situation, nor is it like building a brick wall where each brick is identical to every other one.

The stonemason carefully utilizes his privilege of being deliberate, personal, and distinctive. Thank God that this is His method. The process is one by one. It is not by groups. It is an individual selection that involves choosing and accepting, or choosing and rejecting.

Second, the stones in the building are not identical. Each one is different. We do not see many stone buildings or walls today. Whenever we do, three things are noticeable: all the stones are of different sizes and shapes; they are "harmoniously fitted together;" and they have a majestic appearance.

The individual stones can be seen and identified. They each perform a function, even if it is only as a filler, which enables it to support, or to be supported by, at least one other stone. Each stone has a function to perform. It is marvelous to know that God knows each human stone, from the least to the apostles and prophets.

Third, there is the process of preparing and shaping the stones. When a stone is placed in a wall, it must be fitted in with the other ones. Therefore, the stonemason not only selects the stone, but he shapes it, trims it, fashions it, and places it. If it does not fit just right, then either he works with it some more, or he puts it down and uses it later. Then he stands back and looks at it to make sure it fits together properly and harmoniously.

The same principle works among the community of believers. How is the selecting, shaping, trimming, fashioning, placing, and all the rest achieved?

By preaching and teaching on the foundation of the apostles and the prophets, with Jesus Christ Himself as the chief corner stone. There is a lot of chiseling, shaping, forming, polishing, and cleansing that needs to be done through the exposition of Scripture and by the Holy Spirit.

Believe me, if you are in this building, or are going to be in it, you will be formed and fashioned. It is God's building. He is the one selecting and placing the stones. He has a mighty chisel and hammer, and He knows how to use them.

WHOM THE LORD LOVETH HE CHASTENETH, AND SCOURGETH EVERY SON WHOM HE RECEIVETH [Heb. 12:6].

We must be made conformable, if we are to be placed in this building and *fitly framed together groweth unto a holy temple in the Lord*. Amen!

27

Being Members of Christ's Body

> *In whom all the building fitly framed* (being joined) *together groweth unto a holy temple in the Lord:*
> *In whom ye also are builded* (being built) *together for a habitation* (dwelling place) *of God through the Spirit* [Eph. 2:21–22].

Studying Ephesians presents an interesting paradox concerning the church. On the one hand, we have the impression that God already dwells in the building, or temple, and truly He does. On the other hand, there is the realization that the building is still being built, and it is a habitation in which He is going to dwell when it is completed, and He will. This paradox is true of the building containing the community of believers, and of all who are in Christ.

If the building groweth, then there are questions to consider: How are the stones prepared? For the most part, they are prepared in secret. This truth expresses the great New Testament principle that before any of us can be real members of the community of believers (and I am distinguishing between having our names on a church roll and being in Christ), the mighty work of preparation must be accomplished. It is a work performed by the Holy Spirit, and it is performed in the depths of our souls. It happens where people are and occurs while they are doing their normal chores or tasks. It is not something superficial or external. It occurs on the inside, where it counts.

Paul states it succinctly, *. . . ye are . . . the epistle of Christ . . . written not with ink, but with the Spirit of the living God: not in tables* (tablets) *of stone, but in fleshy tables* (tablets) *of the heart* [2 Cor. 3:3].

The work of the Holy Spirit occurs internally! Often the Spirit of God works within us for a period of time before we even recognize and accept what is happening. It may not be understood, but it is taking place, and He is preparing the stone for its place in the building where the results will be seen. The stone is in the wall or the building, but one does not know how it got there.

Becoming a member of the community of believers means we are subject to a power beyond our full understanding. I do not mean that Christianity is irrational. Being in Christ is anything but irrational. On the contrary, there is nothing so rational as being members of Christ's body.

If you are on the outside looking in, you will not fully understand it. It may seem overly simple, strange, or mysterious. Why? Because it is God's work! He acts in His own way. The princes of this world did not know Christ, they saw him as a carpenter, they were amazed at His knowledge and understanding, and they did not know who He was.

The Apostle says,

> But God hath revealed them unto us by his Spirit; for the Spirit that searcheth all things, yea, the deep things of God.
> For what man knoweth the things of a man, save (except) the spirit of man which is in him? even so the things of God knoweth no man, but the Spirit of God.
> Now we have received, not the spirit of the world, but the Spirit which is of God; that we may know the things that are freely given to us of God [1 Cor. 2:10–12].

The Apostle amplifies on this statement, saying, *But the natural man receiveth not the things of the Spirit of God: for they are foolishness unto him: neither can he know them, because they are spiritually discerned* [1 Cor. 2:14].

These verses say that a person *in Christ* is a dilemma, or an enigma, to the person who is not a member of the community. When Jesus was present on earth and performing His tasks, He generated many comments. The authorities and people said, Who is this? He has not been trained as a Pharisee. He is not a scribe, and He is not a priest. The people of that time did not know who He was.

The person who is *in Christ* is someone who cannot really be understood except by a member of the community. As someone once said, the Spirit's work is not irrational, but beyond reason. The great Blaise Pascal said, "The supreme achievement of reason is to bring us to see that there is a limit to reason."

A person who is *in Christ* is one who has been fashioned, formed, and made to fit as a stone in this wall which is going to be *a holy temple in the Lord*. It is someone who has been changed, renewed, and regenerated; in effect, it is someone who has become a new creation!

As members of a Christian church, we are identified as believers, though we may only be on the church rolls and not accept the truths expressed in Scripture regarding the great doctrines of the Christian faith or Jesus Christ as God's only begotten Son as well as our Lord and Redeemer.

When we are *in Christ*, we are true believers in the true sense of the meaning, Christians. Why? Because we believe the Bible is God's revealed word, we accept the essential doctrines of the Christian faith, and we believe that Jesus Christ is our Lord and our Redeemer.

The community of believers consists of those who are *in Christ*. It does not consist of those who hope they are Christians, or who hope they may become Christians, or who are church members because that has been their practice for whatever reason, and they have never thought of not being a church member. This is a tremendously important point.

Luther taught that the real church is the community of believers; Calvin taught that the real church consists of the elect of God. The Puritans subscribed to the principle that the real church consisted of the gathering together of the saints. They did not accept the idea of a state church and that everyone was a member if they lived within its borders. They asserted that the community consisted only of those who had been prepared, regenerated, redeemed, and renewed. They are the ones who are God's chosen people, both then and now. The Puritans, the early Baptists, and others placed their emphasis upon what they called "the gathered Church." The emphasis was upon the community of believers, the elect of God, the called out, and the gathered church.

It is important to know and understand the relevance of this teaching as well as how the early Reformers interpreted and applied it, especially in today's environment with looser and looser interpretations, vaguer definitions, and the belief that everyone is a Christian.

Paul wrote to Timothy about the foundation and the materials in the building, saying *Nevertheless the foundation of God standeth sure, having this seal, The Lord knoweth them that are his. And, Let everyone that nameth the name of Christ depart from iniquity* [2 Tim. 2:19]. Calvin amplifies upon this saying "Thus any man who calls on God's name, that is, professes to belong to God's people and wishes to be numbered among them, must put far from him all ungodliness."

Paul says that some of the people professing to be Christians deny faith in Christ, deny His resurrection, and though they seem to be followers in the Way, they are not. Paul assures them that God's foundation stands sure, God cannot deny Himself, God knows what He is doing, and God is the architect of the building.

God is not interested in size, numbers, or programs. He desires holiness in His people. Therefore, we should give ourselves to obedience, regeneration, holiness, and the power of the Holy Spirit. Remember, *the building . . . groweth unto a holy temple in the Lord* [Eph. 2:21].

What does our Lord Himself have to say on this subject? Did you ever notice that He seemed to refuse people or make it difficult for them to follow Him? Two men came to the Lord Jesus intent upon following him. He said to the one *The foxes have holes, and the birds of the air have nests; but the Son of man hath not where to lay his head* [Matt. 8:20]. To the other He said *Follow me; and let the dead bury their dead* [Matt. 8:22].

Our Lord said to those two men: Go and think about what you are saying. I do not want you seeking excitement and thrills, and seeing great things; think about what it may cost you. To another He said *No man, having put his hand to the plough, and looking back, is fit for the kingdom of God* [Luke 9:62]. He tests the person; he makes him stop and think.

When the multitudes were with Him, He turned, and said unto them,

> *For which of you, intending to build a tower, sitteth not down first, and counteth the cost, whether he have sufficient to finish it* [Luke 14:28]?

> *Or what king, going to make war against another king, sitteth not down first, and consulteth* (considers) *whether he be able with ten thousand to meet him that cometh against him with twenty thousand* [Luke 14:31]?

Jesus says stop, look, listen. Consider what it will cost you before proceeding.

He seems to be rejecting men, but he is really showing His love and His concern for His Father's house. He is concerned about the holiness of those in the building, not the size or the number.

Consider what Christ did when He left this world with a handful of people to continue His work: ordinary people, some illiterate, some untutored, and some ignorant. That was His way.

God chooses to dwell in a pure church with a pure body of believers, pure in doctrine, and pure in life. Do not forget, His Son came to save sinners that we may have fellowship with Him and the Father now and forevermore. In that holy fellowship we are clothed with Christ's righteousness.

God works in mysterious and surprising ways. Maybe His purifying procedure is for the Presbyterian Church at large to experience a decline in membership so that He can purify it.

Scripture teaches that God dwells among His people and uses them when the vessels are fit and meet for Him to use. This teaching is substantiated and proved by history. Consider what God can do through vessels like Martin Luther, John Calvin, John Knox, and others.

When the Holy Spirit dwells among the community of believers, there is much that can be done. We should realize there is a very delicate and difficult point in this building process. *And the house, when it was in building, was built of stone made ready before it was brought thither: so that there was neither hammer nor axe nor any tool of iron heard in the house, while it was in building* [1 Kgs. 6:7].

How are we to apply this teaching today? There should be no disagreement or debate about the basic doctrinal truths regarding our being in Christ. The preparation of the stone by chiseling, forming, hammering, and fitting it are finished before it is placed into the building. There should be no disagreement about the person of Jesus Christ; the condition of man in sin; substitutionary atonement; regeneration; the person of the Holy Spirit; and the Doctrine of Grace.

When saying this, do not misunderstand. It does not mean that doctrine should not be discussed. We should feed one another, support one another, and help one another to grow. We should remember what the early believers did as revealed in Scripture, *And they continued stedfastly in the apostles' doctrine and fellowship, and in breaking of bread, and in prayers* [Acts 2:42]. John adds to this, saying, *That which we have seen and heard declare we unto you, that ye also may have fellowship with us: and truly our fellowship is with the Father, and with His Son Jesus Christ* [1 John 1:3].

There should not be disputes over who and what Jesus Christ is, or arguments about His person, and whether His death on the Cross was a crime or a supreme tragedy. Some say, what difference does this make? Some say Christ's death was moving and wonderful. Some say we can interpret it in different ways, and it does not matter, since we are trying to be like Him and follow Him. Some say that we are all Christians since we live in a Christian nation.

However, Scripture reveals otherwise. We see this when considering the characteristics of the early believers:

- the Holy Spirit descended upon the followers in the upper room when they were of one accord;
- the early followers continued steadfastly in the apostles' doctrine (teaching), fellowship, breaking of bread, and prayers;
- there was no debate, since they knew Jesus was the Son of God;
- they were witnesses to the resurrection, and Jesus had explained His death to them;
- there was not any disagreement about doctrine among the early followers; and
- the early church grew.

Unfortunately, in recent years so-called leaders have been arguing about fundamental doctrines. This has had a negative impact.

The community of believers was not meant to be a place where there is fighting, arguing, debating, and disagreeing over the vital truths of Christ and His work. The church is the gathering place for those who know whom they have believed and what they believe, who are living on *the foundation of the apostles and prophets*, and who come together to wait upon Him, to worship Him, and to ask Him to fill them with His own presence, power, might, and strength.

Do not misinterpret this; the emphasis is on fundamentals. There are some matters about which there is not complete agreement: the Lord's Supper, certain details of prophecy, and the mode of baptism. These and similar issues should be discussed with respect among the believers. Some people believe that doctrine causes divisions. It may, and it has.

However, it also produces unity. The unity worth talking about is the unity of the Spirit, which produces the same belief in the same Lord, in the same faith, and in the same baptism. It is the unity of those who do not espouse their own personal convictions or ideas, but rely upon Jesus Christ, the Son of God, and His perfect work.

Let there be unity in what Paul has discussed in this second chapter:

- Man *dead in trespasses and sin*, but *quickened* (made alive) with Christ;
- raised by God's grace, through Christ's shed blood;
- reconciled unto God, therefore regenerated and renewed;
- *built upon the foundation of the apostles and prophets*, and joined to Christ;
- Christ is *the chief corner stone* of our faith and may we walk with Him as we travel on life's journey; and
- we are *fitly* (harmoniously) *framed together*, and *a habitation* (dwelling place) *of God through the Spirit*.

May God bless our relationship with Him, and may He continue to reveal Himself to us as we mature in the faith.

Amen!

Outline Questions

Chapter 1

THE DOCTRINE OF SIN

> AND *you hath he quickened (made alive), who were dead in trespasses and sins:*
> *Wherein in time past ye walked according to the course (age) of this world, according to the prince of the power of the air, the spirit that now worketh in the children of disobedience:*
> *Among whom also we all had our conversation* (conducted ourselves) *in times past in the lusts of our flesh, fulfilling the desires of the flesh and of the mind; and were by nature the children of wrath, even as others* [Eph. 2:1–3].

Why does Paul pray for the followers of Christ and instruct them?

How can we acquire a true conception of God's power in salvation?

Why do we need to know the Doctrine of Sin?

What are the reasons for man being as he is?

What is the biblical point of view?

What is Paul saying in the first three verses of the second chapter?

For what is Scripture profitable?

What is man's condition, or state, in sin?

What does Paul say to Timothy?

What is meant by *itching ears*?

Why are we called the *children of disobedience*?

Why is a person ignorant of spiritual things?

What is man's condition in sin?

How would God have us live?

Why does the person of the flesh dislike Scripture?

What happens when you receive the gift of salvation?

Why is the devil able to persuade people that he is not dominating, guiding, or leading them?

Why does Paul say, *Be not conformed to this world*?

How can we stand against the evil one"

Why do people say in various ways, "Do you mean you believe in the devil and his powers?"

With whom do we wrestle?

Chapter 2

DEATH BY SIN

AND you hath he quickened (made alive), who were dead in trespasses and sins:

Wherein in time past ye walked according to the course (age) of this world, according to the prince of the power of the air, the spirit that now worketh in the children of disobedience:

Among whom also we all had our conversation (conducted ourselves) in times past in the lusts of our flesh, fulfilling the desires of the flesh and of the mind; and were by nature the children of wrath, even as others [Eph. 2:1–3].

How did Paul change on the road to Damascus?

What does Paul say to the Ephesians and us?

What does Paul want for the Ephesians and us?

What should be our understanding of the sinfulness of man?

What does the Doctrine of Original Sin declare?

What does John Calvin say about sin?

Why must we contend with the prince of the power of the air?

What does Otto Weber say about Original Sin?

What does Christ know about Satan?

How does a sinner become right with God?

What keeps people from having a positive relation with God?

What changed the life style of the Ephesians and people today?

Why has sin been in the world since Adam and Eve?

What is meant by the *children of wrath*?

Why don't people like the *children of wrath* doctrine?

What changed Paul's heart and mind regarding the Doctrine of Sin?

What is sin?

Why were the Pharisees greater sinners than the Publicans?

What is worse than committing a sin of the flesh?

What are the three great sins of the spirit?

Chapter 3

TRESPASSES AND SINS

> *Wherein in time past ye walked according to the course* (age) *of this world, according to the prince of the power of the air, the spirit that now worketh in the children of disobedience:*
> *Among whom also we all had our conversation* (conducted ourselves) *in times past in the lusts of our flesh fulfilling the desires of the flesh and of the mind; and were by nature the children of wrath, even as others* [Eph. 2:2–3].

What does Paul want us to understand?

To whom is Paul writing?

What was true of Paul's life?

Why did Paul want the Ephesians and us to increase in faith?

What impact did Paul's letter to the Romans have on Martin Luther?

Why do people have trouble with being justified by faith?

Why are we to glory in tribulations?

Outline Questions

Why do people have difficulty in accepting the phrase, *in due season Christ died for the ungodly*?

What does Calvin say regarding God demonstrating His love toward us?

What is meant by trespasses and sins?

Why did Jesus speak of the state of sin?

What is meant by the term *flesh*?

What is the dynamic hostility between the flesh and the spirit?

What does Paul say regarding the *wages of sin* and *eternal life*?

What happened to Adam when he fell?

What is the function of the law?

What was Paul aware of after his conversion?

What can be said about the lusts of the flesh and mind?

What choices does the Apostle John give us?

Chapter 4

THE DOCTRINE OF GOD'S WRATH

> *Among whom also we all had our conversation in times past in the lusts of our flesh, fulfilling the desires of the flesh and of the mind; and were by nature the children of wrath, even as others.* [Eph. 2:3].

How does Paul deal with sin?

Why are we all under the wrath of God?

Why should we deal with these truths?

Why did Christ come?

What did Paul say to the Athenians?

How is God's wrath revealed?

Why does man become subject to the wrath of God?

How is the biblical term *wrath* interpreted?

What does Lloyd-Jones say about God's wrath?

What do the Old and New Testaments say about the wrath of God?

What is our responsibility regarding the Word of God?

What does Paul mean when he says, *children of wrath*?

What is meant by the phrase, *the law worketh wrath*?

What are we to consider with respect to God's grace?

What is the relationship of grace to wrath?

How can God's wrath best be understood?

How can we bridge the gulf between God and ourselves?

What is our relationship to Adam and to Christ?

What does Paul say about sin and wrath in the fifth chapter of Romans?

What does Paul want us to understand regarding sin, the law, and wrath?

Why are we *all by nature the children of wrath*.

Why must we have faith?

What did God do to reconcile us to Himself?

Chapter 5

BUT GOD, RICH IN MERCY

But God, who is rich in mercy, for his great love wherewith he loved us,

Even when we were dead in sins, hath quickened (made alive) us together with Christ, (by grace ye are (have been) saved;)

And hath raised us up together, and made us sit together in heavenly places in Christ Jesus:

That in the ages to come he might show the exceeding riches of his grace in his kindness toward us through (in) Christ Jesus.

For by grace are ye (you have been) saved through faith; and that not of yourselves: it is the gift of God:

Not of works, lest any man should boast.

For we are his workmanship (creation), *created in Christ Jesus unto* (for) *good works, which God hath before ordained* (prepared) *that we should walk in them* [Eph. 2:4–10].

Why does Paul us the phrase, *But God* when introducing new truths to believers?

When can the purpose of Christian teaching and preaching be understood?

Why does the Bible start with God, not man?

What does Paul say about man being essentially good or under the influence of the Holy Spirit?

What is true of man in sin?

Why are there wars, killings, terrorism, and other crimes?

What will change in the future if man continues in his sinful condition?

Why does the Bible say man cannot change while he remains unregenerate?

Why does Paul say, *But God, who is rich in mercy*?

Why is it that we cannot expect Christian behavior from people who are not Christians?

What does the Bible say God has done regarding the unbelieving world?

Should we place our confidence in the natural world or in the Gospel?

Why is the Christian not surprised by what happens in the world?

Why does the Christian know the exceeding greatness of God's power?

What does the real believer know?

Chapter 6

RAISED UP TOGETHER

> *But God, who is rich in mercy, for his great love wherewith he loved us,*
> *Even when we were dead in sins, hath quickened us together with Christ, (by grace ye are (have been) saved;)*
> *And hath raised us up together, and made us sit together in heavenly places in Christ Jesus:*
> *That in the ages to come he might show the exceeding riches of his grace in his kindness toward us through (in) Christ Jesus* [Eph. 2:4–7].

What has God done regarding man's condition in sin?

What truth is Paul never satisfied proclaiming?

What is the greatness of God's glory?

What does our salvation include in addition to the forgiveness of sins?

From whom does everything in our salvation come?

How are we joined to Christ?

Why does what happened to Christ physically happen to us spiritually?

What did the Lord Jesus do for us when He died on the Cross?

Why are we no longer dead in sins and trespasses and no longer *the children of wrath*?

How do we know God was satisfied with Christ's offering?

Why are we no longer under the law but under grace?

What does being *dead to sin* mean?

What eight things are true of the person who is *alive unto God through our Lord Jesus Christ*?

What is true of a person when he or she has been transformed?

How does the new man show himself?

What is meant by having a new mind?

What does the Christian desire?

Chapter 7

CHOSEN BY GOD

> *Even when we were dead in sins, hath quickened us together with Christ, (by grace ye are* (have been) *saved;)*
> *And hath raised us up together, and made us sit together in heavenly places in Christ Jesus* [Eph. 2:5-6].

Why will we be with Christ in the *heavenly places*?

How are we alive unto God?

What three things have happened to us by God's grace and power?

What was our condition beforehand?

What is meant by *in the heavenly places*?

What does it mean to be *alive unto God*?

Where is our citizenship or tenor of life?

What happens when we are under the control of the Holy Spirit?

What are the characteristics of the *heavenlies*?

Why did Jesus sit down at the right hand of God?

How do we realize that we are with Christ?

Why are we to draw near to God?

Chapter 8

GOD'S KINDNESS TOWARD US

That in the ages to come he might show the exceeding riches of his grace in his kindness toward us through (in) Christ Jesus [Eph. 2:7].

Why did God intervene when we were in a helpless condition?

What would we concentrate upon if we had a true scriptural conception of ourselves?

What is the primary objective of salvation?

Why do we need to think in terms of evil in the world?

What does the Bible consider sin to be?

Why did Satan tempt Eve and Adam?

What is salvation?

Why can't Satan affect the character of God?

Why did God send His Son into the world?

Why did God allow man to fall into sin?

Why is the free calling of the Gentiles regarded as "an astonishing work of divine goodness"?

Why do we need to know about our sinful condition?

What was Paul called to do?

Where and how does God work?

How are people redeemed by God?

What plan did God have?

What is the guarantee of our salvation?

Who are the chosen ones?

Chapter 9

SAVED THROUGH FAITH

For by grace are ye saved through faith; and that not of yourselves: it is the gift of God:
Not of works, lest any man should boast [Eph. 2:8–9].

Why did Paul write to the community of believers in Ephesus?

Why does Paul want us to know what it means to be a Christian?

How does one obtain a true understanding of what makes a Christian?

What is "God's way of reconciliation"?

What is your appraisal of the scriptures as our one and only foundation?

How do we become Christians?

How did Noah find *grace in the eyes of the Lord*?

What is the reason for the continued existence of the Israelites in the Old Testament?

What is the result of Christ's death in breaking down the partition between the Jew and Gentile?

What do the Old and New Testaments continue to emphasize?

Where is salvation found?

Why is boasting excluded in our relationship with Christ and God?

Why is there *none righteous, no not one*?

Why are we *His workmanship, created in Christ Jesus unto good works*?

How is the word *faith* used in Scripture?

How do we obtain faith?

What is a Christian?

In what should we glory?

Chapter 10

CREATED IN CHRIST JESUS

For we are his workmanship, created in Christ Jesus unto good works, which God hath before ordained that we should walk in them [Eph. 2:10].

What are the *gifts of God* according to Paul?

What do our works have to do with salvation?

What does Paul mean when he says, *we are his workmanship*?

What is your reaction to the idea of being formed and fashioned by God in Christ?

What does Paul say about God's work in us?

About what does the New Testament continuously remind believers in Christ?

What is the common understanding of being a Christian?

What truths does Paul present about God?

Outline Questions

What does the Bible tell us God has done?

What is creation?

How does God perform His wonderful work?

Why did God give gifts to us?

Chapter 11

GOD'S CHASTENING GRACE

> *And ye have forgotten the exhortation which speaketh unto you as unto children, My son, despise not thou the chastening* (disciplining) *of the Lord, nor faint* (be discouraged) *when thou art rebuked of him:*
> *For whom the Lord loveth he chasteneth, and scourgeth every son whom re receiveth.*
> *If ye endure chastening, God dealeth with you as with sons; for what son is he whom the father chasteneth not?*
> *But if ye be without chastisement, whereof all are partakers, then are ye bastards, and not sons* [Heb. 12:5-8].

Why did the Hebrews grumble and complain?

Why does God chastise His children?

What plan did God design for the chosen ones?

What happens when God begins a good work in you?

How are we able to lead a holy life?

Out of what was the world created?

Of what does God's gift to us consist?

What does salvation include?

What is usually emphasized regarding our salvation?

Why has God given us a *spirit of power, love, and a sound mind*?

Chapter 12

CIRCUMCISION AND UNCIRCUMCISION

> *Wherefore remember, that ye being in time past Gentiles in the flesh, who are called Uncircumcision by that which is called the Circumcision in the flesh made by hands;*
>
> *That at that time ye were without Christ, being aliens from the commonwealth of Israel, and strangers from the covenants of promise, having no hope, and without God in the world:*
>
> *But now in Christ Jesus ye who sometimes were far off are made nigh by the blood of Christ* [Eph. 2:11–13].

How is the greatness of God's power shown?

In what tense does Scripture usually speak?

Why are people not amazed or impressed regarding Christianity?

What conditions existed in the first century?

Why does Paul raise the issue of circumcision and uncircumcision?

How did God overcome this issue?

What is one of the tragedies of our time regarding the Gospel?

What factors did Paul want the Ephesians to consider in resolving problems or difficulties?

What do men usually do when they have differences?

What were the Jews to be as God's people?

What factors contribute to erecting barriers?

Where do the lusts of the mind usually lead?

What other factors cause divisions?

What can help us, change us, and cure us?

What does Christ make us do and see?

What can Christ do with friend and foe?

How can man's nature change and be controlled?

Chapter 13

ALIENS FROM THE COMMONWEALTH OF ISRAEL

> *That at that time ye were without Christ, being aliens from the commonwealth of Israel, and strangers from the covenants of promise, having no hope, and without God in the world:*
> *But now in Christ Jesus ye who sometimes were far off are made nigh by the blood of Christ* [Eph. 2:12–13].

What causes us to act differently or to change for the better?

Why do we need to examine Scripture and ask what God has been doing and is now doing?

What was the purpose of God's covenant with Abram?

What was the Ephesians status before the incarnation?

Why does Paul use tough, straightforward phrases?

What truths does Paul want the Ephesians to understand?

What happens if we take away the covenant of salvation?

How can we see what we were before Christ was in us?

What has God in Christ done?

Who are those without God?

How do we come to God?

What determines whether or not we are Christians?

What does the *blood of Christ* remove?

What happens when we are made *nigh by the blood of Christ*?

What other things are *made nigh*?

What are we to remember?

Chapter 14

BY THE BLOOD OF CHRIST

> But now in Christ Jesus ye who sometimes were far off are made nigh by the blood of Christ.
> For he is our peace, who hath made both one, and hath broken down the middle wall of partition between us;
> Having abolished in his flesh the enmity, even the law of commandments contained in ordinances; for to make in himself of twain one new man, so making peace;
> And that he might reconcile both unto God in one body by the cross, having slain the enmity thereby:
> And came and preached peace to you which were afar off, and to them that were nigh [Eph 2:13–17].

How can we understand the greatness of our salvation?

Why does Paul want us to grasp the greatness of our salvation?

What monumental fact changed the believers in Ephesus?

How are people *made nigh*?

What is one truth in which all the apostles are united?

What are various ways by which people think they can come close to God?

How does the Apostle Paul say we are *made nigh* to Christ?

What does the blood of Christ mean?

What did the Pharisees believe?

How are we drawn nigh to God?

How was the new covenant ratified?

Why did Christ die on the Cross?

What is the essence of Scripture?

Why are we able to come into the presence of God?

Chapter 15

MAKING PEACE

> *For he is our peace, who hath made both one, and hath broken down the middle wall of partition between us;*
> *Having abolished in his flesh the enmity, even the law of commandments contained in ordinances; for to make (create) in himself of twain one new man, so making peace;*
> *And that he might reconcile both unto God in one body by the cross, having slain the enmity thereby* [Eph. 2:14–17].

How does Christ reconcile us to God?

How does the New Testament describe the *community of believers*?

How does the *community of believers* have unity with Christ Jesus?

To whom must the *community of believers* always point?

What does *peace* mean in the New Testament?

What is the Shiloh of which Jacob speaks?

What suggestions are proffered for attaining *peace*?

What causes man's trouble with man and with God?

With which commandment must you start in order to attain *peace*?

What does the saying *for he is our peace* mean?

How does Christ make *peace*?

What does Calvin say regarding the phrase *who hath made both one*?

What is the *middle wall of partition*?

How is the *middle wall of partition* removed?

How does God make *peace*?

What ceremonies that had created a 'wall' between the Jew and Gentile were abolished through Christ?

What is the only way by which the forgiveness of sins can be obtained?

What is meant by *having slain the enmity thereby*?

Chapter 16

RECONCILE BOTH UNTO GOD

> *Having abolished in his flesh the enmity, even the law of commandments contained in ordinances; for to make (create) in himself of twain one new man, so making peace;*
> *And that he might reconcile both unto God in one body by the cross, having slain the enmity thereby* [Eph. 2:15–16].

What do the words *in himself* mean in the phrase *for to make in himself of twain one new man*?

What does the word *reconcile* mean in the phrase *That he might reconcile both unto God*?

What truth is the Apostle Paul conveying in this verse?

What breaks our fellowship with God?

For what was man made?

How can our fellowship with God be restored?

How are we to think of our sinfulness regarding our relationship to God?

How does God reveal Himself?

How can we walk in fellowship with God?

How is reconciliation with God achieved?

Why does Paul point to the Cross and the shed blood of Christ?

How has the enmity between God and man been removed?

What command did Paul give to the elders in Ephesus?

Chapter 17

HE CAME AND PREACHED PEACE

And came and preached peace to you which were afar off, and to them that were nigh [Eph. 2:17].

What are the two possible interpretations of Paul's statement *and came and preached peace to you which were afar off and to them that were nigh*?

To whom was our Lord's primary ministry?

What was preached through the apostles to the Gentiles?

How did Christ proclaim the Gospel to the Gentiles?

What happens when one does not apply the Gospel?

What made possible Christ's ministry through His apostles, disciples, evangelists, and servants?

What truths are contained in the verse about Christ preaching to those *afar off*, and *to them that were nigh*?

Why did the Jews need the message of God's *peace*?

What reaction do people have to the fact that Jesus preached the same message to them *afar off, and to them that were nigh*?

What was true of Paul and the Philippian jailer?

What is true of both those *afar off* and *nigh*?

Who is able to provide the *peace* of God and fellowship with Him?

How are we reconciled to God?

What faith and confidence are we to carry in our hearts and minds?

Chapter 18

THROUGH HIM BY ONE SPIRIT

For through him we both have access by one Spirit unto the Father [Eph. 2:18].

Through whom do we have access to the Father?

What does *access* mean in the original Greek?

For what reasons do people attend a Christian church?

What does the Christian, not just churchgoer, realize regarding *access by one Spirit unto the Father*?

How does the Doctrine of the Trinity differentiate the Christian faith?

For what reason is the Holy Trinity interested in us?

Why must we consider the Doctrine of Sin, when considering the Doctrine of the Trinity?

What is the chief object of our salvation?

What significant points does Paul make about access to the Father?

What does Peter say about access to the Father?

What does the New Testament explicitly teach regarding how a person may know God as their Father?

How do we have access to the Father?

Why should believers in Christ have confidence in their prayers?

What is absolutely essential to prayer?

Chapter 19

CHRIST'S RIGHTEOUSNESS

For through him we both have access by one Spirit unto the Father [Eph. 2:18].

Upon what principles is praying to God based?

What approaches to prayer are not based upon a scriptural foundation?

Why are we to focus on the words *through Him* in the verse *through Him we both have access by one Spirit unto the Father*?

Why do we have access to God?

Who is our great sin bearer?

What makes reconciliation with God possible?

What is the result of Christ dying upon the Cross and shedding His blood?

What is the great stumbling block to reconciliation?

What are the results of Christ dying upon the Cross?

How does Christ become our righteousness?

Why do we have access through Christ?

Who was able to *unlock the gates of heaven and let us in*?

What happens when we realize our complete dependence upon Christ?

Chapter 20

MAKING INTERCESSION ACCORDING TO THE WILL OF GOD

> For through him we both have access by one Spirit unto the Father [Eph. 2:18].
>
> Likewise the Spirit also helpeth our infirmities (weaknesses): for we know what we should pray for as we ought: but the Spirit itself maketh intercession for us with groanings which cannot be uttered.
> And he that searcheth the hearts knoweth what is the mind of the Spirit, because he maketh intercession for the saints according to the will of God [Rom. 8:26–27].

Who provides access to God the Father?

Why is it difficult to pray?

What are certain fundamental truths about prayer?

What was the very essence of prayer to the New Testament writers?

What do we learn about prayer from Paul in this portion of Scripture?

What do we learn from the Lord Jesus about prayer?

Why is prayer a matter of the Spirit?

Why is the Holy Spirit vital to communicating with God?

What is the essence of prayer in the Old Testament?

How does God speak to man and man speak to God?

What positive impact did the period of exile have on the Israelites and their prayer life?

Chapter 21

HAVING FAITH IN PRAYER

> *For through him we both have access by one Spirit unto the Father* [Eph. 2:18].

> *Blessed be the God and Father of our Lord Jesus Christ, who hath blessed us with all spiritual blessings in heavenly places in Christ* [Eph. 1:3].

When did prayer begin to influence the daily life of the Israelite people?

Where must we begin when considering prayer in the New Testament?

What is to be the primary purpose of our prayers to God?

Why is there a need for importunity in prayer?

What does Scripture say is needed in offering our prayers to the Father?

When is the answer to prayer certain?

How does the Spirit itself make intercession for us?

Why did the prayers of the patriarchs and prophets have special power?

What impact did the prayers of Stonewall Jackson have on his fellow members of the First Presbyterian Church in Lexington, Virginia?

What supports every prayer offered with the right intention?

What does the Holy Spirit do in our prayer life?

How does the Holy Spirit reveal our need of God?

How does the Holy Spirit reveal God in His glory?

How does the Holy Spirit lead us to an understanding of God's promises?

Chapter 22

UNITY IN CHRIST

> *Now therefore ye are no more strangers and foreigners, but fellow citizens with the saints, and of the household of God;*
> *And are built upon the foundation of the apostles and prophets, Jesus Christ himself being the chief corner stone;*
> *In whom all the building fitly framed together groweth unto an holy temple in the Lord:*
> *In whom ye also are builded together for a habitation of God through the Spirit* [Eph. 2:19–22].

Why does Paul use the terms *strangers* and *foreigners*?

Why does Paul remind the Ephesians of their former condition as well as their current one?

How does Paul summarize God's workmanship?

How is unity among believers achieved?

Why are all those who are truly Christians one?

With whom do we have unity?

Why does Paul allude to their previous condition?

Why does Paul use the word *quickened* in describing the Ephesians?

Why does Paul repeatedly talk about *With Christ, In Christ, and Through Christ*?

Why does Paul say, *For they are not all of Israel, which are of Israel*?

Why are we to conform to the laws of God?

Why do we say *His commandments are not grievous* and also *O, how love I thy law*?

What does Paul reveal under the influence of the Holy Spirit?

Chapter 23

FELLOW CITIZENS WITH THE SAINTS

Now therefore ye are no more strangers and foreigners, but fellow citizens with the saints, and of the household of God [Eph. 2:19].

What does it mean to be *fellow citizens with the saints, and of the household of faith*?

What benefits and privileges come to these people?

What does the Greek word *Theios* mean?

What changes are brought about by Christ's divine power?

Why does Paul want *the eyes of their understanding to be enlightened*?

What are the peculiarities of the fellow citizens or those who are in Christ?

What is significant about the call of Abraham, Moses, and the Ten Commandments?

Outline Questions

Why did Jesus teach about the kingdom of God and the people entering it?

What did Jesus say to Nicodemus?

What did Jesus say to the chief priests, elders, and Pharisees when he encountered them?

To whom is God's dreadful vengeance proclaimed by Christ?

Who will spare God if He does not spare the natural branches?

From whom will Christ remove the kingdom of God?

Chapter 24

ABRAHAM'S SEED

> *But ye are a chosen generation, a royal priesthood, an holy nation, a peculiar people* (his own special people); *that ye should show* (proclaim) *forth the praises of him who hath called you out of darkness into his marvelous light:*
>
> *Which in time past were not a people, but are now the people of God: which had not obtained mercy, but now have obtained mercy* [1 Pet. 2:9–10].

What thought provoking verses should command our attention?

What does Paul, under the influence of the Holy Spirit, bring together?

How do we define the church and its membership?

To whom are we to separate ourselves?

What is one of the great tragedies since Christ walked on the earth?

Where is Christ's kingdom?

What are the privileges of being *in Christ*?

Outline Questions

Who are our fellow citizens?

What is the glory of God's kingdom?

How does Daniel describe the kingdom of God?

Chapter 25

GOD'S DWELLING PLACE

> *And are built upon the foundation of the apostles and prophets, Jesus Christ himself being the chief corner stone;*
> *In whom all the building fitly framed together groweth unto a holy temple in the Lord:*
> *In whom ye also are builded together for a habitation of God through the Spirit* [Eph. 2:20–22].

What progression does Paul use to describe membership in the community of believers?

Of which truths should we be aware that Paul clearly presents?

What honors does Paul bestow on the Ephesians?

What does Paul teach that should be the foundation of our faith?

Why are we to seek the Word of God in the prophets and apostles?

How does Paul describe the church in his letter to the Corinthians?

What process does God use in building His church?

What does Paul say about the church of God and its members?

What is needed for a building to *groweth unto a Holy Temple in the Lord*?

What is the first priority in building a church?

Where does God dwell?

Chapter 26

THE FOUNDATION OF THE APOSTLES AND PROPHETS

> *And are built upon the foundation of the apostles and prophets, Jesus Christ himself being the chief corner stone;*
> *In whom all the building fitly framed together groweth unto a holy temple in the Lord:*
> *In whom ye also are builded together for a habitation of God through the Spirit* [Eph. 2:20–22].

What two great principles are we to grasp and retain?

What are the different types of unity?

Why does Paul use the term *chief corner stone*?

What is an apostle?

What is a prophet?

How were the apostles and prophets used?

What is the foundation?

What makes us members of the *community of believers*?

What are the ingredients of this foundation and its essential parts?

What does the Word teach?

What do the apostles teach?

What does the person *in Christ* believe?

What deductions may be drawn from the doctrine and teachings of the apostles and prophets?

Why must we know in whom we believe and what we believe?

What is the basis of our faith?

How do we fit into this building that is *a habitation of God through the Spirit*?

How does the stonemason proceed to construct a building or a wall?

Chapter 27

BEING MEMBERS OF CHRIST'S BODY

> *In whom all the building fitly framed together groweth unto an holy temple in the Lord:*
> *In whom ye also are builded together for a habitation of God through the Spirit* [Eph. 2:21–22].

How are the human stones prepared that contribute to the growth of the church?

Where does the work of the Holy Spirit take place?

What does the Holy Spirit reveal to us?

Who is the person that is *in Christ*?

What does Pascal say about reason?

What did Luther, Calvin, and the Puritans teach?

What did Paul write to Timothy about the foundation and the materials in the building?

Why does Jesus say to potential followers stop, look, listen?

What does Jesus mean when he says this?

How do we apply this teaching today?

What was true of the early church?

What truths continue to provide unity among believers today?

Bibliography

Barth, Markus. *Ephesians 1–3*. Garden City, NY: Doubleday, 1974.
Calvin, John. *Calvin's New Testament Commentaries*. Grand Rapids, MI: Eerdmans, 1973.
———. *Calvin's Sermons on The Epistle to the Ephesians*. Carlisle, PA: Banner of Truth Trust, 1973.
———. *Institutes of the Christian Religion*. Philadelphia, PA: Westminster.
Lloyd-Jones, Martyn. *God's Way of Reconciliation*. Grand Rapids, MI: Baker, 1980.
Paxson, Ruth. *The Wealth, Walk and Warfare of the Christian*. London and Edinburgh: Oliphants, 1941.
Presbyterian Hymnal. Louisville, KY: Westminster John Knox, 1990.
Vine, W. E. *Vine's Expository Dictionary of New Testament Words*. McLean, VA: MacDonald.
Weber, Otto. *Foundations of Dogmatics*. Volumes 1 & 2. Grand Rapids, MI: Eerdmans, 1983.